*Mother
Love,
Deadly
Love*

Mother Love, Deadly Love

Anne McDonald Maier

A BIRCH LANE PRESS BOOK
Published by Carol Publishing Group

A Birch Lane Press Book
Published by Carol Publishing Group
Birch Lane Press is a registered trademark of Carol Communications,
    Inc.
Editorial Offices: 600 Madison Avenue, New York, N.Y. 10022
Sales and Distribution Offices: 120 Enterprise Avenue, Secaucus,
    N.J. 07094
In Canada: Canadian Manda Group, P.O. Box 920, Station U, Toronto,
    Ontario M8Z 5P9
Queries regarding rights and permissions should be addressed to
    Carol Publishing Group, 600 Madison Avenue, New York, N.Y. 10022

Carol Publishing Group books are available at special discounts for
bulk purchases, for sales promotions, fund-raising, or educational
purposes. Special editions can be created to specifications. For
details contact: Special Sales Department, Carol Publishing Group,
120 Enterprise Avenue, Secaucus, N.J. 07094

Manufactured in the United States of America
10   9   8   7   6   5   4   3   2   1

Library of Congress Cataloging-in-Publication Data

Maier, Anne McDonald.
    Mother love, deadly love : the Texas cheerleader murder plot / by
Anne McDonald Maier.
        p.   cm.
    "A Birch Lane Press book."
    ISBN 1-55972-137-5 (cloth)
    1. Attempted murder—Texas—Case studies.   2. Cheerleading—Texas—
Case studies.   3. Holloway, Wanda Ann.   I. Title.
HV6533.T4M34   1992
364.1'523'09764141—dc20
                                                                    92-21345
                                                                    CIP

For Max and Nick

Contents

*Mother
Love,
Deadly
Love*

Prologue

Wanda Ann Holloway had not a care in the world as she drove home
from her son's high school in Channelview, Texas, the afternoon of
January 30, 1991. Although the day was cold and dreary, her spirits were
light and sunny. Christian music blared from the stereo in her shiny
Jeep Grand Wagoneer and she hummed along with the tune as she
smiled contentedly to herself.

Everything will be fine now, she mused. It's all going to be okay. As
she foresaw it, all the problems of the last several years would evaporate
and her dearest dream would finally come true: After all her hopes and
prayers, her precious daughter Shanna, fourteen, would surely get to be
a cheerleader at last. She had certainly done everything in her power to
help that effort! Hadn't she just spent the whole day down at that darn
Channelview High working as a teacher's aide—really just sucking up
to the teachers who would help choose the next year's cheerleading
squad—and not getting one red cent for doing it?

That's the kind of crap you had to do, though, she thought. That's
what that damned Verna Heath had been doing for her daughter

Amber for years, and it sure paid off there. That prissy little Amber had been cheerleader the last two years at her junior high, beating out Shanna both times! The little bitch, thought Wanda. She was the reason Wanda had to waste three days a week down at that dumb old high school, working her butt off for nothing, smiling and acting nice as pie all the time. Well, anything would be worth it if it helped Shanna get elected cheerleader when the elections were held in the spring.

Wanda grimaced as she recalled how she was once actually friends with that Heath woman. It had started when Shanna and Amber had been classmates in fourth grade at Channelview Christian Academy. Wanda and Verna Heath had socialized to some extent, carpooling to gymnastics classes for their daughters, going together to the local swim club. But all that had changed over the last two years, ever since Amber beat out Shanna for cheerleader.

Wanda giggled to herself as she remembered how cute little Shanna had looked when, as a three-year-old in a miniature cheering outfit, she had jumped and bounced for her older brother Shane's team at the local Y years ago. Wanda had worn a look-alike cheering outfit to match her young daughter's. Over the years the two had practiced and planned together for the day when Shanna would eventually emerge into the real spotlight, the one that mattered most, the one that could establish her position for the rest of her life. That day was nearing, thought Wanda. Shanna would finally get to be a cheerleader for Channelview High School!

In a town like Channelview, Texas, that would be no small accomplishment. A working-class community, Channelview is home to thousands of blue-collar refinery workers and dockhands from the nearby Houston Ship Channel. The bustling industrial world that provides the economic life's blood for most of the town's residents also renders it undesirable as a place to live or visit for most other citizens of Southeast Texas. The spew of rank pollution from the oil refineries and the toxic chemical wastes that seep into the ship channel serve as an effective barrier to outsiders. Not many people come to Channelview because they want to; they come because they have to, and those who stay find themselves isolated from the mainstream of modern American society.

In this insular community, little things can come to mean a lot. Although not far from Houston, one of the nation's largest cities, Channelview retains the aura of a tiny, rural town, a place where people are born, raised, married, and buried within the same five-square-mile area. People know each other here. The neighbors down the street are likely to be the folks you knew in grade school, or at least in Sunday school. The people who work together also play together and pray together. And in a town that doesn't have much recreation to offer, folks tend to do a lot of praying.

As in many small towns, the churches of Channelview provide one of the main social forums; residents speak proudly of belonging to the Truth Tabernacle Pentacostal group or the Missionary Baptist church. The alternative social forum is found in the beer joints and ice houses (run-down taverns) along Sheldon Road and Market Street, Channelview's two main drags. The former is more upscale, littered with fast-food franchises and motor banks while Market Street is home to seedy bars and prostitutes, and the clientele such entertainments attract.

Interstate 10, the huge highway running east out of Houston toward Louisiana, neatly bisects Channelview into two distinct geographical regions—the good side of town and the bad. North of the artery is the side where the schools, churches, hospital, and restaurants are located. South of the highway is the notoriously rough Market Street area and the fetid, sludgy ship channel. The society of Channelview is almost as neatly divided into two groups as well—those who have made it and those who have not. The criteria for determining who is in which group include the usual outward signs of material rewards, but also the more elusive badges of social prominence that only honors like being the high school cheerleader or band major can bestow.

Wanda Ann Holloway had started out on the wrong side of Channelview as a child, but through determination and opportunistic marriages had finally wound up where she wanted to be: on the right side. Married to her third husband, a wealthy construction company owner twenty years her senior, at age thirty-seven Wanda at last had some of the finer things in life: a nice brick home in one of the town's nicer subdivisions, a big shiny new car, and lots and lots of nice clothes and jewelry. There was, at last, money for extras—modeling school for Shanna, gymnastics classes for Shanna, clothes and makeup for Shanna. Wanda could have her nails sculpted weekly and her hair permed, colored, and coiffed as often as desired. Since her marriage to C. D. Holloway five years earlier, Wanda hadn't had to worry much about money. At last she could concentrate on what she was really interested in, seeing her daughter win a coveted spot on the cheerleading squad.

It had been her goal almost from the time Shanna was born in 1977. The pretty blond daughter arrived at a time when Wanda's marriage to her first husband, Tony Harper, was already crumbling. Tony and Wanda had grown up just blocks from each other, both from the "wrong" side of Channelview. They attended Channelview High together, and wed shortly after graduation. Within a short time there were problems, and the problems got worse as more time passed. In a last-ditch effort to save the marriage, the couple decided to have a second child. Their son Shane (named after the legendary Western movie hero) was then four and the couple didn't want him to be an only child.

Although the new baby girl didn't save her parents' marriage, she did provide her mother with a focus for her prematurely terminated drive and ambition. With no higher education, no professional outlets, and soon no husband, Wanda Ann Harper turned to tiny Shanna Nicole to fulfill herself as a woman. She kept the child immaculately dressed in frilly pink dresses, her blond hair curled to perfection. She tirelessly drove Shanna to dance classes and gymnastics and church play rehearsals, even if it meant skipping activities Shane was involved in. Wanda's son was always treated as kind of an afterthought. All the preparation and practice was aimed at the ultimate title Wanda hoped Shanna would win when she was older—high school cheerleader.

In a town the size of Channelview there are not a lot of stages on which to shine. So the platform of high school sports for boys and high school cheerleading for girls becomes the ultimate proving ground of who is worthy of admiration and who is not, more by the process of elimination than because of any more complex cultural issues. The competition for such spots of glory becomes fierce, especially for the girls who would be cheerleader, since there are only eight available places on the high school squad, as opposed to dozens of athletic openings for boys.

Shanna had never been a "real" cheerleader. Yes, Wanda thought as she drove down Sheldon Road that Wednesday, Shanna had cheered for her brother's teams when she was younger. But that didn't really count; that was a make-believe, dress-up kind of cheerleading. Now was when it really mattered. Wanda fretted to herself as she recalled how Shanna hadn't ever even made the cheering squad at Alice Johnson Junior High in Channelview, although not for want of trying; she had tried out the last two years with no success.

She'd come close, though, thought Wanda. She could have made it. She WOULD have made it, thundered Wanda's inner voice, if it weren't for that damn prissy little Amber Heath, that awful child who not once but *twice* beat Shanna out for the squad. All the teachers and the coaches had implied as much—if Amber hadn't been trying out, Shanna would have been chosen for the squad. It was all that damn goody-goody mother's doing. Amber's mother Verna was always sashaying herself down around the school, kissing up to the coaches and running to the school board to lobby on her daughter's behalf.

"Oooooh," Wanda said aloud through clenched teeth. "Makes me sick. Makes me want to bash her face in!"

But then, almost as suddenly as her anger had swelled, Wanda's fury began to evaporate. She smiled smugly to herself as she turned left off Sheldon Road onto the street that would lead to the subdivision of Sterling Green and her home. "Everything is going to be okay now," she said aloud.

As she turned into her drive and reached across the seat to open the glove box to press her automatic garage-door opener, Wanda didn't notice the plain sedan parked across the street from her house on Mincing Lane. She stopped the car, glanced up at her face in the rearview mirror and patted her large cascade of curled, long brown hair. Her thin lips twisted in a smile as she opened the car door. She straightened her tight black skirt and walked down the drive to the walkway leading up to the house, wobbling only slightly on her high-heeled shoes. It was then she noticed the car across the street, the car with two men emerging from its front doors.

One of the men, the driver of the auto, called her by name. "Wanda Webb Holloway?" he inquired. "Yes," she answered forthrightly in her sharp nasal twang. "What do you want?"

As the man continued to approach, Wanda noticed he had pulled out an identification badge of some sort. "I'm Detective George Helton from the Harris County Sheriff's Department," he said. "You're under arrest for the solicitation of the capital murder of Verna Heath."

One hour later on that evening of January 30, 1991, just around the corner from Wanda's home on Mincing Lane, Verna Heath arrived home with her daughter Amber in tow to a house almost identical to Wanda's; in fact, it had the same floor plan. She was greeted in her driveway by the same pair of Harris County sheriff's deputies Wanda Holloway had seen earlier, the ones who had taken her down to the jail. Detective Helton and Sergeant Flynt Blackwell asked to speak privately with Verna for a moment. Totally bewildered, Verna sent Amber and her two younger sons into their bedrooms and hastily began picking up the children's toys scattered all over the living-room floor. "Please, ma'am," said Detective Helton, "You don't really need to be doing that. Just sit down and we need to talk."

After settling the pretty young mother on the couch, the two men somberly told her their mission. "Are you acquainted with a woman named Wanda Holloway?" Helton asked. Verna said she was. "We just arrested her this afternoon," Helton explained, "for hiring someone to murder you."

Verna sank back into the couch and gasped. "Why," she managed to stammer after minutes of stunned silence, "why did she do that?"

"It had something to do with cheerleading," Blackwell said slowly in his Texas drawl. "She did not want your daughter to get cheerleader again, and she figured if something happened to you that your daughter would not want to try out this year."

Verna sat in shock for several minutes. Tears began to trickle down her face. As the detective handed her his handkerchief, she began to sob. "Why, why would she do this? Someone who has been this close, who lives right around the corner....Who would do such a thing? Why would a cheerleading position be so important! My children—that would leave my children without a mother. Who would raise them? To not have a mother—over cheerleading?"

Detective Helton and Sargeant Blackwell exchanged helpless glances. They had no answer for Mrs. Heath. After years of professional law enforcement experience, working with criminals of every variety, neither man had ever heard of anything like this. They, like Verna, were at a loss. No one understood why Wanda had done what she had done, arranged the contract murder of her former friend and neighbor.

Nobody understood except Wanda. And she wasn't talking.

1

Growing Up and Liking It

There was certainly nothing in Wanda Holloway's past to suggest she would ever plot the murder of a friend, over cheerleading or for any other reason. Born and raised in Channelview, she had led a simple and uncomplicated life as the younger of two children born to Clyde Cleven Webb and his wife Verna.

The Webbs had come to Texas from rural southwestern Louisiana shortly after the end of World War II, when all of the Houston area was bustling with postwar economic enthusiasm. Channelview, built as it was on the banks of the Houston Ship Channel, soon became a community ideally suited for industrial development. With the postwar boom in manufacturing, the petrochemical industry mushroomed also, and as more and more plants and refineries were needed, the environs around Channelview sprouted more and more spires of steel and spewing smokestacks. The huge manufacturing facilities, many covering hundreds of acres of land, added an other-worldly look to the area, with their tangles of pipe and mazes of lights and flares that lit up the nighttime sky.

They also provided thousands of jobs for men freshly back from the front. Dirty jobs, yes, but jobs just the same. So it was that country boys and girls like Clyde Webb and his young wife Verna, who came from a Louisiana Cajun family, found themselves on the edge of the big city of Houston, in the town of Channelview. It had become a sort of company town for the major oil companies that had refineries ringing the area. Clyde went to work at a cement-testing plant. Verna stayed home when the babies started coming, first Wayne in 1953, and then little Wanda Ann in February of 1954. They may have left their rural home, but their values stayed those of the countryfolk. The Webbs were avid church goers—Missionary Baptists—and believed in the good old-fashioned virtues of hard work and clean living.

Eventually the Webbs were able to buy a home, a simple, wood-frame house on the southside of the highway leading out of Houston toward Louisiana. The narrow asphalt lane on which the house sat was even named Channelview. Back in those days, Channelview definitely had the flavor of a small, country town. The two main roads through town, Sheldon Road and Market Street, were both two-lane, and few red lights impeded the flow of the scant traffic. There were only one or two hamburger stands and a smattering of grocery shops and beauty salons.

There were quite a few churches, however, and still more road houses and taverns, where the workers from the area refineries could cool off and unwind at the end of their shifts. Refinery work can be long and demanding. It is not unusual for workers to do what are called "six-tens": six ten-hour days, one day off. Many worked rotating shifts at plants that never closed, even for Christmas. It is not hard to understand why the ice houses often stayed full.

Clyde Webb was not among those swilling chilled longnecked beers. Didn't believe in it, never would. Instead, he spent whatever spare time he had hustling a way to make extra money to help provide more for his family. In back of his house he built an extensively stocked workshop and was known throughout the town for his expertise at a variety of semiskilled tasks such as car repair, vacuum-tank work, and the like. He eventually saved up enough for a tractor-mower, which he used on weekends and days off to contract out mowing and shredding work in nearby pastures.

From all accounts, Clyde Webb was a stern man not much given to frivolity or foolishness. He didn't even waste much time shooting the breeze with friends or neighbors. He concentrated his energies on work, God, and family and expected his children to do the same. He had strong ideas about right and wrong and seldom gave in when his beliefs were challenged.

For example, at the Baptist church he and his family attended in Channelview, he had a falling out with the church leaders over the propriety of "mixed bathing." Mixed bathing referred to men and women, boys and girls, going swimming together at the same time. Wasn't right, he thought, for the opposite sexes to see each other in such scanty attire. Might lead to impure thoughts or even acts. When the elders thought him a mite too out-of-date for the modern Baptist church, Clyde left the congregation with a splinter group and founded a rival Missionary Baptist church in the community.

There he took his children three times weekly—twice on Sunday and once on Wednesday night. Wanda Webb grew up indoctrinated in the teachings of this fundamentalist Baptist sect. It was in this environment she learned to sing and pray and play religious music on the piano, an instrument she was taught from a young age with money earned from her father's extracurricular endeavors.

Those who remember Wanda as a child recall a neatly dressed, well-mannered and hard-working student. Raised as she was by a strict father, Wanda had learned early on not to ask too many questions or make too many waves. Schoolmates recall her as quiet and on the shy side. Once in high school at Channelview High, her main extracurricular activities were related to the Future Homemakers of America. Although she longed to audition for the high school drill-team, a squad of girls who marched at halftime during football games, friends say Wanda's father refused to allow his only daughter to try out because he disapproved of the short skirts the drill team members wore.

"He just didn't want her parading around in front of a football field in skimpy clothing," says a family friend and fellow church member, adding, "I can see why a father might feel that way. Clyde just thought the costumes were whorish."

Wanda's best subjects in high school were in the Vocational Office Education division, where she studied typing and other secretarial skills. Her years of piano playing no doubt contributed to her keyboard speed and dexterity. One of her VOE classmates remembers Wanda Webb as "a giggly girl. She didn't talk much, but she giggled a lot. And she was real good at secretarial stuff."

Wanda and her mother, Verna, were always close. "As close as a mother and daughter can be," her mother later said. When Wanda entered high school, Verna took a job as a cafeteria worker in the school's lunch line. Many fellow high school students recall that Wanda was somewhat embarrassed by her mother's lowly position. Others say it made no difference to them or Wanda. If nothing else, the job enabled Verna to visit with Wanda daily at lunch.

Back in those days, most Channelview residents were on a more equal economic level than they are today. Most residents, like the Webbs, had come from rural roots with little education and ended up in low-level blue-collar jobs. There were no upwardly mobile brick subdivisions with names like Woodforest or Sterling Green. The neighborhoods had no names back then, and almost everyone lived in the same kind of modest middle-class home. Instead of competing against each other, the people of Channelview aspired to be like the rich bosses of the companies where their fathers worked, the executives of the oil companies and manufacturing plants, who for the most part lived twenty miles to the west in more upscale Houston neighborhoods.

From all accounts, Wanda was a typical high school girl. Acquaintances do not remember her being either unusually popular or unpopular; she was just kind of there, blending in. "She was kinda average," says one classmate. "She wasn't really one of the in crowd, but she wasn't the town slut either, and we had our share of those out in Channelview, believe me."

A slender, petite girl with brown hair and eyes, Wanda was somewhat sharp-featured and thin-lipped. She wasn't exactly ugly, but wasn't especially pretty either. In 1970, during a time when most of the youth of America were sporting love beads and long, straight hair, Wanda still favored the over-sized bouffant hairdos of the early sixties and sported a bubble-shaped mass of hair that dwarfed her small face.

When Wanda was fifteen and a sophomore in high school, she took an interest in a senior named Tony Harper. Tony's family, like Wanda's, had been in Channelview "forever," as some describe it. The Harper family, which included two younger boys besides Tony, lived just blocks from the Webbs in a similar modest middle-class home on Harding Street. Many of the streets in this part of Channelview bear presidential names like Coolidge and Hoover, reflecting the era of the thirties in which most were built.

R. E. Harper, Tony's dad, had come to Channelview as a teenager during the forties, seeking his fortune. His family had moved from Alabama to Huntsville, Texas, some seventy-five miles north of Channelview. But R. E. (his name is Roscoe Earl, which he detests) struck out on his own at the age of fifteen because of family problems. After doing a stint in the service, he wound up in Channelview at the age of twenty-one. There he met seventeen-year-old Peggy Fincher, whose own family had moved to Channelview in 1942 from the little North Texas town of Ennis.

The couple met at a dance hall called the Pea Farm because of its proximity to nearby vegetable fields. They married soon after and built a little house on property next door to Peggy's parents' home in Channelview. R. E. went to work as a welder, and Peggy soon gave birth to their first son, Tony, born in 1952. Two more sons came later; Terry Lynn, born in 1955, and Tracy ten years later. Eventually, R. E. saved enough money to buy his own convenience store/gas station in Channelview.

Some time later, Tony's mom, Peggy, bought her own lingerie store. It was called Peggy's Cameo Boutique, and offered, by appointment only, fine lady's underthings to the women of Channelview. The Cameo Boutique specialized in underwear for the hard-to-fit, but also offered a considerable array of titillating lacy black baby-doll pajamas and the like.

Compared to many in Channelview, the Harpers appeared to be fairly prosperous. Peggy drove a Cadillac and sported several large diamond rings. R. E. ended up with a couple of other small businesses and the freedom to schedule his own time instead of punching a clock at a plant.

The Harpers were a devoutly Christian family. They were of a different denomination from the Webbs, however, and went to the Channelview Church of Christ. Most everyone in Channelview was a regular church goer; even today the town is liberally dotted with churches of all denominations, although the most common are fundamentalist-oriented faiths like Missionary Baptist, Pentecostal, Seventh

Day Adventist, and that ilk. One reason church going is popular in towns like Channelview is that few atheists live on the edges of potentially poisonous and explosive petrochemical plants.

Explosions and death are almost a way of life in the petrochemical industry. In 1947, the worst industrial accident in U.S. history occurred in nearby Texas City when a small malfunction on a docked ship caused a fire that set off a horrific chain-reaction explosion along a string of plants ringing Galveston Bay. Five hundred and seventy-six lives were lost and over five thousand people were injured. Years of safety precautions implemented since that disaster, most mandated by Occupational Safety and Health Administration rules, haven't stopped reoccurrences on a lesser scale. During the summer of 1990, an Arco plant right on the edge of Channelview went up, causing seventeen deaths. And just two years before that, a Phillips Petroleum plant along the Houston Ship Channel exploded, killing twenty-three and maiming hundreds more.

If the constant knowledge of potential peril doesn't account for the filled churches, perhaps that awareness explains why so many Channelview citizens seem to marry in their teens and start families right away. As Tony Harper explained it later, "You grow up, you get married, you work, you have kids. Then you wait for the grandkids and try to give them the things you did without."

And so it was that Tony and Wanda began talking of marriage shortly after they began to date in high school. In those days Tony, like Wanda, was described by classmates as being somewhat nondescript. Short, with sandy hair and black-framed glasses, he was said by some to be "pretty much of a nerd." Wanda liked him just the same. Some say she was impressed by the Harper family's apparent prosperity. A few of Wanda's friends from high school recall her saying that some day she would drive a Cadillac like Tony's mom.

Like any teenage couple in love, they made out at almost every opportunity, sometimes on the living-room sofa at the Webb house, and they once even sneaked into Tony's bedroom at the Harper house. Despite her strict Christian upbringing, Wanda consented to sex with Tony before marriage, he says, but only after marriage had been discussed.

And so they followed through with their plans. Tony graduated in 1970 but waited for Wanda to finish school. One week after her high school graduation in 1972 the two married in the Channelview Missionary Baptist church. Wanda Webb became Wanda Harper.

Shortly after the nuptials, as so often happens, Tony began to wonder just what sort of family he had gotten himself into. He had known Wanda was close to her parents; he hadn't known that meant command performances at each and every Webb Sunday dinner. Not only that, Clyde Webb, so entrenched in his own religious beliefs, began questioning Tony about his faith's different credo.

"Mr. Webb constantly bombarded me with questions about my religion," Tony later said. "Why did I think the Church of Christ did this? Why did I think they did that? No matter what explanation I tried to give, he'd say he couldn't imagine why they did it that way." In other matters, too, Tony began to see that Wanda deferred to her parents at his expense.

"Her mom and dad were right equal with God," Tony recalled years later. "We'd be at the table eating supper, and she'd ask me a question like, 'Is there going to be Monday night football?' I'd say, Yes.' Then she'd turn to her daddy and ask, 'Is that right?' It got kind of irritating after a while."

Just thirteen months after the wedding, on July 11, 1973, Wanda gave birth to the couple's first child, Anthony Shane. Wanda named him after her husband and her favorite movie character, from the 1953 movie *Shane*, which starred Alan Ladd. She had never forgotten that touching scene at the end of the movie when the young Brandon DeWilde tearfully begged his hero to stay, crying out over and over, "Shane! Shane! Please come back, Shane!" And so she called the baby by his middle name.

By this time Tony was working two jobs to support the family. In addition to working as a clerk for Missouri Pacific Railroad, he also worked part-time selling insurance. Wanda stayed home and tended Shane in the couple's rented apartment. She made a little extra money working as a maid for her mother-in-law, Peggy Harper. On weekends Tony often begged Wanda to leave the baby with her mother so she could go out with him on one of his frequent hunting or fishing jaunts, but he says now that Wanda always refused.

Another more serious marital problem soon loomed. Tony Harper says now that he began to realize that Wanda just plain didn't like sex. "I did," he says now. "But she was raised so religiously that she was very repressed that way. She was the kind of girl who wouldn't make love with the lights on and didn't believe in ever doing it on Sunday. We used to have frequent arguments about that last one."

After years of wrangling about what was right and what was wrong about sex, Tony finally persuaded Wanda to go with him for counseling. He says that helped temporarily, but he still felt he wasn't getting his fair share of sex. He next tried calling Wanda's gynecologist, who, according to Tony, suggested that Wanda should try having a second child. "He said something about how a woman's hormones increased after her second pregnancy," Tony recalls.

Shanna Nicole Harper was born August 10, 1977, partly as a result of this effort on Tony's behalf. Wanda was immediately enamored of her baby daughter, but showed no increased interest in having sex with the child's father. So much for conventional medical wisdom. Tony Harper says he reached the end of his rope after going to a doctor because of a persistent backache.

"The doctor told me my prostate gland was getting crusted over from lack of use," Tony recalls. "He said a boy my age should be having sex more often." So it was that Tony embarked on a series of extramarital affairs, all purportedly designed to improve his health.

During this time the couple acquired a house, built by Tony with Clyde Webb's help, on a piece of land adjoining R. E. and Peggy Harper's homestead, which, in turn, was next door to Peggy's parents' home. As in most rural areas, the people of Channelview believed in the principle of do-it-yourself. All of the Harper family homes were on a heavily wooded tract on the south side of the interstate near Market Street. The area bordered several small lakes and tributaries of the Houston Ship Channel, all of which flooded heavily during rainstorms. In earlier years, says Peggy Harper, the area was tranquil and peaceful, but after industry moved in the constant clanging of heavy metal equipment spoiled the serenity.

There wasn't much serenity in Tony and Wanda's home, either, but not because of noise from the factories. Family members now recall how the young couple frequently bickered and often insulted one another in front of others.

Peggy Harper says, "Wanda would tease him and call him 'nigger butt,' because his rear end kind of stuck out as the result of a childhood accident. I had run over him with my car on the driveway when he was three; it was awful. He would call her 'beak nose.' It wasn't friendly teasing at all; it was hateful. You could tell they meant it." Peggy adds that both her son and her daughter-in-law frequently came to her seeking advice about their marital woes. "I had them coming from both sides. He would tell me one thing, she would tell me another, and I couldn't tell either one that the other had already talked to me."

Peggy says Wanda admitted that sex was a problem. "She came right out and told me, 'I don't like sex!' I tried to console her, and I told her that I had always had the same problem. It was just the way we had been raised, I told her, to think that sex was dirty and bad. But I told her that I had learned that the right thing to do about it was to go to a psychiatrist or somebody to try to get over it." Peggy notes that Wanda reacted strongly against that suggestion. "She got real upset and said, 'Never! I'm not crazy!'" And so the trouble continued.

By 1979, while Wanda stayed home with Shane and Shanna, Tony had started taking other women with him on his weekend excursions. Eventually, the inevitable happened—Wanda found out. And according to those who witnessed her reactions, she was none too pleased. For perhaps the first time in her life, the young Christian woman showed some hint of the terrible rage she was capable of.

Learning of the location of one of Tony's rendezvous, Wanda reportedly grabbed a pistol and raced to the scene, which happened to be in front of a scuba diving shop. Wanda leapt from her car, brandishing the pistol, and lurched toward Tony and his girlfriend. The girlfriend screamed, and Tony jumped out of the car and disarmed Wanda. Tony Harper says Wanda then calmed down and said meekly, "I've decided to come with you." When he told her it was too late for that, he remembers her saying, "You'll be sorry."

When Tony came home at the end of the weekend, the locks had been changed and his belongings were neatly packed in boxes in the garage. "One thing about Wanda," Tony now remembers, "She was very fastidious." Even in the heat of anger she had taken the time to carefully pack his things. Cleanliness is next to Godliness, perhaps.

The marriage between Wanda and Tony was essentially over. Although the couple would try several times over the next year to reconcile, they finally divorced in May of 1980. As a parting shot, Wanda ratted on Tony to the railroad company where he worked, reporting that he had pilfered goods. She was ecstatic when he was fired.

Wanda Webb Harper wasted no time in getting on with her life alone. In the divorce settlement, she got to keep both the kids and the modest house Tony had built with Clyde Webb's help. She quickly brushed up on her secretarial skills and went out to find a job. In the bustling climate of the Texas oil business of 1980, that didn't take too long. Wanda soon had a position as secretary to the president of American Hose Specialty Company, which was located closer to Houston near the ship channel on Homestead Road. American Hose was a privately owned company that sold a variety of oil-field equipment like hoses and gaskets.

Wanda seemed to enjoy her new-found freedom and career. For the first time in her life she was earning her own money and could spend it however she liked. She began to take special pride in the nice, stylish clothes she wore and to pay close attention to her hair, nails, and makeup. Her mother helped out with the children during the day, and in the evenings Wanda diligently devoted hours to the children's activities.

Little Shanna was still only a preschooler, but Shane was already involved in Little League activities at the local YMCA and had frequent school functions as well. Wanda made sure that Shanna was involved as much as possible and saw to it that Shanna was among the little girls who got to be cheerleaders for their older brothers' Little League teams. She was as careful about Shanna's grooming as she was about her own, and kept the little girl's blond tresses coiffed and the child spotlessly attired in nice dresses.

Wanda dated her ex-husband a few times after their divorce, but soon took up company with a man she met at work, Gordon Inglehart. Inglehart was a co-owner of American Hose, a position that did not fail to impress the twenty-six-year-old financially struggling divorcée. Although he was quite a bit older at forty-four, Inglehart was still handsome and, of course, had lots of money. The oil business was booming, and little companies all over Texas like American Hose were experiencing heady amounts of sales and enormous profits.

Gordon drove expensive cars and took Wanda to the best restaurants, often in the course of entertaining clients. For probably the first time in her life, Wanda was living a life far removed from the restrictive values of her youth. She even went so far as to sip on a cocktail at some of the fancy dinners Gordon took her to. Although Inglehart lived in Beaumont, eighty miles to the east of Channelview along Interstate 10 toward Louisiana, he was frequently in Houston on business. After dating for less than a year, Gordon even gave Wanda a new car: a shiny, sporty Mazda RX7. The couple married shortly after that in 1981.

Inglehart had also been married before and already owned a big, expensive home in one of Beaumont's nicest neighborhoods. Wanda sold the house she and Tony had owned in Channelview, packed up the children, and moved to Beaumont with her new husband. When she put her house up for sale, members of the Harper family recall that Tony wanted to buy it, since it was part of the Harper family compound. Wanda refused to sell to her ex-husband and, in fact, ended up selling the house to people Peggy Harper says were undesirables. "They were awful people. There was always a lot of noise and commotion over there. Finally they lost it in foreclosure."

Once settled in Beaumont, Wanda enjoyed her new life as a well-to-do suburban housewife. She enrolled the children in the Beaumont public schools and even signed up for some interior design classes at Lamar University. Gordon was a generous husband and gave Wanda lots of diamond jewelry and a big clothing allowance. He welcomed Wanda's children into his home, and even went to many of their school and Little League functions. He almost always accompanied the family to church on Sunday and never objected to frequent trips to Channelview to visit Wanda's parents or to their staying in his home whenever they liked.

Tony Harper was awarded twice-monthly weekend visitation in the divorce decree. Every other Friday evening he would make the long drive to Beaumont to pick up his children and repeat the process on Sunday evenings. Sometimes he was late picking up the kids, traffic being unpredictable on Houston freeways, and, on those occasions, Wanda would be furious. Inglehart remembers one evening when he and Wanda had made plans and Tony was an hour and a half late to fetch the children, ruining Wanda and Gordon's date. They were both angry. The next time Harper failed to come on time, they packed the children off to someone else, so that when he arrived, this time only ten minutes late, no one was home. The animosity between Tony and Wanda increased over this kind of custody wrangling.

Aside from that small fly in the ointment, though, Wanda's new life seemed almost perfect. But apparently not perfect enough. Inglehart recalls that Wanda frequently complained that he didn't spend "enough time with the family." He says now, "I understand togetherness, but I felt like I had to be alone sometimes. My big vice is golf, and on Saturdays or Sundays I liked to get out there and hit that ball around. In my business I did a lot of entertaining and I saw a lot of men do a lot worse than play a little golf, but Wanda didn't see it that way."

. Then, too, other problems arose. By late 1982 and early 1983, just a year or so after the marriage to Inglehart, the oil business took a sudden sharp downturn. Thousands of companies in Texas that had made their fortunes supplying the oil industry went under. Bankruptcies hit an all-time high. American Hose was not spared, either. Gordon says by early '83 he was mired in financial problems and also had had to move his elderly mother into his home because of her failing health. It all must have been too much for Wanda, because unbeknownst to her husband she began to make plans to pull out.

"I found out about it by accident," Inglehart says years later. "One weekday morning I was a little bit later than usual going to work. Wanda had left to take the children to school. The phone rang, and it was someone from the school system asking if Wanda was still planning to transfer her children back to schools in Channelview. It was news to me, but I told the lady 'Yes.'" When Wanda returned from her short drive, Gordon confronted her. "She just said that things weren't working out," he recalls.

The following Saturday a moving van pulled up to the house. "I was supposed to play golf that day," says Gordon, "But I stayed home and helped her move. Plus, I wanted to protect my things in the house, to keep her from taking them."

Wanda headed back once again to Channelview, where she moved in with her parents pending her divorce from Inglehart. He says now that Wanda got a generous settlement. "It seemed big to me at the time. Of course, she got the Mazda RX7, and she got some nice diamonds out of it. But I didn't think she ripped me off. I really loved her. It hurt me a lot when she left. She was a very nice woman, a good woman."

That remained to be seen.

2

Our Daughters, Ourselves

In late 1983, back in Channelview, Wanda Ann once more created a new life for herself as a single mother. Using the $40,000 she had saved from the sale of her first home next door to her former in-laws along with money from her divorce settlement from Gordon Inglehart, Wanda bought a new brick house in a "nice" subdivision in Channelview called Sterling Green and moved up the social ladder of her community. This time she would be living on the right side of the interstate highway that served as the proverbial railroad track separating the "good" part of Channelview from the "bad."

By any standards other than Channelview's, Sterling Green would not be a neighborhood to envy. Its brick tract houses are small and placed closely together on small lots. Trees are scarce, many yards are bare of landscaping, and the homes all seem to have a depressing sameness to them. But the people like Wanda who bought homes there were proud of their modern new houses, so different from the trailers and crumbling wooden shacks to the south of the interstate near Market Street. Sterling Green, with its cul-de-sac streets and dishwasher-equipped kitchens, was among the best Channelview had to offer.

Wanda soon found a job in Houston as a secretary for Houston Lighting and Power and settled young Shane and Shanna once more in the Channelview schools. The children were enrolled in a nearby private school, Channelview Christian Academy, which Wanda felt would offer a more sheltered environment and teach the appropriate Christian values.

Wanda became an active member of her community. She rejoined the Channelview Missionary Baptist church, which had a newly built modern brick sanctuary on nearby Dell Dale Road, and acquired the position of church organist. She made friends with many of her neighbors in Sterling Green and enrolled her children in numerous activities—sports and band for Shane, gymnastics and dance lessons for Shanna. Both children studied the piano, as Wanda had as a child, and Shane took guitar lessons as well. Shanna was a singer at church services. Wanda became friendly with other mothers at the children's school, especially the mother of one of Shanna's classmates at Channelview Christian, a woman named Verna Heath, whose daughter, Amber, was in first grade with Shanna.

Verna Heath was also a neighbor of Wanda's. She and her husband, Jack, and their three children lived right around the corner from Wanda's house in Sterling Green. The two women had several things in common. Verna, one year older than Wanda, was also an attractive, well-groomed young mother who took pains to dress both herself and her young daughter impeccably. Amber was Verna's only daughter; she also had two sons, Aaron, who was Amber's twin, and Sean, who was born in 1981. Verna's husband Jack worked long hours as the manager of a local grocery store, Gerland's, that was part of a Houston chain. Verna's main work was her home and her children, but she still taught some classes in dance and twirling at her mother's Highlands studio. The Heaths were devout Christians, too, although they attended a different church from Wanda; they went to the Truth Tabernacle Pentecostal church.

Like Wanda with Shanna, Verna was especially close to her daughter Amber. Although Aaron, like Shanna's brother Shane, was involved in numerous athletic activities, Verna most often accompanied Amber to her lessons in baton twirling, dance, and gymnastics. Such female activities were part of a long-standing tradition in Verna's family.

Verna had grown up in the neighboring community of Highlands, to the northeast of Channelview across the San Jacinto River. She was the third oldest of the four daughters and a son born to Joyce and Felton Brown.

Joyce Brown had grown up in a traditional Texas arena of competition, the rodeo. Her family ran a small rodeo in Crosby, Texas, a small town north of Highlands. At an early age, Joyce Brown competed in barrel racing, a rodeo event in which female riders force their mounts to run an obstacle course around barrels. Those who knew her then say she was a young woman of intelligence and fierce determination.

Joyce eventually met and married Felton Brown, a young cattleman, and the couple settled in Highlands, where Felton ran a cattlemen's supply store and raised a small herd of cattle himself. Joyce opened a studio where she taught piano, baton, dance, and gymnastics to the area's girls. With her insistence on her students' hard work and dedication, Joyce proudly produced most of the area's school twirlers, drill-team stars, and cheerleaders.

Her own daughters were among them. Three of her four daughters, Benita, Verna, and Darla, were avid pupils of these gridiron half-time gyrations. Perhaps because of their mother's drill-sergeant approach to training and competition, all three were highly successful. One family friend of Joyce Brown's recalls, "For Benita, Verna, and Darla, the dancing and twirling were like a profession."

As the girls made their way through the public schools in Highlands, all were outstanding competitors, especially at twirling. Twirling is that unique art of spinning a baton in the air while strutting across a field that for some curious reason has always been especially popular in the South. Because they were trained in the art from the time they could walk, the Brown girls were well-known as being the best twirlers around.

One family friend says, "I can see why people might resent them. In whatever they do, they are the best." This friend recalls how Benita Brown, while a student at Highlands Junior High, was the best at everything she did. "And she knew it," says the friend. "She didn't brag or act like she was better than anyone else. She was just the best and she knew it, and so did everyone else. The other Brown girls were the same way."

Indeed, during her senior year at Baytown's Robert E. Lee High School, Verna Brown was not only the school band's majorette, but also won first place in the 1971 national strutting competition. Verna married Jack Heath after high school, and she began assisting her mother in teaching dance and baton at her studio, the Triple Art Baton, Dance and Model Studio in Highlands. The studio's reputation grew, and it soon became *the* place for ambitious mothers to enroll their young daughters. Anyone who was anyone, or wanted to be, enrolled their girls at Triple Art.

Both Verna and her mother acquired reputations for being strict taskmasters. Mrs. Brown often told mothers not to waste their time or hers by bringing their daughters to class if the girls were not 100 percent involved in learning dance or baton. "She was demanding, she was tough, but she was good," recalls one former student of Mrs. Brown.

Verna shared her mother's obsession with the perfection of these feminine skills of football season. Like her mother, Verna was often bluntly honest with mothers whose daughters did not show special talent. "But she was still a very nice, sweet person," recalls one mother. "Still, she wouldn't let the class leave until they got a routine down."

Jana Hornberger, a student of Verna's during the seventies, recalls Verna and her mother, "They both knew how to instill willpower. They are very organized, very competitive, take-charge kind of people, but I guess you have to be to handle little girls and their mothers." Jana adds that some people didn't like the Brown women, but even so, "There was no doubt that the best bet to make it as a twirler or a cheerleader was to study at their school."

Little Amber Heath, born into the third generation of this twirling dynasty, had a built-in advantage over the competition throughout her childhood. Her mother approached Amber's lessons with the same critical eye toward perfection that she used on her other students and insisted that Amber practice her routines daily from the time she was old enough to carry a baton. By the time she was three years old, Amber was winning twirling competitions.

Because Wanda's new job in Houston required leaving her Channelview home by seven o'clock each morning in order to be on the job by eight, Wanda found she needed help in getting the kids to school. She turned to her friend Verna and arranged a carpool. Verna Heath would pick Shane and Shanna up each morning and drop them at school along with her own children. After school, the Harper kids would stay at the Heath home until either Wanda or her mother picked them up after work.

Shanna Harper and Amber Heath became fast friends. They would often sleep over at each other's houses and were involved in many of the same activities. They both took gymnastics lessons and dance classes, and, because they were classmates at a small elementary school, were often in the same pageants and school plays, requiring that they practice together for their roles.

Little girls in Texas seem to be groomed for the stage from an early age, and Shanna and Amber were among an elite group. The mothers of such girls appear to take as much pleasure, probably more, from their daughters' activities as the girls do themselves. And the smaller the community, the greater the importance the mothers seem to attach to positions that might seem trivial in an urban setting. At some point during their early childhood, for example, both Shanna and Amber were angling for a position as cheerleader for a boys' Little League team. The honor was bestowed on the girls whose families had managed to sell the most candy for the league. Wanda made every effort to accomplish that, lobbying friends, family, and fellow church members to buy candy from her. But at the last minute, before the winner was announced, someone else outsold her. That someone else was Verna Heath, and Amber, not Shanna, won the coveted spot as the team's cheerleader.

That loss was not enough to damage Wanda's friendship with Verna. Besides, Wanda still needed her neighbor's help in ferrying the children to school, since she was still working in Houston. From time to time the two women went shopping together at the nearby San Jacinto mall when their schedules allowed it. On occasion, Wanda would accompany Verna to visit her parents in Highlands, and they sometimes took the children swimming together in the summer months. Theirs was the sort of easy friendship where each could ask the other for favors and help whenever needed.

Once, when Wanda planned a trip to the Astroworld amusement park in Houston with her children, she went to Verna's around the corner and asked Verna to braid her hair to keep it out of her face as she rode the thrill rides at the park. In turn, when Verna had her fourth baby, Blake, in 1988, she asked Wanda's help in taking her children to school while she convalesced from the birth.

Shanna and Amber remained close friends, too. But not best friends; that was a title both girls coincidentally reserved for their mothers. Wanda and Shanna had an especially close relationship, perhaps because Wanda had always enjoyed a special closeness with her own mother, Verna. Even as an adult, Wanda saw her mother daily. In turn, she insisted on creating the same kind of relationship with Shanna. The two frequently wore matching mother-daughter outfits.

Verna Heath was extremely close to Amber, as well, but had more distractions since she had three other children and a husband. Still, she usually spoke of Amber's activities as if they were her own, as, "We are going to have to practice today," or "We are trying out for cheerleader again," in that annoying style so many stage mothers adopt when speaking of their children.

During this period of time, the mid-1980s, Wanda's relationship with her first husband, Tony Harper, remained strained. On two separate occasions Wanda threatened Tony with court actions if he refused to give her more child support. By this time he was selling insurance, first for his own agency, Harper Insurance, and later for another agency in a community north of Houston, near the Kingwood area where he had relocated with his new wife, Mickie. In order to avoid a costly legal battle with his ex-wife, Tony Harper agreed to increase his support payments to $550 a month. Tony continued to see his children on alternate weekends and shared them with Wanda on holidays such as Christmas. Aside from the occasional financial dispute, he and Wanda were still able to conduct reasonably cordial discussions about the children's welfare—school grades, activities, and the like.

In 1986 Wanda decided to marry for a third time. Since becoming organist at her church, Wanda had become close friends with the church choirmaster, an older, prosperous businessman named C.D. Holloway. Holloway had already been married three times before and was said to have a weakness for well-turned-out younger women. Wanda, as most everyone knew, was still blatantly ambitious at age thirty-two, and continued to cling to her life-long dream of getting rich. After she started dating C. D. and the relationship became more serious, friends remember she bragged that she would soon be living in River Oaks, Houston's most prestigious neighborhood and home to most of that city's rich and powerful.

C.D. Holloway might have been twenty years Wanda's senior and going gray fast, but he owned a successful oil field construction company, Holloco, as well as his own airplane. He was a tall, stocky man with an imposing presence but quiet demeanor who was given to wearing gold jewelry—pinkie rings and an expensive watch. He also flashed a lot of cash around, frequently keeping as much as eight to ten thousand dollars with him for emergencies. Last, but not least, he always drove a Lincoln Town Car. All of the Holloway family, which hailed from Munroe, Louisiana, drove Lincoln Town Cars; it was a family tradition. It seemed to Wanda that with C. D. she'd finally have all her heart's desires: money, status, a nice home, and a fancy car.

The couple married with little fanfare later that year. Some say the hastily planned wedding occurred after an overnight church outing during which "something had happened" between Wanda and C. D. Pressured by their fellow fundamentalists to do the right thing after their moment of weakness, Wanda and C. D. took the plunge.

But things didn't turn out exactly as Wanda had planned. C. D. didn't rush out and buy her a mansion in River Oaks. He didn't even buy her a two-story house in Channelview. Instead, he moved into her modest three-bedroom tract home with the pink burglar bars, the one she had bought in 1983 after her marriage to Inglehart ended. Friends recall that Wanda was somewhat disappointed by this development, but was soon mollified when C. D. gave her a huge diamond ring—a yellow-tinted canary diamond, valued at more than $175,000. More diamond jewelry would follow. C. D., says one family friend, "had excellent taste in jewelry." Wanda's new husband also bought her an almost-new Jeep Grand Wagoneer, a deluxe four-wheel-drive vehicle with enough room for Shane and Shanna and their friends. Wanda was proud of the fact that, if new, the car would cost near $40,000.

She was also able to quit her job and once more become a full-time housewife and mother. Although C. D. did not allow her complete access to his large bank accounts, he gave Wanda a generous monthly allowance of two thousand dollars to cover routine household bills. Anytime she needed more, C. D. freely produced it. Soon Wanda became known as one of the best-dressed women in Channelview. She frequently took Shanna on shopping excursions to Houston's upscale shopping mall, the Galleria, to outfit them both in designer clothing.

With more free time and more expendable income, Wanda paid even more attention to her always-careful grooming. Her hair was carefully colored and permed routinely; she usually wore it long and full, in many small curls that puffed out around her head in the style known as "big hair" that became passé many years ago in stylish circles, but which the women of Channelview have stubbornly clung to. Her nails were manicured and sculpted into long, red spikes—the surest evidence that she was a lady of leisure, since no one could work with such fingernails.

Wanda maintained a trim, perfect-size-four figure by arduously working out for several hours at a stretch at a local gym two or three times a week. It was even rumored that C. D.'s money had helped here too, providing Wanda with the money for a tummy-tuck operation and other plastic surgery procedures designed to create a better body.

C. D., unlike Wanda's second husband, Gordon Inglehart, was happy to stay home with her and the children. "They were like a real family," recalls one close family friend. "I was always envious of them because they were all so close." Family dinners, attending church as a group, and going out to eat on Sundays became routine for the newly organized Holloway household. Wanda cooked and cleaned for the family and was said to have an immaculate house. "Nothing was ever out of place," says a frequent visitor to Wanda's home. A weekly maid service helped with the heavy cleaning, but Wanda did the rest. And she did her own decorating, which C. D.'s generous allowance helped finance. She even had luxurious Pakistani rugs custom made to match her living-room furniture.

But even with all these advantages, Wanda still had the fiercely set jaw and the hard gleam in her eye of an unsatisfied woman. Having secured an enviable position for herself in the community, she now set about trying to advance her children's. She wanted the same things for them that she wanted for herself: to have the best and to be the best.

When Shanna was in the fifth grade at Channelview Christian Academy, the school arranged to offer gymnastics instructions to its students on the campus. Since Wanda still harbored the hope that her daughter would one day be a cheerleader, and since modern-day cheerleading has evolved into more of an athletic competition than a beauty pageant, she signed Shanna up for the classes in order to better prepare her for junior high cheerleader tryouts. That competition would take place the next year, when Shanna would be in sixth grade. Verna Heath, who had the same aspiration for her daughter, enrolled Amber in the class too.

Both mothers avidly followed their daughters' progress in learning the tumbling, jumping, and flipping that would be necessary for cheering. Although several other girls were in the class, Verna Heath gradually noticed that Wanda seemed most concerned with measuring Shanna's progress by Amber's. She would later reflect, "I saw a competitiveness in her in that she compared the two girls. It just always was Amber that she compared with Shanna. Not the other kids."

Perhaps because of her long history of training under both her mother and her grandmother, Amber, in fact, seemed to have more innate ability at gymnastics than Shanna. This did not escape Wanda's watchful eyes. During practice, she would stand on the sidelines with tightly folded arms and alternately stare at Shanna and then Amber, mentally noting the differences in their skills. Verna Heath recalled that Wanda even took action. "She was upset that Amber could do body work that Shanna could not do," said Verna years later. "Went to the teacher complaining, 'Why can't Shanna do aerial or backflip?'" Amber Heath could.

Wanda decided that Shanna needed practice, and lots of it. She arranged a little platform stage for Shanna in the garage at home, complete with a mirror and light so the child could watch herself perform her routines. Wanda insisted that Shanna practice every day, even if that schedule meant Shanna might have to rush through her homework assignments. Sometimes Wanda even did the homework herself, or had Shane or one of his friends pitch in to get the school work done while Shanna worked out in the garage.

When Shanna finished the fifth grade, Wanda decided to switch her from Channelview Christian Academy to the nearby public school, Cobb Elementary, run by the Channelview Independent School District. Foremost among the reasons for the transfer was that during the sixth grade students from Cobb were allowed to try out to be cheerleaders for the district's junior high, Alice Johnson Junior High, which was attended by the district's seventh- and eighth-grade students. The junior high had two feeder elementary schools, Cobb and DeZavala. Cheerleader elections at Alice Johnson were held each spring for the fall season that followed in next school year; four seventh-grade cheerleaders were chosen—two from Cobb Elementary and two from DeZavala Elementary. The eighth-grade cheerleaders were chosen from girls then in the seventh grade.

Wanda had her mind made up that Shanna would be a cheerleader at Alice Johnson. If she was a cheerleader, Shanna would be guaranteed all the attention and popularity Wanda felt was her due. Wanda herself had always longed for such an outstanding position when she was a student; that had been denied her, both because her father forbade it and also because, quite simply, Wanda would never have made it if she had tried out. She had been neither cute nor popular. And so she was determined her daughter would experience success instead. Wanda couldn't be a cheerleader, but she could at least be a cheerleader's mom.

With the approaching spring of 1989, and the time for Shanna to try out for junior-high cheerleader, friends say Wanda became more and more intense about making Shanna practice. Her son Shane's activities took a distant second place to Shanna's cheerleading lessons, gymnastic workouts, and practice sessions. Shane would later recall how he once asked his mother to attend his open house at school, only to be told she couldn't make it because she had to take Shanna to cheerleading practice.

Wanda was convinced that Shanna was practically guaranteed a place on the Alice Johnson cheerleading squad because of all the time and energy she had spent in preparation. Besides, since Amber Heath had stayed at Channelview Christian for the sixth-grade, and thus would not be among the contestants from Cobb Elementary, Wanda thought the competition was virtually eliminated.

She was wrong. Unbeknownst to Wanda, Verna Heath had gone to Alice Johnson Junior High in the middle of Amber's sixth grade year at Channelview Christian and told the public school personnel that Amber would be attending Alice Johnson for the seventh grade. She wanted to know if her daughter would be allowed to try out for cheerleader, even though she was not currently attending one of the Channelview elementary schools that traditionally supplied the contestants for the seventh-grade cheerleader spots. Because the school officials had seldom been faced with this decision, and could see no reason to refuse Verna, they agreed to let Amber try out with the pool of applicants from Cobb Elementary. They reasoned that since Amber would have attended Cobb if she went to a public school, she should have to compete against that group of contestants. And, after all, the Heaths paid their school taxes just like everybody else.

That meant that Shanna would face Amber in competition. Once again, during practice sessions, Wanda could see that Amber had skills Shanna did not. But she was not overly concerned, not yet. After all, two girls would be selected from the Cobb group to be Alice Johnson cheerleaders; maybe both Shanna and Amber would make it.

Before the time of the actual tryouts, held in March each year, the junior-high cheerleader sponsor, Donna Jackson, held a meeting for candidates and their parents to explain the rules of the competition. Wanda, Shanna, and Wanda's mother, Verna Webb, attended the meeting, as did Verna Heath and Amber. Ms. Jackson outlined how the cheerleaders would be chosen. First, all the girls trying out would perform in front of a panel of judges made up of college cheerleaders. These judges would select six semifinalists, who would then perform before the Alice Johnson student body. The student body would then hold a popular election to choose two of the six to be their seventh-grade cheerleaders from Cobb. They would also elect two from the six semifinalists from DeZavala Elementary. Before the popular election, the semifinalists would be allowed to actively campaign at the Alice Johnson campus, passing out leaflets, putting up posters, and generally trying to win name recognition and votes.

The week before the tryouts, a cheerleading clinic was held at the junior high for all would-be cheerleaders. Each day the girls trying out would go to Alice Johnson and work out with the school's current cheering squad, learning the school's cheers and certain maneuvers. Each contestant would be required to perform one cheer alone, one chant alone, and then one cheer and one chant with a group. During the group cheer, the girls would be allowed to strut their stuff, show their spirit, by executing whatever special "body work", as it's called, that they had learned—flip-flops, aerials, handstands, round-offs. All were special gymnastic moves the girls studied, some successfully. A few of the moves, like the aerial, which is a flip without the use of hands or feet, were too difficult for Shanna. Most of the girls attending the clinic were accompanied by their mothers, who eagerly watched from the sidelines. Wanda Holloway and Verna Heath were, of course, among them.

Verna Heath thinks now that Wanda started openly resenting her and her daughter during this time. "There was a lot of tension at the sixth-grade tryouts," she would later say. "Wanda would watch Amber, with her arms folded, and make little comments, like, 'Oh, well, she's going too fast, she's doing that cheer too fast.' She wasn't watching the other girls, only Amber."

The day of the actual tryouts all of the mothers were in the school auditorium audience at Alice Johnson Junior High. Verna Heath remembers that Wanda seemed especially tense and hateful toward Amber. "When Amber was on the floor, she started yelling for Shanna, when Shanna wasn't even on the floor at the time," Verna says.

Both Amber and Shanna were fortunate enough to be among the six semifinalists chosen by the panel of judges. Wanda was ecstatic; so was Verna. The girls themselves were excited, but seemed, on the whole, to keep the competition more in perspective than their mothers did. It was, after all, just a contest for seventh-grade cheerleader. Nevertheless, they eagerly helped their mothers design campaign leaflets for the upcoming at-large vote by the student body. Some of the parents even bought trinkets and geegaws for their daughters to pass out to the students who would be casting the desperately wanted votes. Pencils, rulers, candies, and gum littered the school's hallways during the two days of campaigning. Verna Heath cleverly bought dozens of Heath candy bars for Amber to pass out.

The election was held at the end of a school day that March. In order to ensure accuracy and fairness, all the ballots were cast on Scantron computer forms, the kind of forms used by most modern schools for standardized tests that call for filling in little circles with a number-two pencil. The forms are then fed through a computer for tabulation. The cheerleader sponsor, Donna Jackson, was responsible for collecting all the ballots and taking them to the school librarian, who would perform the Scantron vote totaling in a short period of time after school.

After all of the girls had performed, and the students were dismissed for the day after casting their votes, the cheerleader hopefuls and their mothers anxiously waited in the school hallways for the election returns. The procedure Alice Johnson used each year was to have the results announced privately to the current crop of cheerleaders, who were then allowed to break the news to the newcomers. The number of votes each girl received was not released; the winners were simply told they had won.

Donna Jackson remembered later that, in her opinion, Wanda Holloway had acted strangely that day. After Ms. Jackson had received the results from the school librarian, and was on her way into the classroom where the current cheerleaders were waiting to hear who would be joining them on the squad, she says she was confronted by Wanda in the hallway. Wanda's lips were tightly pursed and her posture and facial expression suggested she was angry. "I heard you've already told some people the results," she hissed at Ms. Jackson.

Donna Jackson was completely taken aback. She explained to Wanda that she, herself, had not yet learned who the winners were, having just picked up the vote counts from the school library. Jackson later said she was very surprised at Wanda's behavior that afternoon. "It was like she was accusing me of something that I didn't do," she recalled. "I was shocked, because up until then everything had been fine, she hadn't been like that at all."

Donna Jackson then continued into her classroom to announce the results to the eager girls waiting within: The winners from Cobb Elementary were Summer Rutledge and Amber Heath. Shanna Harper was among the losers. Shanna handled the loss well; her mother did not.

Wanda went home with Shanna that day and began to brood. "Something's not right here," she thought to herself, and within a few days she decided to do something about it. She marched down to Alice Johnson Junior High and demanded a meeting with Donna Jackson. She wanted to know what place Shanna had come in, how close to winning her daughter had been. Ms. Jackson didn't know if she could give out that information, so she suggested that Wanda accompany her to the principal's office to ask his permission. After Principal James Barker learned of Wanda's request, he told Jackson to go ahead and release the vote count to Wanda. Wanda was then told that Shanna had come in third. Summer Rutledge had the most votes, around 150. Amber was second with 120, and Shanna was a distant third with 40 votes.

This news didn't sit well with Wanda. The more she thought about it, the more she felt that Shanna had been ripped off in the whole competition. If Amber Heath had not been among the contestants, she theorized, Shanna would have been second and among the cheerleaders. Amber shouldn't even have been allowed to try out, Wanda decided, since she hadn't even been a student at Cobb Elementary but instead had attended a private school. The written bylaws that governed the cheerleading competition clearly stated that two girls would be selected from Cobb and two from DeZavala. No provision was made for girls from private schools.

Wanda talked at length about this injustice to her husband, C. D. She talked about it to her children, to her friends, and to the rest of her family. Before long, she and her mother, Verna Webb, decided to confront the Channelview School Board about the matter and asked for a closed meeting after the board's next regularly scheduled session. There Wanda presented her grievance and asked that the board make a special exception because of the circumstances of that year's election and create another spot on the Alice Johnson cheerleading squad for Shanna. Wanda said she thought that Amber's participation in the competition was a violation of the school's Cheerleading Constitution. But rather than ask that the child be disqualified, she instead asked that amends be made by giving Shanna her rightful place on the squad while retaining Amber.

The board considered Wanda's request but decided they would only grant it in part. They did not add another position to the squad, and they did not remove Amber Heath. Instead, they made a new rule that in future competitions only students from the designated public elementary schools would be allowed to compete. That wasn't much consolation to Wanda, however, who could only sit and wait for the next year's competition.

Later, Verna Heath learned of Wanda's visit to the school board. In a community like Channelview, as in most small towns, news travels fast and gossip spreads faster, like fire ants. Wanda later said she noticed a distinct cooling in the once warm friendship she had shared with Verna. "I thought she was mad at me," said Wanda, "because right after the school board meeting, if I would pass her, you know, in the street, driving by or something, she would just kind of look at me. Before, we had waved, and you know, it was a friendlier situation. But it got kind of cold."

By the conclusion of the next year's cheerleader tryouts, the cold war between Wanda and Verna would gradually heat up to a hot rage, at least on Wanda's part. Throughout the rest of 1989 and the early part of 1990, Wanda insisted that Shanna continue her gymnastics classes and her cheerleading practice in the garage-turned-studio at home so that she would be ready in the spring of 1990 to once more compete in, and this time win, the elections for cheerleader. Wanda even hired a private coach to work with Shanna, a girl who was a Channelview High School cheerleader.

As the campaign season approached, the school cheerleader sponsor once again called a meeting of all interested girls and their parents to discuss some changes in the rules of the competition. In addition to the new rule resulting from Wanda's discussion with the school board the previous year, the one barring private school students from trying out, Donna Jackson announced that new guidelines relating to the personal campaigning by semifinalists were being issued.

In 1989, when the girls had been allowed to pass out vote incentives like candy and trinkets, many mothers complained that things had gotten out of hand. Teachers had complained, too, of all the chaos such items had created in the classrooms. The school officials had therefore decided that this time, for the 1990 spring elections (for cheerleading spots for the 1990–1991 school year, beginning the following fall), only posters and fliers would be allowed as campaign materials.

A sheet of campaign rules was passed to each girl and her parents:

> Rule number 1 said that each girl would be allowed to post two poster-board-size signs in a designated area.
>
> Rule number 2 said that the student body could be given small name tags with the candidates' names written on them.
>
> Rule number 3 stated that "candy, gum, cookies, et cetera, are not allowed in any school. Violations will result in your immediate dismissal from the competition."

Like the other mothers, Wanda Holloway was, by her own admission, aware of the rules.

As the time of the campaign drew near, Wanda grew more and more anxious about Shanna's chances of winning. Desperate for any and all advice about how to improve her daughter's prospects, Wanda asked almost everyone she met if they had any suggestions for Shanna's campaigning. She even called her ex-husband Tony who suggested ordering some pencils with Shanna's name inscribed as a vote-getting handout. Because Rule number 3 did not specifically mention pencils in the list of forbidden items, Wanda took Tony's suggestion and ordered several hundred pencils and rulers inscribed with VOTE FOR SHANNA. She and Tony split the cost—two hundred dollars.

As in 1989, Shanna was once again chosen by the judges as a semi-finalist in the 1990 competition. Before the days of campaigning, another parents' meeting was held with the cheerleader sponsor. Wanda decided to play it safe and ask whether the pencils and rulers she had bought for Shanna were allowable campaign materials. No, she was clearly told. Shanna was not to bring either item to the school.

The night before campaigning began, Wanda was busily helping Shanna make campaign posters. She had cleverly designed some signs in the shape of a megaphone, glued and glittered them up, and painted them with her daughter's name. She had previously bought some little sticks to attach as handles for the signs, so they could be held aloft by Shanna-fans. But as the sign making progressed that evening, she realized she hadn't bought enough handles.

When C. D. came home from work, he found his wife fretting over the need for more handles. Wanda asked him if he'd run out and buy some paint stirrers, small flat-wooden sticks, to complete the rest of the megaphone signs she had waiting for handles. Exhausted from work, and probably tired of hearing about the cheerleader competition, C. D. suggested that Wanda could just use the stash of rulers she'd bought with Shanna's name on them as handles. "No sense wasting them," the prudent businessman in him said. Pressed for time, Wanda unthinkingly complied with C. D.'s idea. She used the rulers as handles on fifteen of the twenty-five signs she had made for Shanna. This would prove to be a big mistake.

The next day Shanna went off to school armed with all her campaign materials and passed them out to her fellow students. It wasn't long before one of the megaphone signs with a ruler handle was spotted by Donna Jackson, the cheerleader sponsor. "I couldn't believe it," she said later. "I thought we had settled the issue about the rulers." Donna Jackson was more than a little angry about what she saw as this flagrant flouting of the competition's rules. She went straight to the principal's office. Because he was away on personal business, the acting principal was Ida Gilbert, who usually served as assistant principal. Donna Jackson told Mrs. Gilbert of Shanna's violation of the rules and asked how to proceed. Mrs. Gilbert, in turn, called an assistant superintendent with the Channelview School District for his input. The assistant superintendent held a meeting after school that day with Mrs. Gilbert and Donna Jackson to discuss the problem. Some of the other contestants' mothers, including Amber Heath's and Summer Rutledge's, also had talked to Ms. Jackson.

The school officials later called Wanda and asked her to come to a meeting at the school the next morning. When Wanda had arrived, and was waiting in the principal's office, Shanna was summoned from her classes to join the group. There, in the privacy of the principal's office, Shanna and her mother were told that Shanna would be disqualified from the competition because she had brought the forbidden rulers to school.

The mother's and daughter's reactions to the news were telling. Mrs. Gilbert recalls that Shanna took her disqualification fairly well; there were no tears or recriminations from her. Although she was told she could have an excused absence for the rest of the day if she wished, to go home with her mother, Shanna chose to return to her classes. Wanda, however, was beside herself. She wept openly for several minutes in Mr. Biggot's office. Before she composed herself and left several minutes later, Wanda sobbed, "It was all my fault. Mine and C. D.'s."

It would not be long, however, before Wanda would decide that Shanna's disqualification was not her fault at all, or C. D.'s. Instead she would soon blame it all on Verna Heath. It was Verna, Wanda would conclude, who had manipulated the school officials and robbed Shanna of the chance to be a cheerleader.

_____**3**

Why Cheerleading?

The question immediately arises: What is it about cheerleading that would cause Wanda Holloway to become so determined to have her daughter become a part of it?

There are many possible reasons, all of which only partially explain that one woman's incredible zeal to see Shanna Harper become a cheerleader. While there are undoubtedly millions of mothers who urge their daughters to try out for cheerleading posts, Wanda Holloway may be the only one to go to such extreme lengths to achieve that end.

Cheerleading, especially in the South, represents for many young girls the pinnacle of achievement. Being a cheerleader for one's school is, for a girl, comparable to a boy being chosen first-string quarterback or captain of his football team. It means you are on center stage, with all the spotlights on, and the envy of all.

John Hawkins, the Dallas-based author of the 1990 book, *Texas Cheerleading*, sums it all up. "Being a cheerleader means you have what I call the three Bs," he says. "Beauty, brains, and brawn." According to Hawkins, who researched his subject thoroughly, modern-day cheerleaders must be excellent academically as well as physically fit and attractive because of stringent school rules that forbid failing students from participating in extracurricular activities.

In the last twenty years or so, Hawkins points out, competition for cheerleading positions has become more and more intense, as more and more children seek the limelight it offers. But it wasn't always that way. The practice of having designated cheering sections for school teams began in the 1880s at Princeton University, which had all-male "yell leaders" to inspire support from college students watching the school's football team. Soon universities all over the country copied Princeton and formed similar squads. In the late nineteenth century and early twentieth century few women even attended universities. Thus, at the time, female cheerleaders did not exist. By the 1920s, however, high schools across the land began to imitate the colleges by forming cheering squads, and girls were allowed to participate at that level, though colleges still restricted the role to males.

When high-school girls were permitted to help inspire team spirit, explains Hawkins, they were not called "yell leaders" like their male counterparts. "In those days it would have been unthinkable for a young lady to yell," he laughs. "And so they started calling themselves cheerleaders."

It was not until World War II, when many of the young men went off to war and women assumed roles formerly reserved only for men, that college girls finally got a chance to lead their fellow students in spirit yells and cheers. And the girls took it up with a vengeance.

In the early years of cheerleading, from the late 1940s up through the 1960s, cheerleaders were elected by the student bodies of schools more on the basis of looks and popularity than any particular skill. But nowadays, as officials at the Dallas-based National Cheerleading Association (NCA) are quick to point out, cheerleading is almost more of a sport than a beauty contest.

The NCA was started by a former cheerleader, Lawrence Herkimer, now sixty-seven, who had lead his cheering squad at Southern Methodist University in the 1940s. Herkimer is famous in his own right as being the inventor of the "Herkie" jump, a cheering maneuver in which the cheerleader jumps high in the air with one knee bent and the other straight. After graduating college, Herkimer just couldn't get cheerleading out of his blood. Against the advice of his friends and associates, in 1948 Herkimer took his life's savings and started a cheerleader-supply business.

His business has become so successful that it now boasts close to $50 million in annual sales of cheerleader uniforms, pompons, megaphones, and the like. The NCA is probably the major supplier of such paraphernalia in the United States. In addition, the NCA sponsors annual cheerleading summer camps all over the country for both high-school and college cheerleaders, who gather together with other schools' squads to learn new maneuvers and practice their sport.

Every year the NCA also sponsors national cheerleading competitions, where squads from across the land compete for the titles of best squad and best individual cheerleader. At a recent competition held in Dallas, the NCA's Carol Wagers, who is director of the company's high-school cheering division, explained that nowadays cheerleaders are judged on a lot more than their spirit and their looks. "It really is like a sport," she said. "The judges look at qualities like precision of movement, motion technique, jumps, tumbling, stunts, and creativity." But even Wagers conceded, "It does help to be attractive."

Both Amber Heath and Shanna Harper had been going to gymnastics classes since the fifth grade to acquire the necessary physical skills for cheering. Most of the maneuvers taught are definitely related to tumbling and other gymnastic skills. Some of the pyramids today's cheerleading squads are able to perform would rival a circus acrobatic act.

Much of cheering these days is physically demanding, and can be dangerous, as well. The NCA, for example, has had to limit the height of pyramids that competing teams can build at meets because in recent years, explained Lawrence Herkimer, squads were stacking people five-high into the air. "We were worried about people getting hurt," he said, "And so we had to change the rules." Herkimer credits the popularity of female gymnasts like Nadia Comaneci and Mary Lou Retton with adding the new emphasis on gymnastics to the formerly innocuous activity of yelling on the sidelines.

And it has taken a toll. The Consumer Products Safety Commission tabulated over eight thousand cheerleading-related injuries in one recent year, a dramatic increase over previous years. Injuries range from torn ligaments to broken bones to broken necks. Not to mention the injuries that could arise from jealous rivals plotting against each other.

So why do so many girls, and boys, for that matter, want to be cheerleaders? For girls, the answer seems most related to popularity and attractiveness. "If you're a cheerleader, everybody loves you," said one high-school pep squad member from Las Vegas at a recent NCA meet.

Suzette Derrick, who with her two sisters wrote a book, *Deep in the Heart of Texas*, about their experiences as members of the Dallas Cowboys cheerleaders, said recently, "A girl who attains cheerleader, whether in high school or professionally, is like a pillar of the community. It represents success, it represents the epitome of what a girl wants to be."

Cheerleaders have it all: looks, popularity, physical fitness and prowess, and good citizenship. Derrick, who, like her sisters, has long blond tresses, a great body, and wholesome good looks, said, "I've been a cheerleader all my life." Her mother, she explained, was a dance instructor, like Verna Heath, and made sure that all of her daughters participated in dance and went out for cheerleader whenever possible. "My mom was very strong," admits Derrick, "but she only pushed us because she wanted us to excel. She never allowed us to say 'No.' Whatever our dreams were, she forced us to pursue them."

Suzette insists her mother's efforts paid off. "My becoming a cheerleader changed the whole course of my life. I was a very shy child and didn't have many social skills. When I became cheerleader, suddenly everyone wanted to be my friend." There are other benefits, too, says Derrick. "When you have to get out and perform in front of huge crowds, you have to learn to be a leader, and those skills can help you the rest of your life."

Lawrence Herkimer seconds that opinion. "When you develop the ability to get out in front of a group and speak to them with authority, it affects you your whole life," he says. "You may end up head of a company or something."

Then, too, explains Herkie, cheerleading is a wholesome activity. "You don't have to worry about any of these kids getting on drugs or running around drinking," he said as he pointed to a crowd of cheerleaders at a Dallas competition. "These girls are up on pedestals, and once they get there, they don't want to risk falling off."

Indeed, many cheerleaders refuse to get off, and parlay the skills learned from cheering into successful modeling or acting careers. Many current leading ladies got their start in the public eye by being high-school cheerleaders. Sissy Spacek and Phyllis George Brown were cheerleaders at their Texas high schools. So was former Texas governor John Connally. Meryl Streep, a serious actress, once waved a pompon, as did comedian Steve Martin. Even Hollywood producer Aaron Spelling once did cartwheels in front of football crowds. The list is almost endless. In Houston, almost every major socialite was once a cheerleader. Lynn Wyatt, international jet setter and former close friend of Princess Grace of Monaco, is now married to multimillionaire oil and gas tycoon Oscar Wyatt. Lynn got her toehold in society as a student at Houston's San Jacinto High, where she was elected a cheerleader. Another major social player in Houston is Carolyn Farb, now a wealthy divorcée with a mansion just doors away from Lynn Wyatt's. Carolyn was a cheerleader, too, and now says the skills she acquired then have been invaluable to her in her work as a major charity fundraiser.

Many cheerleaders go on to enter beauty pageants after high school, and many go on to win. Beauty pageants are just one step away from cheerleading competitions, anyway, since many of the same attributes are judged in each: looks, poise, personality, and physical fitness. Former Miss Texas Christy Fitchner, who became a runner-up Miss Universe and an actress, also got her start as a Texas cheerleader.

It only makes sense that cheerleaders, who are usually the cutest and brightest girls in high school, would also be successful after high school. Some choose to continue in cheering and audition for places on professional football or basketball team squads like the Dallas Cowboys cheerleaders or the L. A. Lakers girls. There they enjoy an even broader audience than before. Suzette Derrick explains, "I got to travel all over the world as a Dallas Cowboy cheerleader. I learned so much about handling television and the media, plus I was a celebrity of sorts, and would be asked to sign autographs wherever I went." It was all such a wonderful experience for Suzette that she urged her two younger sisters to follow in her footsteps, and they did.

The Dallas Cowboys cheerleaders, formed in 1972, did much to further the idea that somehow Texas and cheerleading are inalienably linked. Cheerleading, of course, is part and parcel of football, and football has always been big in Texas. As the Cowboys rose in popularity, and were eventually known as "America's Team," the Dallas Cheerleaders, with their trademarked star-studded vests and navel-baring hot pants and white boots, soon became many a little girl's idols. One fourteen-year-old girl told a reporter for the *Houston Chronicle*, "I saw the Dallas Cowboys cheerleaders for the first time when I was three, and I immediately said, 'I want to be like them.'" Ever since, she explained, she has worked toward that goal.

John Hawkins says that many of the girls he met while on the cheering circuit echoed the same idea. "Most I talked to had made up their minds by age six that they wanted to be cheerleaders." But there were many, Hawkins adds, who had some help. "Basically there were two kinds of cheerleaders," he explains. "Those who wanted it because they wanted it, and those who were motivated by their mothers."

Indeed, Wanda Holloway is not the only would-be cheerleader mom in the land. At a recent NCA competition, hundreds of mothers were spotted in the crowd proudly sporting sweatshirts that said, I'M A POM MOM, or I'M A CHEERLEADER MOM. The NCA supply catalog even offers tiny little gold lapel pins that spell out the same sentiment.

Other mothers choose to personalize their important roles as breeders of cheerleaders. At cheering meets, many can be seen wearing specially made pins bearing their daughter's faces, or shirts that say, I'M BUFFY'S MOM. In the small towns where many of them come from, everyone would know who Buffy was—a cheerleader.

Cheerleading is, of course, associated strongly with football. In many small towns in Texas as well as elsewhere, the high-school football teams, and their associated panoply of cheerleaders, drill teams, and marching bands provide the major source of entertainment in the community. H. G. Bissinger, who wrote the best-selling *Friday Night Lights* about how high-school football affects the Texas twin cities of Midland–Odessa, spent a year observing the towns' reactions to the weekly spectacles on the gridiron.

He noted recently, "On Friday, just as the football players would trot around in their jerseys, so would the cheerleaders trot around in their costumes. They stood out and were popular; boys wanted to have dates with them. They are the stars, and they have this incredible year of glory."

Of course, some of the glory is reflected back on the parents of the kids on the field, be they football players or cheerleaders. Bissinger notes, "The parents there are completely carried away with high-school football and cheerleading. They are completely caught up with the status of having a son who is a football player or a daughter who is a cheerleader. And just as there is tremendous glory for the children, there is also glory for their parents." Bissinger points out that in many communities, the parents of kids involved with these activities are treated like VIPs, too. They are often given season passes to the games and invited to the postseason banquets for accolades.

John Hawkins wrote in his book, "If football is Texas's state religion, then cheerleaders are its evangelists, singing proverbial praises for their teams, their schools, and sometimes their entire state."

John Hawkins adds that since many of these same children's parents have led rather dead-end lives since they left high school, often stagnating in boring jobs in the same towns where they were born, high-school days carry more weight than they would in an urban setting. "For many of these people," he says, "there isn't much of a life after high school. Many get married and start having kids right away, and then they immediately start looking forward to when their kids get to high school."

Also, explains Hawkins, in small town environments, anyone who was a high-school campus star, male or female, retains a certain cachet in that town for the rest of his or her life. He adds, "There really is just not a lot after high school. The only venues are church and cheerleading."

Interestingly, Wanda Holloway and her daughter Shanna had already reached the top of their church community: Wanda was the organist and Shanna a soloist. Where else to turn for proof of their worth but cheerleading?

That is not to imply, however, that cheerleading doesn't lure women in big cities as well. It's just that the phenomenon is more pronounced in small towns. When the Houston Oilers football franchise announced plans recently to re-form the previously disbanded cheerleading squad for that team called the Derrick Dolls, over four hundred eager young women showed up for the first tryout. One was scheduled to give birth in five days, but said, "I thought, what the heck. I'd be mad at myself if I didn't at least go for it." The woman in question had formerly been a cheerleader with the Chicago Blitz football team of the USFL.

Most of the other women who showed up said they had always dreamed of being NFL cheerleaders. One young woman who had been on the Dolls several years ago, said, "Those were the happiest two years of my life. You're just an everyday girl off the streets and suddenly people are asking for your autograph. It's kind of neat."

That sentiment seems to be the driving force behind most girls' ambitions to become one of the squad—if you make it, you're special. For mothers, the same thing applies, only with a twist—if your daughter makes it, she is special and so are you.

The competition for such glorious places has become so fierce that the NCA now offers to sell a guide to school officials on how to best coordinate the selection process. It is titled, somewhat ironically in light of Wanda Holloway's clear obsession with the matter, *A Cheerleader Advisor's Survival Kit.* The kit includes details on how to organize the tryouts, as well as sample judging forms, which note the various qualities the girls should be tested on: jumps, voice projection, motion technique, spirit and enthusiasm, appearance, and optional. The latter could refer to anything a school coordinator wants it to refer to, including, perhaps, how active each girl's mother was in coming down and watching the tryouts.

Because gymnastics is such a big part of modern cheering, preparation often begins while girls are still at preschool ages. Many anxious mothers enroll their daughters in dance class by age two or three to ensure that they develop the necessary coordination to do flips and aerials.

One young woman, who quit a high-paying job in Fort Worth to open a private cheerleading school, which now has made her even more highly paid, said she frequently gets calls from mothers of daughters as young as three, inquiring as to what they can do at that early age to make sure their daughters later become cheerleaders.

Such private cheering centers have opened around the country and even form squads that perform at parades and other civic events. If a girl can't make the grade for cheerleader at her school, these days she can always pay to join such a private squad. The centers have catchy names, like Cheers to You and Cheer Energy.

Although the exact prerequisites for cheerleaders are never spelled out, a visit to an NCA national competition clearly shows which qualities seem to prevail. Most of the cheerleaders are blond, for starters. If not naturally, then with some help. Most wear their permed hair up in a top-knot ponytail, most squeal, giggle, and cry frequently, and most have cute names like Buffy, Dodie, Misty, or Christy. And of course they can all flip, jump, and tumble.

There are those who have become disenchanted with the activity. One mother noted, with some pride, that her daughters had no interest in trying out for cheerleader, even though their mom had been one as a teen. "They told me," said the mother, "that they would rather have people out there cheering for them."

One school in Plainfield, Indiana, tired of the extreme competitiveness exhibited toward cheerleading, decided three years ago to have an open cheering squad, as well as open sports teams and bands. Any student who wants to participate in any activity may now do so. As a result, roughly half of the school's eight hundred students are now a part of those activities. Seventy girls make up the cheering squad; boys are welcome, but none have signed up, just as no girls have joined the football team. The school's principal, Jerry Goldsberry, said, "There are so many schools which approach sports as a business. These students have needs that need to be met before we can pressure them with competition and the need to win."

Perhaps Wanda should have thought about that before she forced Shanna to practice her cheering every night. And she definitely should have considered other options before she took her next, more drastic steps, toward making sure her little girl became a cheerleader.

4

Housewives and Hitmen

Wanda Holloway made no secret of her animosity toward Verna Heath and her daughter Amber. Throughout the remainder of 1990, after that fateful day in March when Shanna had been disqualified, Wanda frequently and loudly complained to any and all comers about the Heaths and how they had stolen the cheerleading election from Shanna.

It became an obvious obsession with her. Instead of lessening with time, her outrage and anger seemed to grow as the year passed. One of her good friends from that time, Patrick Gobert (pronounced "Go-bear," in the French fashion), recalls how Wanda talked of little else but the disqualification from the day it happened.

Wanda and Patrick were an unlikely pair of friends who had become close under tragic circumstances roughly two years prior to that spring of 1990. Gobert, a prim and stiff young man in his mid-twenties, had originally made Wanda's acquaintance while he was working at the San Jacinto Funeral Home near Channelview. He was a student at the time at the Commonwealth College of Funeral Services in Spring, Texas, studying funeral directing and embalming. He worked at the funeral home near Channelview as part of a work-study program the school offered. While in the area, the would-be undertaker had also started attending the same church Wanda and C. D. went to—the Channelview Missionary Baptist church.

During the winter of 1988–1989, Wanda's seventeen-year-old nephew, Jerry, son of her older brother, Wayne Webb, went on a hunting trip with some old family friends, the Denmans. The Denmans teenage son, Blake, was a friend of Wayne's son. Because of a tragic error in judgment, Wayne's son was killed that weekend while walking through the woods to his deer-hunting stand. A fellow hunter heard rustling in the leaves and fired, leaving the boy dead.

The entire Webb family was devastated. Because the parents and grandparents of the dead child were so distraught, C. D. Holloway and Wanda volunteered to make the necessary funeral arrangements. They had met young Patrick Gobert at their church, and he seemed to them to be a very pleasant, very Christian man. As a result, they took their unpleasant business to the San Jacinto Funeral Home where Patrick was in training.

Gobert, although not finished with his studies, had already acquired the smooth, supercilious, pseudosympathetic manner of many professional funeral directors. Quiet of voice, unctuous in demeanor, he impressed the Holloway family with his somber efficiency in arranging the dead boy's funeral. Even after the services were over, Patrick continued to call the Holloways frequently to see how they were coping with the grieving process. He made a special effort to counsel with Shane, then sixteen, and Blake Denman, also sixteen, who had been present during the disastrous hunting weekend.

"There's more to being a funeral director than just handling the funeral," Patrick said later. "I felt it was very important to help these young boys through that difficult time of mourning. Grieving, you know, can last for many months." Patrick became especially close to Blake Denman and was soon making almost daily visits to the Denman home in Crosby, a rural community north of Channelview where Roy Denman had moved with his family some years earlier. He often brought small gifts to Blake, items of clothing or jewelry; just small consolations to help Blake forget about the loss of his good friend, Jerry Webb.

Gobert made frequent trips to the Holloway home, too, to visit Shane, and he soon became a close friend of Wanda's as well. He often brought gifts to Shane and Shanna, as he did to Blake, including, on one occasion some gold and diamond jewelry for each. Wanda liked Patrick because, like her, he had an interest in decorating and was very talented at artistic endeavors. He also enjoyed shopping and going out to local restaurants, so the two would frequently have lunch together and catch up on each other's news.

Wanda kept Patrick apprised of both her children's comings and goings and school activities, so he, of course, knew all about Shanna's cheerleading fiascos. In fact, he had often been asked by Wanda to help Shanna with school projects so that Shanna would have more time for cheerleading practice. On one occasion, Wanda asked him to construct a miniature Stephen F. Austin–style Texas frontier village for Shanna's Texas history class. "She just asked me to do those things because I happen to have a talent for things like that," he now says modestly.

On the day Shanna was disqualified from the cheerleading competition for bringing rulers to school, Patrick happened to visit Wanda shortly after she had returned home from the meeting with school officials. He found his friend very upset, slamming items around the kitchen and fuming openly about what had happened. Wanda launched into an hour-long tirade about how the other mothers at the school had conspired against her and Shanna. He recalls, "She seemed to think the other ladies had plotted this thing out. I just stood there leaning on the counter and listening, like I always did when I visited Wanda. I didn't say anything. It was pretty much a one-sided conversation."

At some point, Patrick remembers, Wanda singled out Verna Heath and her daughter as the instigators of the whole plot against Shanna. She vehemently denounced the mother-daughter pair and raged about Amber in particular. "The little bitch!" she hissed to Patrick. "Makes me sick. I can't stand the girl!"

Patrick, by this time, was tiring of Wanda's savage soliloquy. "Oh, Wanda," he said to her casually, rolling his eyes, "Why don't you just have her killed?"

Wanda suddenly stopped her frenzied movements about the kitchen and looked at Patrick sharply for a few moments, silent at last. The young man was surprised, and after an awkward period of silence, said somewhat sarcastically, "I have a number you can call if you're interested."

After Wanda made no response, the subject of cheerleading was dropped. But only temporarily. It would come up again, and again, and again, almost every time Wanda talked to Patrick, or anyone else in Channelview.

Gobert says that a few weeks after the disqualification and his conversation with Wanda in her kitchen, she brought up the subject of the phone number he had mentioned to her previously. "About two weeks later she asked me for the number. I just kind of shook it off, because I thought she was just getting upset again. I told her, 'Oh, Wanda, don't be stupid.'" He never gave her a number because he didn't really know anyone to call who would, on request, kill someone.

Patrick Gobert was not the only person who, after witnessing Wanda's intense hatred of the Heaths, would suggest that she do away with them. According to some reports, even her husband told Wanda that she should just, "blow them away." That suggestion came, in fairness to the man, in the early summer of 1990, after C. D. had had to listen to Wanda's daily disparaging of the evil mother-daughter pair for several months. Most likely he was sick of hearing about it and mentioned such drastic action as a way to shock Wanda into seeing how much she had blown the whole matter out of proportion.

Wanda, however, failed to appreciate the sarcasm in such statements and instead would pause each time to consider the idea seriously.

Throughout that summer, Wanda refused to let the matter of cheerleading drop. All her friends and relations recall how they would run into Wanda as she went about her errands in town. She would stop them and talk ceaselessly about the subject of cheerleading. Her former father-in-law, R. E. Harper, who ran a little convenience store a half-mile from Wanda's home, says that whenever she would stop by the store, "All she'd talk about was that cheerleading stuff. She'd go on and on about it." Since the matter concerned his granddaughter, R. E. would politely listen while inwardly wondering why his former daughter-in-law didn't just let the thing drop.

Peggy Harper, Wanda's former mother-in-law, remembers that she always told Wanda, who visited the Cameo Boutique occasionally, that she shouldn't worry. "I told her Shanna could make cheerleader on her own, that she should just wait for next year. But still she'd just keep on about it."

Peggy's son Tony, Shanna's father, refused to listen to Wanda's castigation of the Heaths. "It wasn't the Heaths that did it," he said. "She knew the pencils and rulers were not on the list of things that Shanna could use, which her mother let her use anyway, which disqualified her."

Sometime in September of that year, Wanda became newly incensed about the cheerleading incident, perhaps because the fall semester had started once more without her daughter jumping on the sidelines of the football field. Her hatred of the Heaths intensified when she saw that awful thirteen-year-old Amber Heath prissing around in her flouncy skirt and ponytail at Alice Johnson football games. It should be Shanna down there, Wanda thought bitterly. One day soon after, while the kids were in school, thirty-six-year-old Wanda Holloway decided to look up her former brother-in-law, Terry Lynn Harper, who was Tony's younger brother by three years.

Wanda hadn't seen Terry in years. Their lives had taken drastically different paths since the time when they had both been students at Channelview High. Terry's own mother would be the first to admit that her second son "has had a troubled life." While Wanda was busy marrying rich men and making a name for herself in the Baptist church of Channelview, Terry Harper had, since the age of twelve, made a career out of fast cars, strong drugs, and loose women.

A short, stocky man with close-set blue eyes and a pugnacious air about him, Terry freely admitted his shortcomings and made no excuses for his many failings. At the age of twelve, he explains, he started smoking marijuana and drinking beer with his junior-high buddies. By age thirty-five, he had been married seven times, convicted of six crimes, and had held too many jobs to count. Considering himself lucky to have graduated from high school, Terry had held dozens of blue-collar jobs in heavy industry in Channelview.

At this point in 1990, he was working as an assistant pipe fitter for various contractors who supplied labor for the area refineries. The work was long and hard, but paid well—$13.50 an hour. His usual workday started at 5:30 in the morning and ended at 5:30 in the evening. The workweek was six days one week, five days the next.

When he wasn't working, Terry Lynn had a tendency to get into trouble. He was the first to admit he would take most any drug offered to him, and he had the arrest record to prove it. Prior to 1990, he had been busted on separate occasions for possession of marijuana, possession of methaqualone, and unlawful possession of a firearm. He had also been arrested several times for public intoxication and had two convictions for driving while intoxicated. Police had been called to his home because of his unruly behavior on too many instances to count.

Most of his problems, he explains, were a result of his own stupidity. "I wasn't too bright," he laughs. "When I got busted for marijuana, I was driving through Jacinto City. I think we was on our way down to Galveston after work one Friday. A cop pulled me over for speeding. We had just gotten through smoking a joint, and I think there was probably twenty or thirty roaches in the ashtray. Of course, when I rolled down the car window, smoke just floated on out around that cop. He said, 'Son, step out of the car, please.' I thought, you know, like, Why?"

His arrests for public intoxication, Terry Harper says, were both because he foolishly mouthed off to cops who had suggested he settle himself down. Instead of heeding their warnings, he would talk back to them along the lines of, Who's gonna make me?

By the fall of 1990, Terry hadn't seen Wanda Holloway in years. She had been divorced from his brother for a decade. Besides, he couldn't stand the woman. She wasn't exactly his type, with all her social climbing and her churchiness and her general air of superiority to people like him. But probably one of the main reasons he despised Wanda was because she had once started trouble for him by accusing him of trying to seduce her while she was still married to his brother, Tony Harper.

One day while Wanda was at the Harper home doing the general maid work her mother-in-law paid her for, Terry, who still lived with his parents, came home from his job at a local plant. He'd been out all night, "doing drugs," and came home to go to bed around ten that morning. The way Wanda told it to Tony later that day was that while she was busy cleaning, Terry had said to her, in a leering way, that she should put baby Shanna down for a nap and come join him in bed.

He swears he never said a word to the woman, but Tony stormed over later that evening and confronted Terry about "messing with his wife." Terry says he told his brother that Wanda's story wasn't true, but that Tony harbored ill feelings toward him just the same for several years after the incident.

"I admit that I'm a flirt," Terry explains now. "I've always flirted with women, but I don't flirt with sister-in-laws." He dismisses Wanda's accusation by saying, "Hell, the woman's got some problems. I know her and Tony had some kind of problems. It was pretty bizarre."

Terry certainly had his share of woman problems. He married for the first time at age eighteen, right after high school, and had been more or less on a marital merry-go-round ever since. By 1990 he was on his seventh marriage—technically. He had had only six different wives, but he had been married to the most recent one twice. She was Marla LaRue Long, a thirty-eight-year-old strawberry blond (with drugstore help) who Terry had met in April of 1989 while on a job site. He was working as a truck dispatcher on a highway construction project; she was one of the dumptruck drivers.

Although Terry was already married at the time of their meeting— to his fifth wife, Sandy—he was so captivated with Marla that he asked her out. Before long he and Sandy divorced and Terry Lynn had a new wife, Marla; he called her Rue.

Marla LaRue had had a troubled past, too. She had grown up one of several children born to a hillbilly-type couple who lived in a semirural area east of Houston. Her mother had divorced her real father when Marla was a small child and married Buster Crosby, who, naturally, became Marla's stepfather. They were a poor, uneducated clan, and often hunted in the woods near their home for extra food for the table—men and women alike toted rifles into the forest in search of squirrels, rabbits, and possums for a family meal. Marla had three sisters and a smattering of half brothers and sisters as well, so there were quite a few mouths to feed.

The Crosby clan led a chaotic, violent life. Marla would later report that her stepfather, Buster, served time in the state prison in Huntsville, Texas, for setting fire to the family home. She also said he had repeatedly raped her from the time she was fourteen years old until her mid-twenties, when she escaped the house by marrying her first husband, James Whited. The way Marla tells it, she has been raped by several other people, too, including one of her half brothers. Her mother, she said, was aware of all the sexual abuse in the home. Marla feels she was a type of rapist, too, because she never took action to stop what was happening to her young daughter.

As a teenager, Marla never told anyone about what Buster was doing to her because, she says, he threatened her. She later wrote a letter to her stepfather, for therapeutic purposes, in which she said to him, "I know you told me when I was grown I had to move from there, that if I ever tell this story and it got back to you one more time, I would go into the woods. Honey, I went hunting a lot and only one of us would come out. Remember this?"

Marla explained later she was making reference here to Buster's frequent threats that when the two went hunting together, only one of them would come out of the forest alive, and it would probably be him, she says he promised.

Because of all the sexual abuse she says she suffered, by age fourteen Marla had already started self-destructive actions calculated to escape the molestations. The first time she tried to hurt herself, she swallowed a whole bottle of her mother's glycerine tablets. She later explained she had done it because her mother, "found out what my stepfather was doing and wouldn't stop it." Marla found out the hard way that glycerine is not a very poisonous susbstance. In fact, it is used as a laxative. "They didn't do anything but just make me sick to my stomach," she later recalled.

With her first husband, James Whited, Marla had two sons, Jimmy and Scott. Both were in their late teens, practically grown, by the time she married Terry Harper, and already they seemed to be maintaining the family tradition of staying just one step ahead of the law. Drinking and carousing were routine parts of their lives. Just as they were for Marla and Terry.

Both Terry and Marla now freely admit that their marriage has been punctuated by frequent, violent arguments, most fueled by heavy consumption of hard liquor. Since their marriage in April of 1989, they had been separated dozens of times. The usual scenario was that the two would get drunk, get into an argument, have a physical brawl, and Marla would leave. She would usually stay with one of her relatives for several weeks until Terry would persuade her to return after promising to reform. There would be a few weeks of peace before the pattern repeated itself.

Marla claims that Terry frequently abused her. She says that before their marriage he had raped her, and that he often raped her after the vows had been exchanged, too. She says he beat her frequently, and once even held a loaded gun to her head for over three hours. For his part, Terry says that Marla doesn't know the difference between fantasy and reality. Indeed, Marla herself has admitted to psychiatrists that she has trouble distinguishing fact from fiction.

On several occasions Marla has sought help for her mental problems. Because of limited finances and lack of medical insurance, she usually would go to Houston's charity hospital, Ben Taub, in the Texas Medical Center. She has been there so often that she refers to the mental ward—One South—as if everyone would know that is the name for Ben Taub's psychiatric wing. "Yeah, I went on down to One South that time," she'll say.

The doctors there would usually keep her a few days, and then give her a pass. She would go home and not come back for follow-up treatment. She shunned the medication they gave her—mainly antidepressants, because she says they worsened the nightmares that often plagued her. Doctors at Ben Taub wrote in Marla's medical records that she told them she often had violent outbursts toward her husband, Terry, and that when she was having one of these outbursts she felt she wanted to kill him. They described her as having flights of ideas, delusions of persecution, feelings of unreality, and loose associations. She says now that she made things up to tell the doctors because she didn't want to have to stay in Channelview with Terry.

On several occasions she inflicted physical harm on herself for the same reason—so that she would have to go to the hospital and thus would be away from her husband. Her right knee still bears a large, angry pink scar from two of those incidents. Not once, but twice, Marla Harper took a can of oven cleaner and sprayed it on her bare leg. The first time she tried it, she got a hospital stay of several weeks. Since it had proved so effective that time, she tried it again later when she was ready to leave home once more.

As Terry's father, R. E. Harper, puts it, shaking his head, "That Marla is a real nut case."

Terry Lynn Harper claims that the worst of his wild days were long over before he ever married Marla. He says that in early 1989 he swore off drugs for good and found religion. He says he became a Christian and an avid pupil of the Holy Bible, assisted by his supervisor at work, Bob Wilburs. The impetus for this conversion, Terry explains, came from the bite of a brown recluse spider.

The brown recluse is a small arachnid indigenous to the southern and western United States. Although the little fiddle-shaped house spider is harmless looking, its venomous bite, in susceptible individuals, can be as toxic as a rattlesnake's. Terry doesn't know where he was when the spider bit him. He had gone out one night after work, drunk heavily and snorted some cocaine, and found when he woke up the next morning that he had some kind of insect bite on his finger, which was red and swollen. He went on to work, he remembers, and stayed on the job until about 3:30 that afternoon, when the swelling in his hand and arm caused such intense pain he could no longer work. He went to the plant's infirmary, where he remembers the doctor told him, "You better hope that's not a brown recluse spider bite, because if it is, you'll be dead by sundown."

The fact is, these spider bites seldom kill anybody. Just the same, Terry recalls that when he looked down at his arm, "There were four lines of blood poisoning up my arm." Brown-recluse venom causes local tissue inflammation and destruction. Untreated, the venom can systematically eat away at muscle tissue and result in lasting crippling and disfigurement. The other main danger from the bite is the body's allergic reaction to the venom—the accompanying swelling can impede blood flow to the afflicted body part, and that, in turn, can cause tissue death and gangrene.

Terry was immediately referred by the company doctor to Ben Taub Hospital, the same institution where Marla was often treated. He says he was hospitalized for two weeks. The doctors there performed an operation on his hand to relieve the swelling and prevent tissue death—they split his left palm open from side to side and left the wound open for two weeks so that the fluid causing the swelling and pressure could drain. Somewhere during the course of this treatment, Terry says, the doctors were still worried that the hand might gangrene. He says they told him they were considering doing more surgery, this time to amputate the hand. "I told them, 'Excuse me!'" Terry relates. "'You had your chance once, when I was out the first time. You ain't gettin' my hand.'"

While hospitalized, Terry admitted he had been doing cocaine daily for some two or three years. When asked how he could afford such a habit on his relatively modest salary, he quipped, "I didn't pay my bills." The forced isolation of the hospital caused him to reflect on his life, he says now. "I decided I had to change or die." He went into counseling, and, he says, "got straight." "I basically started living with a mind three years ago. Before that I always was drinking or on drugs, or on drugs or drinking."

His new resolve, however, mainly referred to his drug use, since his periodic heavy drinking continued on through 1990 and parts of 1991.

He remained, as some acquaintances described him, "a six-pack-a-night kind of guy." Still others snorted at that description and said Terry was, instead, "more like a six-pack-an-hour type."

Such was the life Terry Harper was leading at the time Wanda Holloway decided to look him up. He and Marla were living in a double-wide trailer out off DeZavala Road in Channelview. DeZavala, a narrow, two-lane, black-top street, leads off Market Street through woods and gullies toward the south and the ship channel. Small lakes and streams of sludgy, oily-looking water decorate the landscape, and the neighborhood teems with mobile-home parks. Many have quaint names like Possum Hollow or Lakeside View. Most of the trailers are littered with laundry on clotheslines and one or two rusted, abandoned cars out back. It is the Houston-area equivalent of the more squalid regions of Appalachia.

It was certainly a far cry from Sterling Green, where Wanda had been living for years. But she nevertheless had no trouble finding Terry Harper when she decided she needed his help. Channelview is like a small town that way—everyone knows where everyone else resides even if they haven't had contact for years. If they don't have personal knowledge of someone's whereabouts, all they have to do is ask someone else in town. They'll know.

Terry Harper recalls that one afternoon in late September or early October of 1990, he was relaxing in his trailer when he heard a car pull up and honk its horn sharply several times. He got up from his La-Z-Boy recliner, went to the door, and peered out at the driveway from his front steps. There he saw Wanda, in her midnight blue Jeep Grand Wagoneer, which he recognized from having seen her drive past his dad's convenience store on Sheldon Road near Wanda's home a time or two. He hollered out, "What you need?"

Wanda partially opened her car door and yelled in turn (the distance from the drive to the front door is about one hundred feet), "I need to talk to you."

Terry said, "Well, come on in."

Wanda shook her head vehemently. "No!" she answered, "I don't want to talk to you here. Let's meet somewhere." She either didn't want to cause gossip or else she didn't want one of her mother's friends from the nearby beauty parlor to later remember having seen her go in Terry's trailer. Terry offered to meet her up the road at Bo's Super Stop, a combination convenience store, check-cashing stand, and barbecue joint at the corner of Sheldon Road and Market Street, about a mile and a half from Terry's home. It was a simple little place, the kind of operation that sells fresh-cooked hard-boiled eggs on the cash-register counter and keeps plenty of single beers iced down in chests right by the register for all the thirsty refinery workers who stop by after work.

A few minutes later the two rendezvoused at Bo's. Terry parked his truck and got into Wanda's Jeep. He later recalled, "The first words out of her mouth, 'We've never had this meeting.' I said, 'No doubt.'"

There was no small talk exchanged between this unlikely pair—no mention of how they hadn't seen each other in years. Instead, Wanda told Terry, "I have a problem. But first, I need to know how much you care about your niece and your nephew."

Terry Harper, after all his many wives, was still childless. Consequently, he was extremely attached to all four of his brothers' children—Tony's kids Shane and Shanna, and Travis's babies, Thomas and Travis. He answered his ex-sister-in-law honestly. "I love them with my life," he replied. "I'd do anything for them."

"Good," Wanda interjected rapidly. "Because I've got a big problem."

By this time she had the story down pat, having repeated it throughout Channelview for the last six months. Verna Heath and her daughter Amber, she told Terry, had cheated Shanna out of being cheerleader. Shanna and Amber had been in competition for some time, she explained.

"Well," Terry recalls he responded, "Okay. So what's the problem?"

"I hate this girl," Wanda told Terry. "I want to get rid of her. I hate her mother. I want to get rid of her."

Terry sat upright in surprise but paused before answering. He was dumbfounded by Wanda's intensity. "What are you talking about here?" he finally managed to stutter.

"Don't you know what I'm saying?" Wanda snapped back. "I want these people done away with."

Terry proceeded to explain to Wanda that he had gone straight since she last saw him and was, in fact, on probation at that moment for driving while intoxicated. "I haven't been involved with anyone who would do anything to that effect in at least two years," he told Wanda. "I don't want nothing to do with this. You talking about, you know, killing a little thirteen-year-old girl, and I don't know anybody who would be interested in doing anything like that. I don't want to be interested in doing anything like that, and I don't want to be involved in it."

Terry recalls that Wanda then launched into a detailed history of the problem with the Heaths. She told Terry that Shanna had been disqualified because of these things she had handed out during the last competition, but that the school was rigged, all the votes were rigged, the whole thing was rigged by this other mother. "She told me she didn't know what else to do," Terry remembers. "She just wanted these women out of her life forever."

Terry sat in stunned silence in the passenger seat of Wanda's Jeep, not knowing quite what to say, how to defuse the situation. "I was surprised just to see Wanda again, okay?" he says now. "I hadn't seen the woman in a while. I can't say that she was just a friend of mine who would drive by and say 'Hi'," the self-confessed ne'er-do-well recalls. "But I told her I'd check into it. But I also told her I didn't know anyone that's going to want to kill a thirteen-year-old girl."

Wanda's response surprised Terry Harper even more. The Baptist church organ player, who listened to the gospel at least three times a week, said, "There's such things as car wrecks and houses burning down."

She then went on, says Terry, about her feelings about this other mother and her little girl. "Most of her anger was directed at Amber," recalls Terry. "It seems like every time she said, 'I hate,' it was directed at the girl. But then every so often she'd say, 'I just hate them two. I just can't stand them.'"

Once again, Wanda asked Terry if he knew anyone who could help out. "I just started laughing," he says. "I told her I didn't know what to do. I told her, 'You could always go out here and get you a Colombian drug lord, have the woman kidnapped, taken over to Colombia, take her over there and sell her into white slavery.' That's when everything was going on in Colombia, anyway," he explains.

Wanda didn't catch the hint of humor in Terry's suggestion. "How much would that cost?" she inquired earnestly.

Terry, an admitted bullshit artist, quickly concocted an answer. "Oh, say, five, ten, fifteen, twenty thousand dollars." he quoted.

Wanda seemed shocked. "That's awfully expensive, isn't it?"

Terry says he answered, "This ain't no five-and-dime burglary you talking about. You're talking about a federal offense." Terry says he also suggested to Wanda, again, not seriously, that she ought to forget about killing Amber, since no one would want to murder a child, and instead just get rid of the mom. "I told her that would take the wind right out of the little girl's sails," he recalled later.

The two left it at that—with Terry promising he'd "look into it." He removed himself from Wanda's car completely bewildered. "I thought the woman was just upset," he says. "I mean, I couldn't imagine someone wanting to do this, personally, and I just really wanted to get out of the car and go. I hadn't talked to her in, like, three years, and by that point I was hoping I wouldn't be talking to her again for another three years."

Terry didn't get his wish. By the end of 1990, he had, indeed, been contacted again by Wanda Holloway, with the same proposition—she wanted either Amber or Verna Heath, or both, killed and she didn't seem to care how that came about.

During the intervening months, between early October and late December, Terry sometimes wondered about Wanda's visit. He started worrying about it, mainly because of something he'd told Wanda. "I kept remembering how I'd told her that I loved those two kids, Shane and Shanna, with my life," he says now. "I started worrying that she might try to use that against me, try to hang something on me because of what I'd said." Terry added later that he feared a frame-up. He was afraid Wanda might hire a real killer to do the job and then point the finger at Terry if anyone came around asking her questions.

Because of his concerns, Terry talked to his supervisor at work, Bob Wilburs, the man who had counseled him with his bible studies and his efforts to stay straight. Wilburs advised Terry to be extremely careful with Wanda Holloway, and warned his friend to avoid further contact with her. Terry tried to put the whole strange encounter with his former sister-in-law behind him.

But Wanda wouldn't let him forget. By Christmastime Wanda's obsession seemed to have intensified. Even though almost everyone else was happily distracted by thoughts of gifts and family gatherings, this good Christian woman chose to celebrate Christ's birthday by continuing to tell everyone she met about Shanna's problems getting elected cheerleader. One night near Christmas, for example, a friend of Shane's came to the Holloway home for a holiday visit. Pete Reyes, although four years older than Shane, had a sister who was in the Channelview band with Shane; the two young men had met through band activities and become friends. Pete recalls that he dropped by one night in late December just to wish his friend a merry Christmas.

Instead he became a witness to what seemed to him at the time to be a bizarre conversation. Shane and his girlfriend, Amy Goodson, were sitting in the kitchen with Wanda. Instead of discussing the upcoming holiday, Reyes recalls, the three were "sitting there talking about people they hate."

A truly joyous topic for a season where most folks usually concentrate on good will toward men. Shane volunteered that he hated Nancee Carter, his fellow drum major in the band. It seems he felt as if he should have been the sole drum major, and he resented the fact that Nancee shared the honor. Wanda agreed, and added that she not only hated Nancee, but also her mother, who Wanda felt had "rigged" the drum-major selection, just as she felt the mothers at Shanna's school had rigged the cheerleader election.

This odd conversation triggered Reyes to remember an incident from earlier that fall, when he and Shane were planning to go out "wrapping" houses with toilet tissue on a Friday night. Pete remembers that he and Shane told Wanda that they planned to wrap the Carter home because of Shane's resentment of Nancee. He says Wanda told them, "I wouldn't bother with wrapping the house. Why don't y'all just slash their tires?"

During the conversation near Christmas, the topic suddenly turned from Wanda and Shane's hatred of the Carters to Wanda's hatred of Verna and Amber Heath. For probably the thousandth time, Wanda recounted her reasons for hating the Heaths, and again fretted about how she could ever make sure that Shanna would get elected cheerleader the next time she tried out. She suddenly turned to Reyes and asked, "Would you kill Verna Heath for me?"

Reyes, Wanda knew, routinely carried a pistol. He worked for a Venezuelan export company and often had to travel through rough areas of Houston near the ship channel as part of his duties. Reyes says he just laughed off Wanda's request at the time, not thinking she was serious. Later he would have his doubts.

Wanda, for her part, would keep looking for someone to help her get rid of her rival.

A few days later, on Christmas Eve, the Harper clan gathered at the home of R. E. and Peggy Harper to celebrate the holiday. The whole family was there—Peggy's parents, Tony and his wife Mickie, Terry and Marla, and Travis and his family. A little later in the afternoon Wanda delivered Shane and Shanna there to spend the evening with their father.

Terry Harper recalls that the group had gathered in the living room, waiting for final preparations for the Christmas Eve dinner to be completed. When at last the call to table came, everyone got up to go into the dining room. Terry was one of the last to leave the room. To his surprise, his niece Shanna came up to him at that point and said, "Uncle Terry, I need to talk to you privately." He steered the teenager toward a corner of the now-deserted living room and said, "What is it?" Shanna handed him a piece of paper and said, "Mama wants you to call her at this number. I don't know what about."

Terry answered, "No problem," and pocketed the note. In turn, he says, he wrote down his phone number and gave it to Shanna, saying, "If you ever need me, all you have to do is call, either you or Shane."

Later that night, after Terry and Marla had returned to their trailer, Marla, who was always the jealous type, demanded to know what Shanna had been talking secretively about with Terry. Terry told her about everything, including the meeting with Wanda months before; he may have had many shortcomings, but dishonesty was not among them. Marla, who had been separated from Terry at the time of Wanda's surprise visit, had not heard about it before. She, like Terry, was worried that somehow Terry could get into trouble.

Terry didn't know what Wanda wanted this time; he guessed it was one of two things—either to tell Terry to forget her request from months before or else to renew her request that he help her find somebody to kill Verna and Amber Heath. Terry didn't know what to do. He told Marla on Christmas Eve that he had to talk to his brother Tony about everything before making another move. Tony knew Wanda better than they did and might be able to help figure out what the woman was up to. Since Tony had left the same evening to spend Christmas with Mickie's family in Louisiana, Terry knew the discussion would have to wait. He advised Marla that the best thing they could do at that point was to try to enjoy their Christmas with her sons, Jimmy and Scott, who were on their way over for a late-night visit.

5

Never Trust an Ex-In-law

Terry Harper finally got in touch with his brother Tony on New Year's Eve of 1990 and told him about his contact with Wanda. Tony was in a hurry that afternoon; he and Mickie were planning to go to a New Year's Eve party at the Hyatt Regency Hotel in downtown Houston, and were packing their car for the overnight stay at the moment Terry called.

"What you doing?" Terry asked after Tony picked up the phone. Tony explained he was getting ready for the party. "Well, are you sitting down or standing up?" Terry inquired.

"Right now I'm standing," Tony replied, puzzled.

"Well, maybe you ought to sit down," Terry suggested.

Tony complied and told his brother, "Okay, I'm sitting down now. What you got?"

"You're not going to believe this," Terry started out, "Wanda wants me to go and kill a lady and her daughter."

Tony listened in stunned silence as Terry told him that the mother of his two children, a woman he was once married to, was talking to his kid brother about having some people murdered.

"Why does she want to do it?" Tony queried. "What's this all about?"

"It's because of that cheerleading stuff," Terry answered. "You know, because Shanna didn't make it. Wanda thinks these people were behind it."

"Terry, do you think she's really serious?" Tony asked with a note of disbelief.

Terry answered honestly. "I don't really know, but my gut feeling is that I don't trust Wanda Holloway." Terry related to Tony how he had told Wanda he loved his niece and nephew with his life. He was worried, he explained, that Wanda might somehow use that statement to implicate him if something happened to the Heaths and Wanda was questioned. Terry knew that in the eyes of the law, he, not Wanda, would seem the more likely guilty party, what with his history of petty criminal activity. Wanda's record, he knew, was spotless. Not to mention that he was currently on probation for his second DWI offense; any hint of trouble could land him in prison, and he knew it.

Tony interrupted Terry to ask, "When did Wanda talk to you about this?"

Terry hesitated to answer. Finally, he admitted, "You may get mad at me, because she's been talking to me for a couple of months." Terry knew that Tony had been divorced from Wanda for almost ten years, but he also remembered how angry his brother had been years before when he thought Terry had made a pass at his then-wife. Terry didn't want to reawaken any jealousy that might still exist on his brother's part.

Tony didn't get mad; instead he wondered, "So why are you telling me about this now, if she's been talking to you for months?"

Terry was blunt. "She pissed me off, that's why," he explained. "She had Shanna come up to me at Christmas, at Mom's house, Christmas Eve night. She called me over to the side, said, 'Mom wants you to call her about the deal.'"

Tony was incredulous. "You mean Shanna knows about this?" he fairly shouted into the phone.

"I don't know if she knows or not," Terry answered. "But what do you think I should do?"

Aside from wanting advice, Terry called Tony for another reason: He wanted someone else to know about all this in case he needed a corroborating witness. He had enough knowledge of the law to realize he didn't want to be put in a situation where it was his word against Wanda's. The druggie versus the church organist. He doubted he'd ever be able to win that credibility contest.

After some thought, Tony gave Terry his advice. "If I were you," he told his brother, "I'd go ahead on down to the D.A.'s office, just to be on the safe side." Tony didn't know what kind of trouble Terry could get in, but he figured there was no sense taking any chances.

Terry hemmed and hawed a little, and finally said, "Well, I'll go down there in a few days."

But Tony was adamant. "No," he told his brother firmly, "you need to go down there today."

Terry was reluctant, seeing as how it was the afternoon before a holiday weekend. "Why today?" he asked Tony. Terry explained he was kind of afraid to go to the law right then because he had several unpaid traffic tickets outstanding. He didn't want to spend the holiday weekend in jail.

Tony was impatient, anxious to get on his way to the Hyatt with Mickie. "Look, Terry," he said, "You're the one who's called me and told me this. This is New Year's Eve. Now, if anything was to happen to Verna Heath, you know, I don't want to be any part of this whatsoever. But now you've made me aware of it. If you don't go downtown today, then I'll go on down to the D.A. myself." He then gave Terry his mobile phone number, where Terry could reach him later at the Hyatt, and also the name of a lawyer who had handled some traffic violations for him, just in case Terry needed some help in that department.

Most average citizens are fairly ignorant of the exact letter of the law. Those like Terry, who have had a few run-ins with the judicial system, know a little more than average, but still not very much. Yet they seem intently interested in the subject. It is not unusual, in the bars and beer joints of Channelview, to hear loud and lively discussions among the patrons of just what is and just what is not against the law. One man will argue that burglary of a habitation is only a misdemeanor; he will be hotly disputed by another who says he knows firsthand that, in Texas, it's a felony. As the argument builds steam, the man insisting that burglary is a felony gets angrier and angrier, as he sips from a bottle of cheap whiskey. "Look, man," he finally bellows. "I just did fifteen years in the pen for burglary of a habitation. Don't tell *me* it's not a felony!" End of discussion on that topic, but others ensue. A debate arises about the relative legal liability involved when a driver accidentally runs into a cow on a country road. One man quips, "The last cow I ran into, I married!" Others discuss their personal DWI probation status. One brags that he routinely visits his probation officer while drunk. Another warns that a new law, which he's just studied up on since it will apply to him, mandates drug and alcohol testing for all probationers in Harris County.

Personal-injury law is also always a hot topic in Channelview, since so many of the community's residents work for the huge refineries and industrial plants where on-the-job injuries are so prevalent. Not to mention wrongful death actions when a relative is blown up in an explosion or poisoned by leaking toxic gas.

Still, there are large areas of the law that are complete mysteries to the people of Channelview, and Wanda's proposition to Terry was one of them. Neither Terry nor his brother Tony knew exactly what kind of trouble Terry might get himself into, but they both had a vague sense that trouble was brewing and they didn't want to wait around to see what the exact charge might be if the law was involved.

So Terry called the Harris County District Attorney's Office, the afternoon of that same New Year's Eve rather than going in, and explained to the individual manning the incoming complaints desk what had happened between him and Wanda. To Terry's surprise, the D.A.'s employee seemed unconcerned.

"I don't think the guy understood what I was saying," Terry later said. "Like everyone else up to that point, he just didn't quite grab ahold of it, you know, like, 'This guy is not serious.'" Not knowing what else to do, Terry called Tony to tell him of the lack of interest in Wanda's scheme among the law downtown.

By this time Tony had become somewhat exasperated. He was also anxious to get on with his New Year's Eve celebration. Just the same, he took the time to look up the number to the Harris County Sheriff's Department substation closest to Terry in Channelview. Since the D.A.'s office wouldn't do anything, he figured he would refer his brother to another branch of the law.

Terry had better luck with the sheriff's department. He called the number Tony had given him, which was for the District III substation on Wallisville Road. A Sergeant Leach answered the phone. Once more, Terry explained the nature of his call. Sergeant Leach transferred the call to Detective Marcel Dionne, who was then working in the homicide division.

Detective Dionne listened to Terry Harper's story. He then asked if Harper would be willing to give him a sworn statement. Terry agreed, and an appointment was set up between the two for that same afternoon.

Terry went to the station with Marla by his side to help quell his apprehension. She, at least, would know where he was if he should be tossed in jail for his unpaid traffic tickets. Besides, when they weren't separated, the two were nearly inseparable. "We do everything together," Terry explains.

Detective Dionne took a routine statement from Terry. He did not check into Terry's arrest or traffic record, however. He just wrote down the information as Terry relayed it, in front of Marla and a clerk-stenographer. After the report was complete, and Terry had told everything he had to tell, Detective Dionne read it back to Terry and asked him if it was a true and correct statement of the facts as Terry knew them to be. "Yes, sir," Terry replied.

Then Detective Dionne pointed to the telephone on his desk. "Would you call Wanda Holloway right now, in front of me?" he asked Terry, to see if he was telling the truth about this lady or if he was making the whole thing up. Terry said, "Sure," and waited while Dionne plugged a tape-recording device onto the phone before dialing. After a few rings, Terry heard a click, and a taped voice saying, "Hello, this is C. D. We're unable to take your call right now, but..." He hung up the phone. "Don't guess I ought to leave a message, do you?" he joked with the police officer. Texas law allows clandestine taping of conversations as long as one party to the conversation is aware of the tape.

Dionne's answer was stony silence. He unplugged the recorder and turned back to his paper work. Still, the fact that Terry had agreed to place the call at all added to the weight of his story.

Detective Dionne then explained the department's procedure before allowing Terry and Marla to leave. He would review the report with his superiors and get back to Terry in a few days with their response.

On the next regular work day, Detective Dionne called Sergeant

Flynt Blackwell and Detective George Helton, both members of the
Harris County Sheriff's Department. The two long-time veterans of
the sheriff's department were at that time assigned to a special
multiagency Harris County Organized Crime Task Force, headquar-
tered in Baytown, Texas, not far from Channelview. Led by another
veteran, Captain Charles "T-Bone" Shaffer, the task force had been
created with state grant monies in the late 1980s to specifically target
drug organizations and other gangland-style criminal activities. With
over one hundred personnel, the force was unique among law enforcement agencies in that it was given special license to cross jurisdictional
lines, share information, and call on federal agencies for additional
resources. It was often assisted by the FBI, the DEA, U.S. Customs
officials, and even the IRS. Sheriff's department personnel were joined
by members of the district attorney's office, Texas Department of
Public Safety officers, and members of fifteen separate city police
forces from in and around Harris County.

Its efforts had paid off. In 1990 alone, the task force totalled over
twenty-two hundred arrests, confiscated drugs worth over $250 mil-
lion, and seized cash and assets valued at more than $4 million.

In addition to handling most of the major drug investigations, the
task force had also become the arm of law enforcement most often
called in on contract murder cases, which, by definition, are a type of
organized crime, since they involve considerable planning and end up
with one person paying another to commit a crime.

Detective Helton, called "Grandpa" by his cohorts, had, in his
seventeen years with the sheriff's department, become the agency's
unofficial "expert" on murder-for-hire. In dozens of cases he had
actually posed as a hit man himself in order to secure the evidence
necessary to win a conviction against the person contracting for the
killing. Helton would meet with the would-be contractors, ask what
they wanted done, tell them the price, and see if they would take the
bait. The entire transaction would be tape-recorded, and the resulting
tape would often provide extremely damning evidence of the contractors' intent and willingness to pay for the deed.

Helton's colleagues often joked that he had drawn that unique
assignment for one reason and one reason only: "He looks like a hit
man!" one friend from the D.A.'s office laughed. "He's tall and thin, a
chainsmoker—he just looks like a contract killer."

His partner on this investigation, Sergeant Flynt Blackwell, was almost his opposite. Young and baby-faced, Blackwell was called "Spanky" by the other officers because of his resemblance to the character from *Our Gang*. Small in stature, with big, wide eyes, Blackwell had nevertheless made a strong impression on his superiors with his tenacity and incredible ability to work undercover.

Under Texas law, hiring a killer is officially known as "solicitation of capital murder." There are six categories of capital murder in Texas, all of which can carry the death penalty:

1) The person murders a peace officer or fireman.
2) The person intentionally commits the murder while in the course of committing certain other felonies (kidnapping, burglary, robbery, aggravated sexual assault, or arson).
3) The person commits the murder for remuneration or the promise of remuneration or employs another to commit the murder for remuneration or the promise of remuneration.
4) The person commits the murder while escaping or attempting to escape from a penal institution.
5) The person, while incarcerated in a penal institution, murders another who is employed in the operation of the penal institution.
6) The person murders more than one person while committing one other criminal transaction or while committing several different criminal transactions with the same scheme or course of conduct.

Wanda Holloway may have thought her scheme was simply "getting rid" of some people she didn't like; in the eyes of the law, she was talking about soliciting a capital murder.

When Detective Dionne first talked to Sergeant Blackwell and Detective Helton about Terry's story, he recommended to them that this case needed to be worked. In his years of law enforcement experience, Dionne thought he had learned to recognize when someone was telling the truth and when someone was lying. Terry Harper, in his opinion, was on the level. Without doing a background check of any kind on either Terry or the woman he had accused, Dionne referred the case to Blackwell and Helton because of their extensive practice in both undercover and murder-for-hire cases. Captain T-Bone Shaffer, as head of the task force, supervised all the officers' activities.

On January 9, 1991, Blackwell and Helton drove by Terry and Marla Harper's trailer home in the early evening, when they thought Terry would be home from work. The weather that night was typical for a South Texas winter—cold and rainy. When they arrived at the trailer, they could see that the low-lying yard was already inches deep with water and mud. Sergeant Blackwell was wearing a brand-new pair of cowboy boots. He took one look at the path he would have to tread to Terry's front door, through the water and mud, and decided he and Harper would just have to have their first meeting somewhere else.

He dialed Terry's home from the mobile phone in the undercover police car. Marla answered and told the cops that Terry wasn't home yet but was expected any minute. Blackwell told Marla to have Terry meet them at 6:30 P.M. at the McDonald's at the intersection of Sheldon Road and I–10. That way they could have their meeting and eat it, too, so to speak, as well as keep their boots dry and clean.

Terry showed up not long after the appointed time. The three men sat in a red-vinyl booth overlooking the brightly lit McDonald's parking lot, and Terry once again repeated his story. The officers frequently referred to the report Detective Dionne had turned in as they asked Terry questions. Terry did not waiver in his version of the events of the last few months—he neither added nor detracted from the simple facts he had told Dionne. Another mark in his favor; if he had taken it this far, talking to more than one cop, he must be serious, the two officers thought.

After forty-five minutes or so, Sergeant Blackwell suggested they meet again the next evening, after Terry got off work, so that Terry could try again to place a call to Wanda that the police could tape. In order to determine if they should continue to investigate the case, the police knew it was imperative to hear Wanda herself speak of her desire to have Verna Heath and her daughter done away with.

Terry was working at the time as an assistant pipe fitter at the Phillips Petroleum plant on Highway 225 in Pasadena, not far to the west of Channelview. He was officially working for Brown and Root, but the prevailing practice of the day was for the petroleum plants to hire contract laborers from large employers like Brown and Root, who then shouldered all the responsibility of payroll and employee insurance.

The three agreed to meet at 5:30 P.M. at the Pasadena Motor Lodge at the corner of Highway 225 and South Avenue in Pasadena. Not exactly a high-rent meeting place. Pasadena, like Channelview, was a community often mocked by the more upscale Houstonians to the west, who thought themselves above the blue-collar industrial workers of the smaller communities. Pasadena had become nationally famous as a redneck paradise back in the seventies, when the Hollywood production *Urban Cowboy* dramatized the life of refinery workers who partied after-hours at Gilley's nightclub. Now Gilley's was long-shuttered, but the refinery workers still remained.

One former resident who had risen to prominence as a defense attorney in Houston once joked that folks in Pasadena loved Channelview, because it gave them a place to look down on. He himself was from Channelview, but his remarks were still taken seriously by the people he'd left behind. Many swore they would never take their legal woes to him again.

On the afternoon of January 10, 1991, Terry wheeled his truck into the parking lot of the Pasadena Motor Lodge. The meeting was held a little earlier than the scheduled 5:30 because rain had prematurely ended Terry's workday. He had alerted the officers of the change, and they had agreed to the earlier time. Blackwell and Helton had already designated a certain pay phone near the office as the meeting place from which the call to Wanda would be made. The two officers attached a suction-cup recording device to the receiver of the phone and instructed Terry to go ahead with the call to the Holloway home. He picked up the phone and dialed the number that Shanna had previously given him: 452–7022.

At approximately five minutes to four that afternoon, the phone rang at Wanda's house.

Wanda, busy preparing dinner in her kitchen on Mincing Lane, picked up the phone at her end. "Hello," she said in her sharp Texas twang.

"Wanda," Terry said.

"Yes," she replied.

"This is Terry."

"Um-hum," was her answer.

"How you?" he asked.

"Fine, I was just thinking about you," she giggled a little after speaking.

"Well, I'm sorry it was taking so long to get back at you," he apologized. It had been weeks since Shanna had approached him at Christmas.

Wanda didn't mind. "That's alright, that's okay," she said.

Terry went on somewhat clumsily, "Um, I just been, I just got rained out early today, so I figured, you know, I can't do it at the house."

"Right," Wanda agreed. Her terse answers suggested she may have been worried about eavesdroppers as well. "Well, I was gonna call, too, but you know how I..."

Terry got right to the point. "Uh, well, you still interested in taking care of that problem?"

After only slight hesitation, Wanda responded, "Uh-huh."

"Alright!" Terry said, and Wanda laughed at his enthusiasm. "Uh, I got in touch with someone for you," he continued.

"Okay," was her only answer.

"But," he hesitated, "I need to know exactly what you want."

"When can I get with you?" she asked. "That's gonna be the problem."

"Well, when would be good for you because I'm working six-tens," Terry asked, explaining his busy schedule of long work days.

Wanda was flexible. "I'm free most anytime," she said. "So you let me know when you can."

Terry thought a moment. "Well, what about, do you have a problem with, like, after I get off work or anything?"

Apparently not. Wanda quickly said, "When?"

Terry thought about it. "Well, I guess I'm gonna have to get with him this weekend, and maybe this weekend or next week we could meet," he said, deliberately referring to the hit man he and Wanda had previously discussed him finding for her.

"That will be fine," Wanda answered. "Just call me, you know?"

After arranging the times Terry should call and leave a message for Wanda, Terry told her "I am gonna get with this guy this weekend, get everything set up. Are there any questions you need me to ask him?"

Wanda said no, so Terry went on, hoping to get her to be more specific. "Well, he's gonna have to have some information."

"Tell him I can get what I can," Wanda assured her ex-brother-in-law. "Just find out what the scoop is and how you do it, and get back to me, and then you get back when you get back, right?" Wanda sounded like a pro at these clandestine activities.

"Okay," Terry said. They then agreed to meet Monday night between 6:00 and 6:45 P.M.

Minutes later, after Terry Harper hung up the pay phone at the Pasadena Motor Lodge that afternoon, Sergeant Blackwell and Detective Helton rewound and played back the tape recording just made with Wanda. They exchanged glances as they heard her obvious interest in meeting with Terry. This could be the real thing, they thought. This lady sounded like she meant business. The conversation between Terry and Wanda had lasted only a minute and a half, but it would have repercussions that would last a lifetime.

On the morning of January 11, the day after this first recorded evidence of Wanda's intentions, Sergeant Blackwell and Detective Helton contacted Assistant District Attorney Joe Magliolo.

Now a member of the U.S. Attorney's Office Drug Task Force in Houston, Magliolo was then acting as the appointed liaison attorney between the Harris County Organized Crime Task Force and the Harris County District Attorney's Office in downtown Houston. By early 1991, he had already put in twelve hard years as a trial attorney with the D.A.'s office, and had tried almost every conceivable type of case, from hot checks to drug possessions to child abuse, on up to grisly murders. Like most long-time members of the D.A.'s office, Magliolo had become inured to the daily doses of violence and depravity with which he was forced to fill his brain in the interest of successful prosecution of the crimes. He thought he'd heard almost everything.

In the six months he had been appointed to the task force, though, he had prosecuted mostly major drug crimes—big-time dealers and large possession cases. He had enjoyed the relatively brief respite from the more violent crimes he had previously handled.

A young, bespectacled Italian with curly black hair, Magliolo smiled as the veteran officers came in his office that morning of January 11. "What's going on?" he asked good-naturedly.

Blackwell looked at Helton briefly before saying slowly, "Look, we've got something kinda strange here." Magliolo recalls being told, "We've been told there's a lady out there in Channelview who wants to hire somebody to kill someone."

So what! Magliolo thought to himself, and said aloud, "Happens all the time, doesn't it?" He and the officers all knew that murder-for-hire was an all-too-common crime in Harris County. They had all three personally handled too many cases of that kind to be surprised at man's inhumanity to man.

But Blackwell spoke again. "This one's kind of different," he told Joe. "This lady wants to kill a girl because she beat her daughter at cheerleading."

Still Magliolo failed to be surprised. "Sure it's a strange motive," he said later. "But is it really any stranger than having somebody killed for insurance money? Or because somebody wants a divorce? Or any of the other crazy reasons people kill each other in this country?" Joe Magliolo still had too many vivid memories of really bizarre crimes he had prosecuted to be surprised by this one. His all-time worst memory was of a young woman he had tried for murder. The woman, a drug addict, had killed a man who had burned her on a drug deal by taking up a pickax and plunging it repeatedly into his chest as he lay sleeping. Testimony at her trial revealed that days after the murder, she had bragged to friends that she had had an orgasm every time she sunk the ax in the victim's chest. "After that, what could surprise you?" Magliolo asked later.

At any rate, Joe Magliolo told the officers, the motive for the possible crime at hand wasn't important. What was important was making sure that proper procedures for collecting crucial evidence were followed.

In most cases of this type, Magliolo now explains, the best possible scenario is to have a police officer pose undercover as the hired hit man. Most people looking for a killer don't know where to find one. They usually start out, like Wanda, by asking someone else who they think might know how to go about getting one. If the police are ever going to find out about these schemes, someone has to inform them, and nine times out of ten the informant is the one initially asked to obtain the killer for the person wanting the killing done. In other words, the go-between is the most likely informant. He or she can then tell the contractor that a hit man has been located, and suggest a meeting between the contractor and the hit man. That way, an undercover officer can act as a hit man and collect first-hand, eye- and ear-witness testimony as to exactly what is being solicited.

After Magliolo listened to the first recording Blackwell and Helton had made, he asked them about the possibility of Helton acting as a hit man and meeting with Wanda himself. "Find out if this Harper guy can set that up," he told the officers, "and then we'll decide what to do. Meanwhile, better keep close tabs on the people she wants killed."

Of prime importance in investigations of this nature is ensuring the safety of the proposed victims while the police collect their necessary evidence against the solicitor. They never know, explained Magliolo, how many other would-be hit men the solicitor may have contacted. For example, Wanda may have already hired someone to kill Verna and Amber, even while continuing to deal with Terry Harper, just to make sure the job was done right, just to cover all the bases. If that were the case, an attempt could be made on the Heaths' lives even while the police were investigating the information they had managed to obtain.

The police did not want to warn the Heaths directly of the possible threat to their lives, either, because they might start behaving differently and thereby tip off Wanda or her hired henchmen that something was up. By the same token, any security surveillance of the Heaths would have to be done surreptitiously, again to avoid revealing police involvement that could scare off the perpetrators and spoil the case. It was all a rather complicated, and dangerous, game of cat and mouse.

On the evening of January 14, shortly after he left the plant, Terry Harper once again stopped at the Pasadena Motor Lodge and placed a call to Wanda's home. This time he was alone, and no police were present. The call was not recorded. At their last meeting, Blackwell and Helton had cautioned Terry that he should never act on his own in this case, and should carefully follow whatever instructions he had been given by them. That warning included telling Terry he should not call Wanda unless they were present to record the conversation or had previously wired him for the same purpose.

They had agreed to an exception for this particular call, however, because it was merely designed to confirm the time and place for that night's meeting with Wanda, which would be recorded. Terry placed the call and told Wanda to meet him around 7:00 P.M. at the Grandy's restaurant located at the corner of Uvalde Street and Wallisville Road just a few miles west of Channelview. "I picked that place because it wasn't in Channelview," Terry would later explain. "Too many people know us in Channelview. I didn't think we should meet there."

Wanda agreed to the meeting. Terry hung up and drove to the sheriff's office on Wallisville Road, about a half-mile from the designated Grandy's. There Blackwell and Helton once more reviewed what they wanted Terry to try to elicit from Wanda. They wanted her to say what she wanted done, to whom, and why. They also wanted to see if she would agree to meet with the "hit man" that Terry had said he had located.

Then they showed Terry how to operate the small microcassette recorder they had previously used to tape Wanda on the phone on January 10. They indicated how he should press the RECORD button, and placed the recorder in his shirt pocket. "Just don't forget to turn it on," Helton joked, "but make sure you do it before she gets there." The officers also placed a remote transmitting device on Terry's back, under his shirt, and affixed it with tape. They wanted the conversation broadcast to them as they sat in their nearby unmarked police sedan.

Terry left for Grandy's. The officers followed behind at a discreet distance in their car. They would park some distance away from Terry and observe his meeting with Wanda so they would be able to further corroborate the evening's events later.

Grandy's is a chain of fast-food "home-cooking" restaurants in the Houston area. It advertises COUNTRY COOKIN' and specializes in southern-style entrees of fried chicken and chicken-fried steak, served on styrofoam plates instead of in boxes, with side dishes of vegetables like mashed potatoes, okra and green beans, cream gravy and biscuits. It's sort of a sit-down version of a Kentucky Fried Chicken, but with more emphasis on a homey atmosphere for those who feel guilty about taking the family out for fast-food.

Terry wheeled his vehicle into the lot and parked on the Uvalde Road side of the building, away from the door at the end of a row of spaces. There wasn't much of a crowd; after all, it was a Monday night after seven. Most of the area's residents don't go out on weekdays, and if they do, they dine earlier. Blackwell and Helton parked on the other side of the lot, but in clear view of Terry's car.

Wanda arrived about ten minutes later. When Terry spotted her car turning in the drive, he reached into his shirt and activated the recorder. Wanda parked one space away from Terry, leaving a space between them. Terry hopped out of his vehicle and walked around the back of it to Wanda's. He opened the front passenger door and got in the Grand Wagoneer.

At first there was an awkward silence. Finally, Wanda spoke. "Ready when you are," she said with a nervous giggle, then added, "How come you call me so late? I figured it would be earlier."

Terry explained he'd had to go by his house first. "Are you covered there, too?" she politely asked.

"Yeah, I guess I'm covered," Terry laughed. "I got in a fight before I left the house." Terry was obviously clever at inventing alibis.

Wanda again erupted in laughter. "Oh God," she said in mock-fear. "Let me look around, make sure nobody is following you."

Terry reassured her, "No, there ain't nobody following me."

"There ain't nobody following me either, that I know of," Wanda said lightly.

Terry got right down to business. "Well," he explained. "I got a hold of this guy."

"Okay," Wanda chirped. "What's the deal, tell me the scoop."

"Exactly what do you want done?" Terry asked. "Cause that determines how much money it's gonna cost you."

Wanda thought a minute and said, "That's right, I know, but I just don't know. I just need to get something done. I mean, they're already working on this cheerleader thing, and I think Shanna is stuck again already."

Terry pretended outrage. "Are you serious?"

Wanda got wound up. "Hell, it ain't even started yet, Terry, and they are already down there kissing ass so bad it's unreal."

"Well, can't you go to the school board?" Terry innocently inquired.

"Are you kidding?" Wanda almost shrieked. "I've already been to the school board." She was referring here to her trip almost two years earlier. "It's all politics, it's all it is," Wanda went on. "Now, I'm working down here, here's what I'm doing, you ain't gonna believe what I'm doing. I am working down here at the school now, for free. I am what is called a 'volunteer mother.' It's called a 'Friends Like You,' a volunteer parent."

The distraught mother began to rant, speaking rapidly in an angry tone. "I go down there Tuesday, Wednesday, and Thursday, and I work in the band hall with Mr. P., okay? I got the P.E. teacher is trying to help me, okay? I work down there from nine to three for nothing, three days a week. Now, I'm talkin' about puttin' in some hours, right? They know me, they know who I am, Mrs. Bassett, the cheerleader sponsor, she loves Shane, she thinks he hung the moon, she thinks he is wonderful, okay? She knows who Shanna is, but she knows Shanna has never been a cheerleader because she never had a chance. All those other girls have been cheerleader."

Terry noticed that Wanda's eyes were bugging out of her head. She seemed oblivious to her surroundings, almost as if she were reliving some past event. He tried to calm her down.

"Shanna, she's thirteen now?" he asked, more to change the subject as much as anything.

"Be a freshman," Wanda answered, looking straight ahead. "Now this is a critical year. She don't get it this year, she ain't never gonna make it."

Terry once more tried to defuse Wanda's intensity. "Well," he offered. "You said last time that she might not even want to go out for it."

"Oh, she does!" Wanda interjected. "She said, 'I don't do it this time, I'm not gonna go anymore,' you know. Her little ego can't take anymore. After awhile, kinda kills you, you know."

Terry tried to interrupt. "I thought about this," he began, but Wanda once more cut him off.

"Well, it pisses me off so bad," she hissed. "That Verna. I thought about that Verna, that's Amber's mother I'm talking about now. She's been going down there to the school. She has no reason to go up to that high school unless she is kissing butt, okay? Now, I know Mrs. Bassett has got to see this. I know she knows what's going on. The woman is not stupid, but the woman is not all upstairs, I've been told that, too. She likes to whine and squall, that kind of thing."

Like so many others in Channelview, Terry had become the hopelessly captive audience of one of Wanda's cheerleading mono-logues. All he could do was nod and mutter, "Um hmm."

Wanda went on without noticing. "Well, Verna's been going up there every day at seventh period and sitting around with Mrs. Bassett, watching the cheerleaders. I thought, Give me a break! I guess she just likes going down there at seventh period and watching the cheerleaders. But now, how obvious can you get!"

Terry tried again, "I know, but..."

"I mean, how obvious can you get!" Wanda said, this time louder to drown out Terry's attempt at conversation. "Other cheerleaders' mothers doing the same thing, and there's only going to be two picked, maybe three, maybe three!"

At Channelview High School, where Shanna would be enrolled the next school year, beginning in the fall of 1991, the cheerleading squad was composed of two or three girls from each grade level. Wanda was right—at most three freshman girls would make the squad.

Terry asked quietly, "And you think this is what we need to do?"

"I don't know what to do, Terry!" Wanda sounded angry and exasperated. "I don't know how to get rid of this woman, you know? I mean, what do you do there?"

"Well, it depends on how you want it done," Terry said.

"Well, what can you do?" Wanda asked. "What does this guy do?"

"He does everything," Terry said with confidence. "He can break her legs, he can burn her house...."

"I ain't gonna help him," Wanda interjected firmly.

"He can kidnap her and ship her off to Bumfuck, Egypt, you know," Terry joked. "Send her over there to Hussein."

Wanda finally laughed and quit her strange raving. "Let me ask you something else," she said seriously. "This cannot *ever*, and I know and I realize that you cannot be tied in to it, but Terry, if I ever get tied in to this, Shanna is...Hey, the kid will have to move. She cannot ever live in Channelview ever again. Do you know what the kids will do to her? Do you know what they will say to her?"

"That's another part of the deal we need to talk about," Terry agreed.

"Yeah," Wanda added. "How do you know somebody's not gonna get caught?"

Terry just laughed.

Wanda continued, "I started getting scared. I started thinking about this shit, and I think, Oh, God!, you know?"

Terry expressed surprise at her fears. "I thought that you had made up your mind, that you were 100 percent."

Wanda quickly reassured him of her intentions. "I know I want to do it. I want to do it."

"Because I have already stepped out on a limb here," Terry cautioned. "You know I don't associate with these people no more."

"I know, I know," Wanda said, perplexed. "I know I want to do it. But how do you know you're not gonna get caught? Do they squeal if they get caught?"

Terry tried to calm her fears. "I imagine what they will wind up doing is getting their money and getting gone. These people are professionals—they don't get caught."

Wanda seemd to relax. "Well, what are we talking about here?" she asked.

"That depends on if you want one or both, if you want the mother or..." Terry tried to explain.

Once again, Wanda interrupted. "I thought they didn't do the daughter, I thought they didn't take care of anybody else."

Terry quickly fabricated an explanation. "Well, they do, but it's expensive," he said. "Then again, it depends on what you want done."

"What kind of money are we talking about here," Wanda wanted to know. "Just give me an idea."

"Well," Terry said, "seventy-five hundred dollars."

Both Wanda and Terry were quiet for a second, then both laughed out loud. Terry said, "I told you it was going to be expensive. You can't go around killing people just for a nickel or dime, you know."

"Oh, I know that," Wanda snorted. "I understand that. But I don't have that kind of money that I can just come up with, okay?"

"That's the part I need to know," Terry said.

Wanda thought for a minute. "I've been trying to get rid of some land I got."

"How soon is this going to take place?" Terry asked.

Wanda pondered it. "Let's see. Cheerleader tryouts are gonna probably be in the middle of March."

"Okay," said Terry. "The middle of March. This is the middle of January."

"We got two months," Wanda thought out loud.

"*We've* got two months, but this guy, you know, he..." Terry started.

"You can do it tomorrow, I'm sure, if you need it to be done tomorrow," Wanda replied. "I mean, I understand that he can do it as soon as he's got the money, then he's gonna do it. But what if you give him his money and he don't do it?"

Terry explained how these things work. "That's where I made a little deal with him," he told his ex-sister-in-law. "Half down, and half when it's over."

"Okay," Wanda said, "so you're talking about thirty-five hundred dollars right now, and..."

"That's what I'm trying to say," Terry once again attempted to explain. "Do you want the mother or do you want the daughter or do you want them both?"

"What would be best?" Wanda asked. But in an instant she had arrived at her own answer. "Get rid of the daughter," she snapped. "Then for sure she ain't gonna be doing nothin'."

"That's what I'm saying," Terry responded. "But this is your choice."

"I can't believe I'm talking about this!" Wanda suddenly said with a laugh.

Terry began to laugh too, and added, "Well, I can't believe you and I are talking about this!"

After all, this odd couple had practically been enemies for years. And they certainly were a most incongruous pair. Wanda, as usual, was dressed to the nines in a silky synthetic-blend dress, stockings, and heels, her hair carefully swept out around her face and her makeup painstakingly and heavily applied. Terry Lynn, in his usual work-a-day mode, wore stained denim coveralls and heavy work boots. Yet here they sat, talking like old friends, talking about murder.

Wanda returned to the topic. "Well, how's he gonna do this? How are you gonna get the kid away from the mother?"

Terry said, "That's where you come in."

"A car wreck!" Wanda gleefully guessed.

"No," Terry said impatiently. "I've got to have pictures. I need, right now, names, address, what kind of car she drives."

"I've got all that," Wanda said with a dismissive wave of her hand.

"Well, I need it wrote down so I can give it to him," Terry went on.

Wanda balked again. "Oh, and you think I'm writin' it down in my handwriting? You bullshittin' me!"

"Well, give me a piece of paper then," Terry said. "God, I don't have a photostatic memory, you know."

Wanda turned and rummaged in the backseat of the Wagoneer, where her children's school books lay scattered. She muttered as she searched for a blank sheet of paper, "My husband would shit bricks if he knew I been talking about this."

Finally she located a piece of paper she thought would be safe to give Terry. "I don't want nothin' on there of me, you know. It has to be something like this that don't have anything on it," she said, handing the sheet to Terry.

He got out a pen and prepared to write. "Okay, what's the lady's name?" he asked.

"Verna," said Wanda. "V-e-r-n-a."

"Okay," said Terry.

"Heath," added Wanda. "H-e-a-t-h."

"That's the mom, right?" asked Terry, and Wanda nodded yes. "What's the daughter's name?"

"Amber," Wanda said in the same flat tone. She figured Terry could spell it without her help. "I don't have any good pictures of these people, though," she apologized. "But I can give you an annual picture of the girl. But I don't have a picture of the mother."

"Well, I'm gonna need one," Terry said.

"Maybe I can get one," Wanda thought out loud, then suggested an alternative. "Can't he just look at the car? Can't he just look at who the hell's driving the car, who it is?"

"Well, yeah, I guess," said Terry. "Okay, what kind of car does she drive?"

"She drives about a 1985 Mercury Grand Marquis," Wanda said. "Gray." She pointed out a similar colored car on the lot. "That's about the color of hers, that metallic gray, dark metallic gray, with a light gray vinyl top, landau, a half-vinyl top."

"Light gray top," Terry repeated as he wrote.

"It's got a busted windshield," Wanda added with a laugh. "and I can give you her license number. 475..."

Terry repeated for accuracy, "475..."

"G-E-D," Wanda finished. "Her address is 1355 Wrotham, w-r-o-t-h-a-m."

"Whoa, wait a minute," Terry said, struggling to keep up. Wanda was getting in a hurry. "W-r-o..." he repeated.

"T-h-a-m," finished Wanda. "That's right down the street from me."

"In Sterling Green?" asked Terry, and Wanda nodded that it was.

"Okay, how old is she?" Terry asked.

"She's thirteen," said Wanda.

"I mean the mother!" Terry explained.

"Oh, she's probably thirty-eight," said Wanda, "Thirty-seven, thirty-eight, about my age."

Terry returned to the nature of the job. "This guy told me he could do anything you wanted."

"What would you do, Terry?" Wanda asked plaintively.

"Gollee, Wanda, I can't tell you...." Terry said.

"Would you do it to the girl, or would you do it to the mother?" Wanda asked. "The girl is harder to get rid of. The mother ain't no problem, once you get rid of the girl."

"Well, if that's what you think is the way to do, you know," Terry said in a noncommittal tone. "What I'm saying, is that if something happens to that girl, maybe even just a leg broke, it might not look so good," he explained.

In earlier discussions with Blackwell and Helton, the officers had told Terry to try to sway Wanda away from the child. Even hard-bitten officers couldn't stomach the idea of a child being the subject of a hit. They knew, of course, that this was a sting. However, they still didn't know if Wanda was seeking assistance from others as well. They didn't want the murder of a child to be the result if she was.

"I think if the car wrecked, where they both died, if the car blew up or something, it might be different," Wanda mused. "An impact, an explosion or something, you know what I'm talking about? Then it wouldn't look so obvious. And usually it's just the two of them at night, traveling around, going to the gym and doing things."

"Oh, that's something else I need to know," Terry interjected. "Where does her husband work?"

"He works at Gerland's in Deer Park," Wanda said. Her years of being friendly with the Heaths were certainly coming in handy, she thought to herself. "I think he does shift work," she added, "he goes in at night."

"Can you get me a schedule on that?" Terry asked.

"No way!" said Wanda. "I don't know the woman that well!" She didn't know Verna well enough to know what shift her husband worked, but she damn sure knew her well enough to know her car license number.

"I just know he's at home on Thursdays and Fridays," Wanda went on. "And that's iffy. He's a manager. Not assistant manager. And his name is Jack."

"Okay," said Terry. "What time does she go to school?" he asked, referring to Amber.

"They go to school at 8:20. She probably leaves her house about a quarter to eight. Her mother brings her, her mother picks her up, her mother does everything for her."

"Does her mama wipe her ass?" Terry asked sarcastically.

"Probably!" Wanda said, with a hoot of laughter. Terry laughed, too. "She fixes her hair, you name it," Wanda said with disgust, then continued detailing the Heath family. "She has a twin, the little girl is a twin."

"What?" Terry said in alarm, wondering how they would distinguish the right one.

"She has a brother," Wanda explained. "So they can tell the difference. But, I mean, she is a twin."

"Okay now," Terry said, folding his notes. "I'm gonna have to meet this guy again. If we do something like that, if you just want them dead, you need to tell me, or if you just want them maimed for life."

Wanda faltered, "I ain't...I ain't..."

"Do you want to meet this guy?" Terry asked, following orders from the police.

"Hell no!" Wanda said forcefully. "I don't want no contact!"

"Well, he said he wanted to meet you, but I told him there wasn't no way," Terry said.

"No way, Jose!" Wanda chimed in, "I ain't gettin' my face in nothin'!"

"This is something else I will stipulate when we do the money thing," Terry told Wanda. "But you got to have the money."

"I know that, I understand that," Wanda said.

"Cuz when he comes after me," Terry said. "I'm gonna say, whoops, time out, hold on, let me show you where this woman lives, you know? What I'm saying is, if he does it and you say, Whoops, I don't have the money…"

Wanda reassured Terry. "If I go through with this, he'll have the money. I'm not gonna do that to you. I promise I'm not gonna do that."

"Well, I'm gonna cover my butt," Terry said with a laugh.

"But he's not going to proceed till we give him money, right?" Wanda asked. "He ain't gonna do nothin' by himself?"

"Well, naw," said Terry. "But he's gonna start finding out when they go to school, where they are out and about by themselves. Do you have any times that they are out and about by themselves that you know of?"

"I know on Thursday nights she goes to the gym with Shanna," Wanda said, referring to the girls' lessons at Alpha Gymnastics Studio.

"Well, I don't want Shanna around her," said the girl's doting uncle.

"We don't ride with her," Wanda explained. "It's just the same night."

"Where is this place at?" Terry asked.

"It's on the old Spencer Highway right across from Gilley's," Wanda said. "Where old Gilley's used to be."

"Do you know which way they go?" asked Terry.

"They go down the beltway," said Wanda. "Same as me."

Beltway 8 is a massive outer loop under construction around the city of Houston, some fifteen miles in any direction from the center of town, built to supplement the inner-city Loop 610 and relieve heavy traffic congestion. The construction process has been interminable, with roads constantly rerouted, lanes narrowed, and driving rendered unbelievably hazardous.

"That beltway is a treacherous road," Terry said thoughtfully, as if to suggest it might be a good location for the proposed "accident" that Verna and Amber might have.

"Alright," Terry said with finality. "I am going to give you something to think about here, and you need to get serious with me."

"Okay," Wanda said.

"This guy, he don't like doing children, alright?" Terry explained. "Seventy-five hundred dollars is the most for both of them to be dead."

"Okay, that's for both, that's for both," Wanda echoed.

"It's five thousand dollars for the girl and twenty-five hundred dollars for the mother," he itemized.

"The mother, she ain't worth a crap, is she?" Wanda laughed at her own cleverness. "Only twenty-five hundred dollars for the mother!"

"That's it, half down, half when it's completed," Terry continued.

"Maybe I should go with the mother," Wanda thought out loud. "And the kid, she can just be screwed with the mother. Maybe it would mess with her mind."

"I'm sure it would," Terry said, "but who you lookin' at?" He had noticed Wanda staring out the car window at something. "Why don't you turn out your light?" he suggested to Wanda.

"You ain't gonna expect an answer tomorrow, are you?" Wanda asked.

"I was kind of expecting an answer tonight," Terry said.

"Well, I have to find some money, I need to get some money," Wanda explained.

She then discussed with Terry how she would raise the money. She told Terry she could turn to her husband, C. D. "I'll just tell him what I want it for," Wanda said off-handedly. "He already knows I've been talking about it."

"What!" Terry exclaimed.

"I've been talking about this for two years," Wanda almost boasted.

"Doing this woman in?" Terry asked.

"Killing her kid!" Wanda corrected. "C. D., he's the one put the idea in my head."

"No-o-o-o shit!" Terry was shocked.

"Yeah, no shit," Wanda said. "He say, 'Yeah, we'll just have her blowed away,' and I said, 'Right, we ought to.'"

"C. D. don't know nobody?" Terry wondered, fearing that the police might have been right about Wanda conducting several murder contracts simultaneously.

"No, he really don't," Wanda sneered. "He is so dang straight up and honest, it's ridiculous. It makes you sick."

Terry laughed. "So the second choice is to call Terry?" He wanted to find out if any others had been contacted.

"No," Wanda squirmed. "I mean, I don't know anybody who knows anybody. I have heard that crap that you knew those kind of people, and I said, 'Right,' you know."

"Well, I do," Terry conceded.

The two went over possible times for their next discussion for a few minutes, and Wanda again expressed her concern about the money.

Finally she asked, "What if we told him we wanted to go with the mother, and then things happen that I could get more, and get both of them, would that matter?"

"No," said Terry.

"Okay, then," Wanda decided, "I say the mother. And like I say, during the day the kids are in school all day long and she is by herself. But she has a two- or three-year-old son, and I don't know if he goes to Mother's Day Out."

"I'm fixin' to have to get out of here," Terry said, trying to wind up the long meeting with Wanda.

"I might can come up with the twenty-five hundred dollars," Wanda said. "Much easier than I could seventy-five hundred dollars."

"And to be honest with you, Wanda," Terry said. "Doing kids is just, you know..."

"Yeah, but Terry, you don't know this little girl!" Wanda interrupted, her voice dripping with venom. "If you knew her! Ooooooh! I can't stand her. I mean, she's a bitch! Makes me sick! I mean, I could knock her in the face, you know?"

Terry cut her off before she ranted on again for another twenty minutes. "Look, I'll call you Tuesday between five-thirty and six, and you see if you can come up with the twenty-five hundred dollars, okay?"

"Okay," Wanda agreed. "I'll see you later."

The two exchanged good-byes, and Terry got out of Wanda's car and into his own. Wanda drove out of the parking lot. Terry lit a cigarette and reached down to turn off the tape recorder.

"Ah shit!" he said to himself. He couldn't figure out how to turn the damn thing off. Blackwell and Helton had shown him how to turn it on, but not how to turn it off. "I don't know how to cut this thing off!" he said, knowing the officers could hear it over their radio. "But I'll be there in a minute."

He got out of his car and walked over to the plain sedan and got in the backseat.

Helton congratulated Terry Harper, "You did good, man, I want to tell you!" Both officers were grinning with excitement. "Is it still going on?" Helton asked.

"Yeah, man, it's still going on," Terry said, and shook his head in wonder.

6

Wanda Takes the Fall

Terry laughed to himself all the way home to his trailer. "Holy shit!" he said out loud, and reached forward to crank the country-western music blaring on the radio a little higher. He had never before, in his trouble-filled life, felt so important or useful. For once, he thought, he was doing something right. All those years of being called a drunkard, a drug addict, a bum...Now he would give them something else to talk about.

He skidded his tires as he wheeled his truck into the dirt driveway of his and Marla's mobile-home lot. Marla was waiting supper, none too happily, and glared at her husband as he stomped up the trailer steps and into the prefab home. She was more than a little suspicious about exactly where Terry had really been that evening. This whole business with the sheriffs and Wanda sounded just a little too far-fetched to be true.

Terry ignored his wife's silence and strode straight to the telephone on the kitchen counter. He punched in a number on the push-button dialer. After a moment's silence, Marla, sitting on the living-room couch four feet away, heard Terry exclaim, "Tony! It's Terry." Marla later swore that Terry then launched into an extensive account of that evening's activities, detailing his conversation with Wanda that had been taped by police. He told his older brother everything.

"He was more or less bragging about what he had said," Marla later explained. By her account, Terry first asked, "You've always wanted your children, right? Full custody? Well, now you're finally going to get them." Tony must have seemed intrigued, for Marla says Terry told Tony, "We're gonna burn that bitch," and then explained how.

They had set Wanda up, Marla later remembered Terry saying. Wanda would take a fall, and then Tony would get his kids. After all, if Wanda were in prison, who else besides Tony, the children's father, would be a better candidate to care for them? Marla claims she was shocked by the vindictiveness of this plot. She didn't personally know Wanda Holloway, but she had been in Channelview long enough to know the woman was considered an upstanding member of the community.

Besides, Marla and Terry hadn't been getting along very well lately, if they ever had. Marla was mad because Terry had started drinking again, heavily. Sometimes she joined him. The result was often a vicious argument fueled by the alcohol each had consumed. There had been so many fights lately that Marla maintained a constant feeling of irritation, if not outright anger, at Terry. When she heard him bragging to his brother about how cool he was, with the police, and Wanda, and getting her to say all these things on tape, she felt a flash of hatred.

She kept it to herself, though. She had learned, from living with Terry for the last year and a half, not to mess with him much when he was drinking. If she confronted her husband about what she thought were his true motives in meeting with Wanda, he was liable to flare up, and only God knew what might happen after that. There had been too many times when she had had to call the police because Terry was out with a gun shooting in the air, or worse, at somebody else's trailer. She didn't tell anyone at the time, but she made careful mental notes about everything she had heard Terry tell his older brother.

Terry kept laughing, she later recalled, saying, "I've always hated that bitch." Marla remembers that Terry reminded Tony about the time

Wanda had squealed on him to the Missouri Pacific Railroad, back when Tony and Wanda were still married. Tony had had a good job as a clerk; everybody knew that railroad jobs were gravy trains. But Wanda had ruined it all by reporting Tony as a thief to his company when she was mad at him for cheating on her as their marriage disintegrated. Tony had been fired.

Still, Marla was shocked that after more than ten years, such anger was still brewing toward Wanda in the Harpers. "So," she thought. "That's what this is all about. They're just trying to screw that lady around." As a fellow lady who also felt she had been screwed around, Marla became immediately sympathetic to Wanda's situation.

Terry finished his conversation with Tony and sat down with a self-satisfied sigh in his recliner. He gulped down the dinner Marla had kept warm for him as he watched the color TV. One of his favorite movies, *Lethal Weapon*, was coming on HBO.

Terry had a week to relish his new role in life as a police informant before he had to meet with Blackwell and Helton again. Although he had been cautioned by the officers not to discuss the case with anyone, Terry could barely contain himself. According to Marla he called Tony several more times that week, to talk about the case. And Terry himself admitted talking to his friend and "spiritual advisor" at work, Bob Wilburs.

Marla later said she thought Terry was especially enthusiastic about his new sideline activities because, she says, "He had always been the black sheep of his family." Terry thought that if he was successful at ruining Wanda's life and getting Tony full custody of his children, he would at last be redeemed in the eyes of his family.

Terry insists now that it was never that way. His main concern, he maintains, was the safety of Verna Heath and her daughter. Second in line of importance was his own fear that Wanda would somehow pin this plot on him if he didn't report it to the police.

The investigation continued. The following Monday, January 21, Terry once again met with Blackwell and Helton after work at the Pasadena Motor Lodge to place a call to Wanda. But the pay phone was broken, so the trio traipsed down the street and around the corner to a convenience-store phone booth. According to their prearranged schedule, Terry placed the call to the Holloway home between 5:30 and 6:00 P.M.

Wanda answered the phone, but it must have been a bad time for her. Terry said, "Hey, what are you doing?" Wanda said icily, "I'm sorry?" Terry said, "Hey, Wanda!" Wanda said, "I'm sorry, you've got the wrong number." Terry then asked Wanda if it was a bad time to call, and she responded, "No, I'm sorry. That's not it. Thank you, bye."

"C. D. must have been home," Terry said to the cops as he turned around, hanging up the receiver.

"We'll try again tomorrow," Blackwell suggested.

According to police records: "January 22, 1991, approximately 6:00 P.M. Terry Harper is going to place a call to Wanda Holloway at 452–7022 in reference to a capital solicitation of capital murder."

This time, Sergeant Blackwell came alone. Terry once again dialed Wanda's number. As with the previous calls, Sergeant Blackwell had attached a suction-cup recording device to the phone receiver. A microcassette recorder heard everything that was said.

Wanda answered the phone, but quickly indicated to Terry that she couldn't talk at that time. Apparently her family was within earshot. Instead, she stammered nonincriminating answers to Terry's questions about the planned meeting to exchange money for the hit on Verna. After only minutes of conversation, the two agreed to talk again the following Friday, when Wanda said she would know something about the money.

Once again, when Terry went home to Marla, she says he boasted about his police activities. He called Tony again, she later reported, and laughed repeatedly about how he had scared Wanda with his threats of having the nonexistent hit man come after her if she reneged on the deal.

"He said that he told her that these people don't play games," Marla later reported of Terry's conversation with Tony. "He told her that they play for keeps, and if you try to change your mind or back out, they'll come after you because they know where you live."

The Organized Crime Task Force members were starting to feel pressured. As busy as they were, they couldn't afford to spend week after week on a capital solicitation case that might not even happen. There were plenty of criminals out there for them to pursue without having to wait around for a housewife to turn murderess in Sterling Green. But still, there was something about this case.... Both officers still feared that Mrs. Holloway might have been dealing with other people who would really accept her offer to pay for the Heaths' murders.

They arranged another meeting with Terry for the following Friday, January 25, so he could yet again call Wanda from the Motor Lodge pay phone, or whatever working phone they could find thereabouts.

Terry had a little trouble placing the call. The Pasadena operator kept telling him to deposit another quarter, but he had just done so. He screamed into the phone, seconds before Wanda picked up her end, "Woman, I done put one quarter in there and got a recording! And now I need to put another quarter?"

Just then someone answered the phone at the Holloway home. "Hello," a young female voice said. "Is Wanda there?" Terry asked.

The voice said, "Mom! Phone! I don't know who it is."

Wanda picked up, "Hello."

"Can you talk?" asked Terry.

"Yeah, sure can," Wanda replied.

"Okay, so where do we stand?" Terry asked.

"I got some jewelry," Wanda said, "some earrings. We paid like fifteen hundred dollars for them. They're worth probable twenty-five hundred, maybe three thousand. I'm not sure. That's what he was told."

A long conversation ensued in which Terry urged Wanda to hock the earrings she wanted to use for payment, since cash was much preferred by the hit man.

Wanda indicated she had no knowledge of how to pawn something, so Terry advised her. He suggested she should try a better area of Houston, not only to avoid being seen in Channelview, but also to get top dollar for her jewels.

Finally, Terry asked her when they could close the deal.

"Maybe I can do something Monday or Tuesday," Wanda said.

"Alright, let's do Monday night," Terry decided.

"Okay," Wanda said.

"Same time?" Terry asked.

"Yeah," Wanda said.

"Okay, gal, but we really need to..." Terry again stressed the need for some action, "need to start moving on this, 'cause we're dragging it along about two, two to three weeks." He had already told her of the hit man's impatience and his need to constantly be on the move in and out of the country. In reality, of course, it was the police officers' impatience that necessitated the rush. "You know, I told you before," he concluded, "he is subject to just up and fly at any time."

"Alright, no problem then," Wanda said.

"Okay, bye," Terry said, and hung up the phone. He turned and grinned first at Flynt Blackwell and then at George Helton, who stood on either side of him in front of the pay phone. The two officers exchanged a look over Terry's head, and then Helton said. "Good." He and his partner both knew they had just gotten one step closer to their quarry, the permed and petite housewife from Sterling Green. The organ-playing bible thumper had just described exactly how she was going to pay for the hit on Verna Heath—with her diamond earrings.

That wasn't the way Wanda had wanted it, though. Just a few days before, she had desperately tried to think up other ways to obtain the cash that Terry kept saying the hit man wanted. She had even gone to Terry's dad, R. E. Harper, at his Harper Convenience Store and Check Cashing Stand on Sheldon Road and asked her former father-in-law if he could loan her a couple thousand dollars for awhile.

R. E. Harper recalls a distraught Wanda coming in during a weekday while her kids were at school. "She didn't tell me what she wanted the money for," he later recalled. "Said it was something to do with the kids. I just flat didn't have the money to lend her, else I might would have done it," said the Harper family patriarch, a kind-hearted man who had often been called on to lend his sons money to help them out of jams.

So Wanda had to use her jewels, those hard-won badges of her worth earned from years of pandering to older, richer husbands. It was, in a way, proof of how badly she wanted the job done that she would even consider using such baubles to pay for it.

The following Monday, January 28, Terry Harper once again stopped at the Pasadena Motor Lodge on his way home from the Phillips plant to give Wanda a call. He was met by the same two officers who had been working the investigation for the last two weeks. Sergeant Blackwell and Detective Helton wanted Terry to find out in this call if Wanda had hocked the jewels or otherwise found some cash to make the initial payoff.

At ten minutes to six that evening, the officers hooked up the suction-cup device to the phone receiver at the Motor Lodge. Terry dialed the number. He got the wrong number on the first try and looked sheepishly up at the officers as he redialed the correct number for Wanda's house.

After some initial chatting about the cover story they'd cooked up to explain Terry's calls, the real conversation began. "Alright, here's the deal," Wanda explained. "I haven't got to do that other thing yet, so I'm going to blow it off right now. Tell that guy not to worry about it 'til he gets back into town or whatever at the end of the month. Then we'll see, but I ain't going to be able to…"

"I got a deal for you," Terry proposed before Wanda could finish. "He'll take the rings. I mean, the earrings."

Wanda laughed, and said something that sounded like, "Cause it ain't, okay?"

Terry reiterated their purpose. "Now what are we talking about? Did we ever make that decision?"

Wanda said cryptically, "The first, the first…"

"The what?" said Terry, puzzled.

"What do you mean?" Wanda asked. It was obvious from her vagueness that she must have an audience at home.

"The amount," said Terry. "The mother, or the daughter, or both."

"Yeah, the first," Wanda again said unclearly.

"The mother?" guessed Terry.

"Yeah," said Wanda.

Terry explained to Wanda that the hit man had agreed to take the jewelry in lieu of money, but the cash was what he really wanted. The deal was that the hit man would take the earrings up front, but after the deed was done he would return the diamonds in exchange for the cash that Wanda would manage to acquire by then. There was only one catch, "I've got to have the earrings today," Terry told her.

Wanda jumped right in. "That shouldn't be no problem," she assured her ex-husband's brother. "I was fixin' to be leaving here and pick up Shane's girlfriend at six, and we're going to the Royal Wood Baptist church over there off Uvalde and Highway 90. It starts at seven, so I could drop them off and maybe I could bring you the pictures."

They agreed to meet at Grandy's at 7:00 P.M..

Terry smiled gleefully up at the police officers. Wanda was finally going to make the payoff, this very night. He hadn't been wrong, as the officers had surely thought during this investigation. He had known what he was talking about. Wanda Holloway wanted someone dead and was willing to pay for the job. That very night they were going to have their final meeting, and Terry would prove to the cops that she meant business when he walked away with two gleaming diamonds in his pocket.

There in the Pasadena Motor Lodge parking lot, Blackwell and Helton showed Terry a second time how to operate the pocket microcassette recorder they had loaned him for his previous meeting with Wanda at Grandy's. This time, they not only showed him how to turn the tape on, but also showed him the OFF button. They loaded the machine with a fresh cassette, and Officer Blackwell taped an introduction.

"This is January 28, 1991, Sergeant F. E. Blackwell. It's approximately 6:20. Now there's going to be a meeting, set for seven o'clock this date between Terry Harper and Wanda Holloway in reference to a solicitation of capital murder at the Grandy's parking lot, Wallisville at Uvalde," he said in a businesslike monotone.

As they did the last time Terry met Wanda in person, the officers planted a transmitter under Terry's shirt so they could listen by remote on their cruiser radio while the conversation was in progress.

Wanda was a little bit late for the meeting. In fact, Terry was beginning to wonder if she had decided not to come. Shortly before seven, as he sat under the mercury vapor lights of the Grandy's parking lot, he thought he saw Wanda drive south on Uvalde, without stopping. It looked as if she had some other people in the car, too.

But then, a few minutes after seven, she was back, and alone. She had just dropped her daughter off for a church meeting and was now going to resume her discussions about killing with Terry Harper. She wheeled her Wagoneer into the parking lot next to Terry, who had driven one of his dad's trucks. As he had done at the first meeting, Terry got out of the truck and got into Wanda's car.

After a brief conversation, Wanda said, "Okay, look," and reached into her purse and pulled out a Ziploc sandwich bag with two sparkling earrings inside. "Here," she said, proffering the goods to Terry. "You can see 'em. They're like point seventy-five each, right at between seventy-five and eighty, which is a carat and a half."

Terry, who didn't know diamonds from dog doo, pretended to study the jewels in the dim light from outside. "Okay," he finally said, putting them back in their protective plastic. "You'll get these back."

"Well, listen," said Wanda. "How is he going to do this?" Her voice had a sharp nervous edge to it. Both Terry and Wanda then began to talk at once, and the tape recorder was unable to record either's voice clearly.

Finally Terry was heard saying, "I was lucky I got a hold of this guy."

Wanda added in a rush, "Well, see, I didn't even get to go look at those. Then I got to thinking that day, and I thought, screw it! I mean, I am tired of this hassle and hassling Terry, and that guy don't understand. And also, I hate to admit it, but I didn't want to tell him I don't have it til the end of February. If you can't do it, and come back, then that's fine. And if he don't, well, I just got screwed is all I can say." Wanda seemed afraid she was about to be ripped off by the hit man. She was, of course, about to be ripped off, but not the way she feared.

"Alright then," Terry tried to calm her. "This is what's gonna happen. This is what you call D-Day. This is it." His years of watching *Godfather*-type movies had finally paid off—he had the patter of a gangland operative down to a tee.

"When is it gonna happen?" asked Wanda tensely.

"Well, I ain't gonna tell you that," Terry said smugly, with an all-knowing air, as if Wanda must be horribly naive about how "these things" worked.

Terry then told Wanda the big problem she faced was that if she did not come up with the money owed the hit man, he would come after her. She said she would by February 28, a month hence.

Then Terry asked, "And this is what you want to do?" As he had throughout his conversations with Wanda, Terry was once again offering her the chance to back out. She didn't take him up on it.

"Oh yeah," she said, her voice dripping venom. "I got to have her. I can't afford to do her, I can barely give up twenty-five, okay? And I can't afford five. But I'd love to have seventy-five, and I could do them both in, okay?" Wanda laughed almost hysterically before continuing. "The mother's done more damage than the daughter, though," she rationalized. "The mother is the one that screwed me around. She's the one that got Shanna kicked off last year, got her disqualified!"

"Yeah," Terry pretended to agree, although he truly was amazed at the level of Wanda's hatred of the Heaths.

Wanda continued to rail against her nemesis. "The mother's the one that done all the damage! Now, if you stop her...that's another reason I hate to wait til February because she gonna have all the little things made. Amber gonna have all that to hand out, even with her mom here or ain't here. She still gonna have all that shit to hand out."

At the high school, where both Amber and Shanna would be trying out soon for the upcoming fall cheerleader positions, the rules allowed students to hand out trinkets and favors. Eager mothers like Wanda and Verna planned their daughters' treats and began making them well before the actual campaign.

"Call me on Monday the twenty-eighth," Wanda said. "Like we been doing."

"Okay," Terry agreed. "Ah, I guess, you know, if anything happens, I guess you'll know when it does." He giggled.

"Yeah, I sure will," Wanda said.

"Cause she won't be around no more," laughed Terry, referring to Verna Heath's imminent disappearance.

"I mean, I won't know right when it happens, but I'll know eventually, a day or two later or something," Wanda clarified. Then she started wondering. "Now, what is he...I don't want her ass showing back up in Channelview."

"No," agreed Terry. That would be a mess.

"Okay then," said Wanda, just making sure. "I just don't want her, two weeks later, coming up and pointing the finger at Wanda and accusing me, even though..."

Terry promptly interrupted. "How is she gonna do that when she is gonna be dead?" he asked.

"I don't know, Oh, I don't know about that anyway," stammered Wanda.

"I mean, that is what you want, isn't it?" Terry pressed. Hadn't the woman just seconds before said she didn't want Verna's ass back in town? The surest way to guarantee that would be to kill her, wouldn't it?

Wanda didn't know and didn't care. "Well, I just want her out of here," she said. "I don't care if they ship her to Cuba and keep her there for fifteen years, okay? I just don't want her showing back up here in five years." Her voice had the same hate-filled tone it always had when she talked about "those two."

"Well, I mean, that's what you told me," Terry explained.

"I want her gone," Wanda said forcefully. "I want her gone."

"So..." Terry began, but Wanda kept talking.

"Well, you said if he didn't kill her he would take her to Cuba or something, but she wouldn't be around, finally."

"Well, whenever I talked to him, he said okay," explained Terry.

"I don't want to know what he's gonna do," said Wanda. "The less I know, the better off I am."

They finished up their conversation and Terry moved to get out of Wanda's car. The door handle stuck and delayed his progress.

"I hate that door," Wanda said with a laugh. Terry laughed, too, but not about the door. He knew he had just helped set Wanda Ann Holloway up. That bitch was history.

By prearrangement with Blackwell and Helton, Terry left Grandy's and drove a short distance south on Uvalde Street to a meeting place selected earlier by the police officers—a doughnut shop, of course. He waited until the officers pulled in, then left his vehicle and entered the backseat of their car. He excitedly handed them the baggie with the earrings in it and his pocket recorder, which was still running. He still didn't know how to turn it off.

Blackwell and Helton took the earrings and congratulated Terry on a job well done. "That should do it," Helton told him. "This should be enough for us to move with." He then told Terry they would be in touch when they needed him. The two officers told their informant goodnight and headed for home.

Terry headed for home too, after stopping for a few cold ones on the way. When he got back to Elspeth Street, and the trailer where he thought Marla was waiting, he felt jubilant and excited. Marla did not share his enthusiasm because she was not there. The police may have thought Terry was a hero, but she damn sure didn't. That very day, she had packed her bags and left. She had had enough of Terry and his braggadocious talk. She had heard him boast to Tony just one time too many about how good he was at conning Wanda, and how great he was for helping Tony get back his kids.

She later said of her decision to go, "That was the day I knew things were so out of hand it was unreal. This whole situation with Terry and Wanda, this whole fabrication. I was scared because of what I had been through and because I just didn't have anyplace to go, really, I thought I'd do it as long as I could, you know. Just go along with things until it gets to be too much, and then I'd leave. That day he was supposed to have met with Wanda and been wired is the day I left."

She left Terry a letter that read:

Terry, you told me when we went back together and everyone else that if you ever, for any reason, brought a gun back in this house for any reason, you wanted me to leave you. Well, you've got it. You're a very dangerous person and everyone knows it. Only difference is no one else has to live with you. For my family's peace and safety, I am not contacting them.

If you so much as call or have them call, I will be forced to make some calls myself, the D.A., for one. Remember when you lied to the police about calling Tony and discussing the case and when you were bragging about setting Wanda up?

I taped you and your conversation with Tony. I did this for my safety. I want a divorce. I don't love you. I'm tired of being lied to and used and controlled. My attorney knows everything. When my divorce papers come final in the mail at this address, 14337 Hillsboro, Houston, Texas, I will call Detective Dionne and return this gun you ordered me to go get. Goodbye and God Bless. Marla

P.S. I hope you can eventually straighten out your terrible life.

Marla went to stay with one of her sons at an apartment in another part of town. She did not call the police, she later said, because she was afraid of what might happen. According to Marla, she and Terry had had another one of their ugly confrontations not long before. As Marla described it, "Terry had held a gun at my head for about three hours one night. The police were called, and eighteen officers showed up out in the yard, and he shot at them. When I called them," she continued to relate, "I told them that he was going to shoot at them, because he told me if I called the law that there would be a shoot-out, because he wasn't going to go alive. He said he would go to Honduras first."

Colombia, Cuba, Honduras—the people of Channelview seemingly had many dreams of visiting exotic Latin America.

After the police came, Marla related disgustedly, not much happened. "They ended up arresting Terry, handcuffing him, and then letting him go." A typical Terry Harper escapade.

This incident happened sometime before Terry's final meeting with Wanda Holloway, and apparently Sergeant Blackwell and Detective Helton were unaware of it. The day after Terry's second rendezvous with his former sister-in-law at Grandy's Country Cookin', the two officers took their evidence back to the main office to see Captain Shaffer and Assistant District Attorney Joe Magliolo about obtaining a warrant for Wanda Holloway's arrest.

Magliolo briefly reviewed the newly gathered evidence with the officers. He and the officers could all clearly hear on the tapes exactly what Wanda wanted—Verna Heath "gone," either by killing or shipment to Cuba or by whatever means necessary. They could also clearly see the diamond earrings Wanda had used as a down payment for the deed she wanted done. But, as a lawyer, Magliolo knew that Wanda's actions needed to be described in terms that matched the Texas penal code's descriptions of criminal activities. Hiring someone to kill Verna was solicitation of capital murder, Magliolo knew, which was a felony in the first degree in the eyes of Texas.

Magliolo knew that this case wasn't as clear cut as many other murder-for-hire cases. For one thing, the undercover operative was not a police officer, as the task force generally preferred. For another, they hadn't carried their pretenses through as far as they often did. In many cases of this nature, the undercover officers liked to go so far as to pretend to the solicitor that the murder had in fact been carried out. They would usually do this by approaching the solicitor after the "killing" with dummied-up photos of the dead body. When the contractor expressed his satisfaction with the job, and payed up the rest of the fee promised upon completion of the murder, the resulting evidence of intent to have another killed would be incontrovertible.

This case was a little trickier. Because of their fears for the Heaths' safety, none of the task force members wanted to play the game that long. After some discussion, they all agreed they had enough evidence against the little church lady to move ahead without going the extra distance they usually preferred.

Without hesitation, the task force liaison attorney quickly drafted a warrant for the officers to take before a magistrate for execution. It met all the requirements of the Texas Code of Criminal Procedure—it was issued in the name of "The State of Texas," it named Wanda Ann Holloway, it charged the commission of an offense, and it outlined the "probable cause" the officers were acting under in seeking the warrant: the evidence they had collected in the last two weeks that indicated Wanda had committed this solicitation.

On the morning of January 30, 1991, Sergeant Flynt Blackwell and Detective George Helton both appeared before an appropriate magistrate. In Texas, any magistrate may issue an arrest warrant. Magistrates include all state and county judges, including justices of the peace, as well as mayors and municipal court judges. Both officers signed an affidavit swearing that, to the best of their knowledge, the information contained in the warrant was true. One bit of information contained in the warrant was, in fact, not true, but the officers nevertheless signed the document. That part said that their informant, Terry Lynn Harper, had no known criminal record. In the warrant, Terry Harper was described as "a credible person with no known criminal history." His long track record of petty crimes and misdemeanors was, for that one moment, obliterated. The investigating officers had simply not bothered to ask or check.

The magistrate signed the warrant, authorizing the officers to arrest Wanda Ann Holloway without delay. Blackwell and Helton got in their car and headed for Channelview.

7

Legal Eagles and Beagles

Wanda Ann Holloway was, at that very moment, on her way home from Channelview High School after having put in a long day working in the school office. For once, at least, she thought to herself, I'll be getting paid for putting in those hours up there. That day, Wednesday, January 30, had been Wanda's first day on her new temporary job as a substitute worker in Channelview's principal's office. Her "Friends Like You" volunteer work had actually led to something a little more worthwhile. Of course, it didn't hurt that Ann Goodson, the mother of Shane's girlfriend, Amy, worked as the school secretary and had helped Wanda get the paid position.

Since it was after four o'clock, Wanda knew that Shanna was probably already home, alone, from Alice Johnson Junior High, so she hurried through her shopping stop at Gerland's grocery—not the one where Jack Heath worked—on her way back to Sterling Green. She only needed a few supplies for that night's dinner.

Because she was hurrying, Wanda didn't notice the unmarked car parked across from her home on Mincing Lane. She had no idea who Sergeant Blackwell and Detective Helton were as the men approached her. Nevertheless, she turned and faced them squarely when they called her name. "Yes, I'm Wanda Holloway," she said, her chin thrust up in the air with pride.

"You're under arrest for the solicitation of the capital murder of Verna Heath," Detective Helton said in his usual deadpan manner. Wanda remained motionless and her expression did not change.

Helton continued with the required Miranda warnings, not wanting to take any chances of screwing this case up. "You have the right to remain silent," he intoned from memory. "Any statement you make may be used against you. You have the right to an attorney. If you cannot afford an attorney, you have the right to have an attorney appointed by a court of law to advise you."

Wanda still stood silently as Helton finished his recitation. She did not resist or act surprised. Instead, she quietly asked if she could check on her daughter before being taken away. Her second major concern, according to arresting officer Helton, was what she should wear. No matter what circumstances she found herself in, Wanda Holloway always wanted to appear the perfect lady.

"The officers were very nice," she later related of her arrest. "They let me go in and call my mother to come stay with Shanna, since she was alone. And they let me take off my jewelry before going to jail." The jailhouse was certainly no place for canary diamonds; even the police knew that.

Wanda was taken to the Harris County east-side lockup and booked on the charge of solicitation of capital murder, a felony in the first degree. The punishment for her crime could be five years to life in prison if she were later found guilty. She did not cry, she did not plead. She was a proud woman, but meekly complied with the jail matron's requests. Wasn't much sense in fighting now, she thought. Save that for later.

Her one allowed phone call was to her husband, C. D. He would know what to do since he often had to bail out some of his employees on trucking violations and the like. C. D. Holloway had been around the law enough to know that the first thing he had to do was get his wife a lawyer, and a good one. As the old saying goes, if you don't know the law, know a lawyer.

"Don't worry, honey," he told his young wife. "Just sit tight, and don't talk, and someone will be there to help you as soon as possible." He had had his share of legal disputes, but he had never had big trouble like this. Nevertheless, he vowed to stand by his wife throughout her ordeal.

Holloway first called a young attorney he knew from his business dealings, Harry Herzog, in Houston. Herzog was not a criminal attorney, but immediately told Holloway he would help find a good one. As it happened, one of Herzog's classmates from the South Texas College of Law in Houston, Troy McKinney, had recently affiliated with one of the better known defense attorneys in Houston, Stanley Schneider.

Schneider was well-known in Houston, primarily for his success in handling appeals. He might not win at trial as often as some other attorneys, but hardly anyone could beat Stanley when it came to developing clever grounds for reversals at higher judicial levels. At least that's the way he always told it. Still in his early forties, the New York native, who had studied law at St. Mary's University in San Antonio, was said to be an ace at keeping up with all the latest rulings of the Texas Court of Criminal Appeals. He kept his opponents from the D.A.'s office constantly on their toes with his fancy legal footwork.

In one case, for example, the bearded, dark-haired Schneider was defending an infamous murderer known as the Austin Strangler. Because of the case's notoriety (the defendant was accused of brutally murdering several women), the district attorney's office chief of felony trials, Rusty Hardin, prosecuted the case for the state. Hardin had long had the reputation as one of the best trial lawyers in the Harris County D.A.'s office. During voir dire, though, Stanley Schneider threw Hardin for a loop.

During a typical voir dire, or jury selection, in Texas, the prosecuting and defense attorneys pick their jurors from a panel of possible jurors ranging in number from thirty to sixty, depending on the nature of the case. More jurors may be sent over for selection if the first group fails to yield an unbiased jury of twelve plus an alternate. The panelists are assigned numbers, and interviewed in consecutive order beginning with number one. Under the Texas criminal procedure rules then in use, before selection began either side could ask that the panel be shuffled, or assigned new numbers. Such a shuffling might be requested, say, in a case involving the murder of a nurse if the first twenty panel members all turned out to be nurses. For obvious reasons, the defense would not want such people on their jury, and might request a shuffle so as to get a more objective audience.

In the case of the Austin Strangler, though, Schneider tried to pull a fast one on Hardin. Unbeknownst to Hardin, the Court of Criminal Appeals had just that week issued a slip opinion, a brand-new law that had been unpublished except on fliers mailed to D.A.'s and other interested parties. According to this new law it was now permissible to request a shuffle at any point in the voir dire process, not just at the beginning. Even the most scrupulous legal scholar would have difficulty keeping up with each and every new rule that the courts routinely issued. Midway through voir dire on the strangler case, Schneider stood up in the courtroom and respectfully requested that the judge allow a panel shuffle.

Hardin looked completely dumbfounded. He had never heard of such a request. But he knew Stanley Schneider well enough to realize that it might be best not to object and insist that the rules, as he understood them, be followed. Although Stanley often had a rather hapless, befuddled air about him in a courtroom, he knew his rules. Hardin told the judge he had no objection to the shuffle, and it took place.

Later, after winning a conviction, Hardin was glad he'd followed his hunch. Schneider knew when he made the request that a new rule was now operative. If the prosecutor had objected to the shuffle, the judge, who was also unaware of a rule change, would have granted the objection and refused to allow Schneider the shuffle. Schneider was no doubt counting on that. He would then have had instant grounds for an appeal if he lost the case on the technicality that the new rule had not been followed.

Of course, as often as not he would lose his appeals, but still he maintained his reputation in the legal community as a tenacious, intelligent, and dedicated advocate for his clients. He would try most anything to get them off, even putting forth incredibly far-fetched arguments explaining why his client was innocent. He had been in the news a lot because of his high-profile cases, including one in which he had won an acquittal for a notorious black gangster charged with promoting prostitution and organized crime activities in a Houston ghetto. Schneider proudly displayed in his office a smiling photo of himself arm in arm with the known pimp and crack-cocaine kingpin.

His new associate, Troy McKinney, shared Schneider's bent for statutory skill as opposed to great courtroom demeanor. A tall, thin, gangly young man in his early thirties, McKinney had graduated near the top of his class at South Texas. He did not cut an impressive swath with either his looks or his laconic style in court. His shock of curly blond hair and scraggly mustache, together with his strong Texas twang, made him seem more like a country and western singer than an attorney. But McKinney could quote section and verse of the Texas statutes with the best of them.

Because Herzog placed the call for help to McKinney first, Troy drew the job as lead attorney for Wanda Holloway, with Stanley Schneider sitting a close second chair. The pair immediately met with C. D. Holloway to discuss how bail could be met. Because it was already late in the day, the attorneys warned Holloway his wife would probably have to spend the night in jail. At least she was lucky enough to have been taken to the smaller, substation jail, which was a much cleaner, less violent place than the huge jungle of the main Harris County jail in downtown Houston.

Later that evening, Wanda's bail was set at ten thousand dollars, a relatively low amount for a first-degree felony. The court had originally set the amount at twenty thousand dollars, but her attorneys successfully argued that it should be reduced. After all, this was her first offense, and the little lady from Channelview certainly did not seem to be a threat to the community. However, Wanda did have to spend the night in jail—in a private room—because by that time all offices and banks were closed and the paperwork simply couldn't be done before morning. Wanda remained stoic throughout this ordeal and later thanked her jail tenders for their kindness to her. Early the next morning, C. D. brought the bail money—in cash—to win his wife's release. Most people would have had to use a bondsman to raise that much cash, but not C. D. Holloway. He always kept large amounts of cash handy.

Word of Wanda's arrest spread like wildfire. The tiny *Baytown Sun* newspaper was the first to trumpet the news of Wanda's arrest for this bizarre crime. The paper's police reporter, Jane Howard, had been among the first in the media to hear of it. A young blonde who had grown up in the area, Howard had been working closely with the

Harris County task force since its creation and had developed the kind of rapport with its officers that led to them giving her inside tips. Captain T-Bone Shaffer of the task force talked to Jane before anyone else about the so-called cheerleader murder plot.

By that same evening, however, all the major news outlets in Houston were on the case, too. The six o'clock television news on all channels carried the story the evening of January 31, and the international media flurry began in earnest after that. The community of Channelview was besieged with reporters from all over, anxiously interviewing the locals about their town, looking for someone, anyone, who could shed some light on the strange motive for Wanda's alleged crime. Everyone was at a loss as to why anybody would want to have someone killed over cheerleading.

No one was more puzzled than the Heath family. Just the evening before, right after Wanda had been taken into custody, Verna Heath had been visited by Sergeant Blackwell and Detective Helton. The two officers had quietly informed her that her neighbor had been arrested for trying to hire someone to have her killed.

Verna's reaction was shock and sorrow. Tears streamed down her face as she begged the officers to help her understand why it had happened. "Why would she do this?" she pleaded. "Why, why, over cheerleading? To leave my children without a mother?" she asked.

Verna would have been the first to admit that she was serious about her daughter's and other students' competitions. Winning was important, she knew, and she liked to win, perhaps even more than most people. But never, in her whole life of involvement with twirling and strutting and dancing and cheering had she ever come across any competitiveness that approached this level.

The officers couldn't help her grasp the rationale, either. They didn't have a clue. Captain T-Bone Shaffer would later say, "All murders-for-hire are about love or money. This one, although it was hard to figure out, was about love."

George Helton repeatedly characterized Wanda Holloway as "the ultimate stage mother" in his comments to reporters. He added, "She would go to any length, apparently, to further the career and popularity of her daughter. She's an overachiever-type mother. The impression I got is the mother is living her life through the daughter."

As Wanda herself had said in one of her conversations with Terry Harper, "The things you do for your kids!"

Needless to say, most of the people in Channelview who had ever known Wanda Webb Holloway were shocked at the news of her arrest. The church piano player? That nice little lady who volunteered down at the schools? The one with the rich husband? They were all dumbfounded; they didn't think it could happen.

The day after the news of Wanda's arrest broke, the principal at Alice Johnson Junior High went on the P.A. system first thing in the morning to explain what had happened to the bewildered classmates of Shanna Harper and Amber Heath.

After relating the facts, Principal James Barker said, "Children, we must understand that parents sometimes do things that embarrass us. But we must not hold the children responsible for the actions of their parents. These girls, Shanna and Amber, both need your support."

In conclusion, he added that counselors were available for any student who felt the need to talk about their feelings regarding a mother who would kill over cheerleading. This was the biggest thing that had ever hit the school district. As Principal Barker later explained, prior to the cheerleader-murder-plot scandal, "Our biggest, most persistent problem in this school has been gum chewing and tardies to class," he said, "and we've had about four smoking cases this year."

One of the biggest problems the schools in Channelview soon faced was the press. Reporters of all descriptions and types began their steady, relentless attack on the town. All were eager to get the gritty details of the case of the Pompon Mom, a moniker almost instantly bestowed on Wanda Holloway.

The same day the story broke, swarms of reporters descended on Alice Johnson Junior High the very second the dismissal bell rang at the end of the day. Children were accosted as they attempted to leave the grounds. They were asked questions about Shanna and Amber, and what they personally thought. Many were offered cash—as much as fifty dollars—for their copies of the Alice Johnson school annual, from which the reporters could obtain photos of the girls in question.

Before long, a sort of siege mentality prevailed among the denizens of Channelview. At first the residents were kind of flattered by all the attention they were getting from the media. But they soon tired of being constantly questioned and kept from their day-to-day business by hordes of reporters who kept getting in the way.

Among the first to bar the gates, naturally, were the Channelview schools. After all, children had to get their education, regardless of what

Wanda Holloway might have done. Guards were posted at the gates of the high school and the junior high. School officials politely referred all phone inquiries to the Channelview Independent School District part-time public relations flack, Sam Ogden, who politely attempted to steer reporters in a direction other than sensationalizing the Channelview area as a whole.

"This has made my job hell, frankly," Mr. Ogden told one reporter. "No one wants to come down here and find out about a young lady we have who is a National Merit finalist. No one wants to talk about our support for the troops in Desert Storm. All they want to know about is the cheerleader lady."

Principal Barker added, "This has been challenging because there are so many good things that happen out in these twenty square miles." He went on about how many Channelview students have good college entrance exam scores, win appointments to military academies, and are involved in antidrug programs. "But there's no coverage of that!" he lamented. "But, you know, put out a hit contract and—wow!—Paris and London want to know about it!" By the end of the first week after the scandal broke, Barker said he had heard from "Everybody from Geraldo to Oprah, the *London Mail*, Bowling Green. Even Johnny Carson made a joke about it."

The folks in Channelview weren't laughing, however. They began to take it personally, and withdrew into a tight group. Members of Wanda's church, Channelview Missionary Baptist, were the next to circle the wagons after the schools. Jesus loved the sinners as much as the saints, they reasoned, and Wanda was one of their own. They refused any comment on their fallen sister. But even the folks sipping beer down at the Sheldon Road Ice House grew wary of the interloping reporters who kept stopping by. They resented the way most accounts of Wanda's crime cast a shadow on the community of Channelview. "They're blaming the whole town for the actions of just one person," said more than one plaintive drinker.

Perhaps most harrassed by inquisitive reporters was the Heath family. Unwillingly thrust into the limelight as they were by their neighbor's heinous deed, the Heath home was soon surrounded by reporters seeking interviews. Early on in their ordeal with the press, the Heaths sought the advice of Houston attorney Bob Shults. Before a week had passed, the Heaths had received numerous inquiries from Hollywood producers promising big money for the rights to the Heaths' exclusive story—*How I survived the attempted cheerleader murder plot.*

The Heaths were offended by the lighthearted, almost joking way the case was handled by much of the media. Many newspaper and magazine articles concluded that the town of Channelview itself was somehow to blame for the aberrant actions of only one of its citizens, inflaming the locals, who were angry at being tarred with the same brush used on Wanda Holloway.

The last straw for Verna Heath, which induced her to get some legal help, came when a team of reporters from *A Current Affair* ambushed her one afternoon as she was busy cooking supper. The doorbell rang and Verna answered it, opening only the solid wood door and leaving a screen door between herself and her caller. A *Current Affair* reporter stood there and began a barrage of questions. Verna was flustered and answered the best she could. She said of Wanda, "She's a mother who will go 150 percent for her child." Unbeknownst to her, a cameraman was hidden in a bush near the door, taping the whole encounter, which later played to a national audience, billed as an "exclusive" interview. Verna resented this unwarranted intrusion into her and her family's privacy, and she and Jack decided to consult an attorney.

Before long, with professional advice, they were acting like the most reclusive of Hollywood celebrities. Interviews, if granted at all, were carefully orchestrated and monitored. Their attorney would spell out the ground rules, including the allowable topics for discussion. Any deviation from his guidelines would result in an immediate termination of the interview. Any reporters who continued to call or otherwise contact the Heaths were told in no uncertain terms that legal action would be taken against them if they persisted.

The Heaths' lawyer also helped field the hundreds of offers from Hollywood producers, eager to snap up the Heaths' story rights for development into a television *Movie of the Week*. Attorney Bob Shults later joked about how he decided which producers to take seriously. "I reject outright anybody who calls me 'Baby,'" he explained. Small town Texas folk don't take kindly to the fast-talking smarm that riddles the entertainment business.

Although surprise was the most common reaction in Channelview to the news of Wanda's arrest, there were at least three people from Channelview who were not the least taken aback. Terry Harper, of course, knew it was in the works. He had, in fact, helped orchestrate the lady's fall. His brother Tony Harper also knew of the police investigation into his ex-wife's activities, because Terry had called him repeatedly throughout that January and given him a blow-by-blow account of his intrepid undercover work.

After hearing of his ex-wife's arrest, Tony Harper told the press, "I was shocked, but I wasn't really surprised. Wanda is a very determined lady." He remembered that trait all too well from his eight years of marriage to the woman. And it was not news to Marla LaRue Harper, who, like Tony had been privy to all the details from Terry.

Marla was still staying with her son at his apartment when the news first came on the television that Wanda Holloway had been taken into police custody. Marla watched the screen in horror, she later said. She was still convinced that Wanda was the innocent victim of a plot by Terry and Tony Harper to discredit her so that Tony could win back his kids and Terry could become a hero in his family's eyes.

When she heard that the "plot" had apparently been successful, Marla took immediate action. She went right to the phonebook and looked up the number for the household of C. D. Holloway, and then called it.

She later said that a female voice answered. "I asked to speak to C. D. Holloway," Marla explained. When C. D. came on the line, Marla said her name and who she was married to, and then told C. D. that she wanted to talk to the D.A. and to the Holloways attorneys, because, she said, she knew that his wife was being set up for something she didn't do. "I told him I had wanted to tell them before, or to tell the police, but that I was scared of Terry, and I had to get to a safe place before I could call him back."

The very next day, the day after Wanda was released from jail, Marla called again, and this time C. D. persuaded her to talk to Wanda's attorneys. One of Stanley Schneider's investigators was sent out to Channelview to pick Marla up and bring her to Schneider's office in Houston's Greenway Plaza. There, in front of Stanley Schneider and Troy McKinney, Marla recited her story of how Terry and Tony Harper had been talking and plotting about Wanda ever since New Year's Eve, and about how Terry had laughingly told Tony that he was going to "burn that bitch." She mentioned the discussion about Tony getting his kids back. Marla even told Schneider how Terry had bragged about the way he had scared Wanda with his references to the hit man coming after her if she didn't come up with the money.

Wanda's two attorneys exchanged a long look between them. Marla Harper had just provided them with the perfect defense for Wanda Holloway! She had not only been lured into a trap, but coerced into staying in the murder plot because of Terry's threats! Under the law, acting under duress or out of fear for one's life can sometimes be a successful defense.

Troy McKinney asked Marla if she was willing to repeat her story to the D.A.'s office as well as at any trial that might occur in the future. The attorneys were hoping they might be able to avoid a trial if they could convince the officials that Wanda herself had been an innocent victim of a plot by her ex-husband and brother-in-law. Marla said she would do all she could to help. "I've never met Miz Holloway," she told them. "But it isn't right what Terry and Tony done to her."

Wanda had others willing to vouch for her, too. Her young friend Patrick Gobert told the lawyers he would gladly take the stand and swear that all the allegations against Wanda were hogwash, that he had never seen or heard any evidence of this so-called plot in all his visits to the Holloway home.

Back in Channelview, Wanda kept a very low profile. Outside the door of the family home on Mincing reporters and photographers camped twenty-four hours a day, hoping to persuade the well-dressed little lady with the big hair and the murder-plot rap against her to grant them an interview. Around the corner at the Heath residence a similar scene was in progress. The Heaths came and went as usual, ignoring shouted questions and hiding their faces from the cameras.

But Wanda's house stayed oddly quiet, with no discernible activity. Many in the waiting crowd speculated that she and her kids had gone to stay elsewhere, to escape the commotion and the notoriety. By the end of that first week, dozens of reporters' business cards were jammed in between the iron gates that barred access to the front door. All went unanswered. Troy McKinney told the press that his client was handling her problem "remarkably well. I think she has to be that way," he explained. "But I'm sure there must be moments when she's not all that composed."

Friends close to Wanda say that even within the closed family circle, Wanda's predicament was not discussed at all. Patrick Gobert, who was still a daily visitor at the time, said, "We talked about the media and how crazy they were, but her arrest and the charge against her were never talked about."

Pete Reyes, Shane's friend, remembers being at the Holloway home shortly after Wanda came home from jail. Pete and Shane's girlfriend, Amy Goodson, were at the house to wait for Shane, who was on his way home from an out-of-town trip. According to Reyes, Wanda mentioned what had happened, but only obliquely. "She told us she had made a mistake, and that she had to live with it, but she couldn't discuss it any further," he said. "So we didn't ask anymore."

Not long after she'd met with Wanda Holloway's attorneys and told of the "plot" by Terry and Tony Harper against the mother of Tony's children, Marla Harper reconciled with her estranged husband. Terry had called her repeatedly during the weeks she'd been staying with her son, promising to reform and begging her to return. As she had done all the times before, Marla eventually relented and decided to give the marriage one more try. She later said of her decision, "I thought I still loved him, and I wanted to make my marriage work. And I just— stupidity."

Once more she settled into the trailer on Elspeth Street. After a day or two of reunited bliss, however, things began to turn ugly again. Because Marla and Terry had always been relentlessly honest with each other, Marla promptly told her husband of her call to C. D. Holloway and her subsequent visit with Wanda's attorneys. Terry didn't take the news at all well.

"He couldn't believe I had done it," she later said. "He just hovered over me and would just scream and yell and get drunk and knock me around and make threats about how I had ruined his character."

Terry, after all, had felt like his involvement in this case was his one chance to expunge the sins of his past. Now Marla was trying to spoil it all by making up stories to tell against him. The way he saw it, Marla was trying to ruin his life. He had worked hard for the last two and a half years to straighten himself out, only to have his own goddamned wife go and try to mess it all up.

Marla claimed later that Terry had threatened to get even with her if she didn't recant. "He told me he was going to mess me up so bad my own momma wouldn't recognize me," she said. Still, she held fast to her version of the events of that fateful January.

Marla's divorce from Terry became final during this time, but she kept on trying to work things out with him. She later reported that she and Terry continued to have frequent arguments about the story she told to Wanda's attorneys. They went back and forth and round and round about it, but she refused to give in.

Trouble was brewing on other fronts in Channelview as well. During the week immediately following Wanda's arrest, Tony Harper became intent on seeing that his children received counseling because of the ordeal their mother had created for the entire family. He called Wanda's house several times that week, and asked C. D. if he and Wanda had any plans to get some help for Shane and Shanna. No, he was told repeatedly. "They seem fine to us," C. D. explained. Tony was incredulous. How could these people not see how devastating it was to these kids to be thrust into the center of a national scandal?

He called the attorney who had handled his divorce from Wanda in 1980 and asked what he could do to make Wanda get the kids to a counselor. His attorney explained that since Wanda had been given the powers of managing conservator of the children in the original divorce decree, she alone had the right to decide what medical treatment, if any, her children required. Tony was merely a "possessory conservator," with weekend visitation rights, and would only be allowed to make treatment decisions in case of a dire emergency while the kids were with him. If one of the children were to suffer an accident like a broken leg while they were with their dad, he could take them to an emergency room and authorize treatment. But nothing more.

Nevertheless, the next time Tony had Shane and Shanna over, he called the offices of Dr. Kit Harrison, a forensic psychologist with offices near Houston's Galleria, to see if he could bring his children in for a meeting. Forensic psychology refers to that subspecialty of the field that deals with the interrelation between the law and psychology. Such specialists are often called in by various courts to assess the mental status of individuals caught up in a variety of judicial situations. They are asked to assess a criminal defendant's mental competency to stand trial, for example, or, in a guardianship proceeding, whether an elderly person is competent to manage his or her own affairs.

Forensic psychologists are also often asked to evaluate parents involved in a custody battle to decide which would provide the best environment for the children at issue. Knowledgeable of the statutory requirements that judges must follow in such cases, they are often called in to render an opinion in court to assist a judge or jury in making their ultimate decision. Most, like Dr. Harrison, also have more traditional practices in family or individual therapy.

Kit Harrison was well qualified for his role as a courthouse psychologist. A native of Wisconsin, he had received his B.A. and M.A. in psychology from the University of Wisconsin. His specialized training in the forensic fields came with his Ph.D. program at the University of Missouri. He moved to Texas for his internship, which was conducted at the world-famous Texas Medical Center in Houston, the huge Veterans' Administration Hospital in Houston, and the Houston Child Guidance Center.

But when Tony Harper asked the doctor if he would see the children, Dr. Harrison politely informed him that he could not. He knew the law, and he knew that Tony did not have the right to authorize such treatment. He also knew that he could be left open to liability if he agreed to see Shane and Shanna without their mother's permission.

After Dr. Harrison explained it all to Tony, Tony decided to do what he could to make sure his children were properly cared for. His former attorney suggested another family law specialist in Houston, Paula Gavrel Asher, as someone skilled in the field of child custody. Tony Harper soon met with Ms. Asher, who explained that under the Texas Family Code, because of the changed circumstances in the children's lives, Tony could seek to have the original custody order that granted Wanda the lion's share of parental rights modified to allow Tony the right to obtain medical treatment. He decided to go for it.

On February 14, 1991, Wanda Holloway received an unusual valentine from her first ex-husband. Tony's lawyer, Paula Asher, filed a Motion to Modify in Suit Affecting the Parent-Child Relationship in the Harris County Family Courts. Therein she asked the court to award Tony complete custody, or managing conservatorship, because of the fact that the children's circumstances in their mother's home had been, "materially and substantially changed since the date of rendition of the order to be modified." According to the Texas Family Code, custody arrangements, once made, are not to be disrupted unless such material and substantial changes have occurred.

Further, Asher stated in her motion that the appointment of Tony Harper as managing conservator would be a "positive improvement," and that "retention of the present sole managing conservator would be injurious to the welfare of the children." The motion asked that in the alternative, Tony could be named joint managing conservator of the children, a move that would give Tony and Wanda equal "rights, privileges, powers, and duties" as parents.

An affidavit was attached, signed by Tony Harper, stating the events of that January in which Wanda had been arrested for soliciting the capital murder of one of Shanna's classmates as well as the classmate's mother. The affidavit concluded that, "To leave the children, Anthony Shane Harper and Shanna Nicole Harper, in their current environment, will continue to result in unnecessary emotional trauma to them and would continue to be an ongoing danger to the emotional and personality growth of these children, thereby creating serious, immediate questions as to their safety and welfare."

Wanda was outraged upon learning what her ex had done. As if she didn't already have enough to worry about, now she had to face the prospect of losing Shane and Shanna! Her lawyers tried to calm her, and assured her they would do everything in their power to help her keep her children.

A court hearing was set for March 6, only weeks away. Family Court Judge Henry Schuble ordered a psychiatric evaluation of the children to determine what, if any, emotional jeopardy they might be in. Once again, Tony Harper called Dr. Kit Harrison. This time, the handsome young doctor agreed to meet with the children. It would be his task to decide if a genuine emergency existed in the Holloway home that would endanger the children's welfare.

On several occasions over the next two weeks, Dr. Harrison met with Shane and Shanna in his plush westside offices. Wanda even brought them on one occasion, although she herself was not interviewed by the doctor. After his meetings with the children, Harrison gave a deposition to Paula Asher, Tony's attorney, about his findings.

He later said of his work, "The disorder in this family was obvious. Wanda had a symbiotic relationship with both of her children, although the disorder was much stronger with the child of the same sex."

A symbiotic relationship, Dr. Harrison later explained, is one in which one individual, usually a parent, fuses his identity with another's, usually a child. The results are extremely detrimental to the functioning of all parties involved. This ego fusion usually occurs when the child is very small, earlier than age two, according to psychology textbooks on the subject, and leaves the child in a lifelong servitude of sorts to the involved parent, who is usually the mother. Harrison says 70 percent of these cases occur in women. "Men are usually symbiotically attached to their work," he explains, "whereas women become so attached to their children."

The child learns early on in life that it exists only to please the mother, who gets her gratification from the child's successes in life. Various degrees of the disorder are extremely common in our society, according to Harrison. "After all, how many stage mothers are out there?" he asked. But it was definitely rare for the disorder to progress as far as it had in this case. In fact, Harrison says he has never before heard of a case where this type of dysfunctional ego fusion resulted in a felony against a third party, although it often leads to child abuse.

Symbiotic relationships, according to Dr. Harrison, are usually transgenerational, or passed on from one generation to the next. When people become parents, they tend to repeat the parenting style in which they themselves grew up. Thus, if a woman was raised by an overly involved mother, she, in turn, is likely to become overly involved with her own children.

Dr. Harrison explains, "Usually there is some spousal abuse of some sort in the family of origin which causes the mother to withdraw from her spouse. That abuse is often of substances like alcohol or drugs, where the father is, say, an alcoholic, so the mother turns away from him."

When children enter the picture, he adds, "The mother gloms onto the kids to 'protect' them from the father," and also for the emotional closeness lacking in her marital relationship. Typically, says Harrison, children raised in these environments will later involve themselves in abusive relationships, like their mother's, and repeat the process with their own children. This lifestyle can repeat itself ad infinitum unless some crisis calls a halt to it and intervention is employed.

Harrison describes the typical family dynamics in symbiotic relationships. "There is always some kind of persecutor," he says, "an external threat of some kind which the mother uses to draw the children to her. The implied threat operating there is that the mother says, in effect, to the child, 'Do as I say and I will protect you. If you remain attached, clinging, dependent, vulnerable, and fused to me, I will give you everything that you need,'" he explains.

"The other side of the equation is, 'If you should reject me, I will destroy you.'" Harrison explains that with young children the way to destroy them is to abandon them, either physically or emotionally. When children are older, he says, such parental rejections in skewed relationships of this type are sometimes the motivation for infanticide. "In many cases where parents have murdered their children," he says, "symbiotic relationships are found to be the root cause."

The whole system, he explains, "is based on an elaborate quid pro quo that is unspoken but clearly understood. As the child grows older, it usually takes the form of the parent implying to the child, 'If you do things that reflect well on me and make me look good, I will give you love. But if you screw up, forget it.'"

According to Harrison, there are many variations in the intensity of symbiotic relationships, from mild to severe. All parents, after all, want their children to be happy and successful. But in extreme examples, the child's entire existence serves only one purpose—to further the parent's goals. Often this takes the form of the parent attempting to live his or her life, which to date has been unsatisfactory, through the child. The father who was never good at sports but who pushes his son to excel at them, the mother who has led a life of menial drudgery who urges her daughter on to a professional career, are typical examples. When the child fails to achieve the desired result, says Harrison, the parent experiences depression and then anger. "Rage is always an inherent part of symbiotic relationships," Harrison explains.

The effect on a child in such a system can be devastating emotionally, Harrison says. "There are no age-appropriate task acquisitions," he explains. "Everything the child ever accomplishes is done with the parent's help, so the child fails to acquire a sense of mastery and feels helpless and dependent."

Because the parent usually turns to the child, not her spouse, for emotional support, the child becomes the mother's major confidant, and often feels stressful pressure to emotionally support the parent, when it should work the other way around.

Harrison said after evaluating the Harper children that both suffered from this dysfunctional relationship with their mother, although Shanna was more involved in it than Shane. He noted the anger Wanda had felt toward the girl she felt had "beat Shane out" for band major. But unlike Shanna, Shane had reached the point where he had had enough of it. "He was just counting the days until he could leave that house," Harrison said.

Apparently, Wanda's intrusions into the boy's privacy had become intolerable. Harrison learned that on one occasion, for example, Wanda had managed to tape record a conversation between Shane and his girlfriend in which they were discussing some activity Wanda felt they had no business discussing—something of a sexual nature. She sat Shane down and lectured him about his impropriety and also threat-

Tony Harper and Wanda Webb, the way they were at Channel-view High School the year their ill-fated romance began.

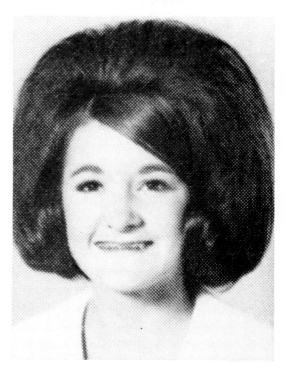

Wanda wanted Verna Heath "gone" because she always won everything. Here Verna struts her stuff as National Twirling Champ in 1971. She hoped her daughter, Amber, would carry on the family tradition.

A scenic spot in Channelview. Refineries and manufacturing plants line the Houston Ship Channel as it cuts through the community . . .

Don Hueske

. . . Which perhaps helps explain why God plays a big role in the lives of Channelview folks. Here is one of the many local houses of worship.

Terry and Marla Harper's mobile home, not far from a trailer park called "Possum Hollow." Wanda came here looking for Terry when she decided she needed a hit man.

Don Hueske

From left to right: Stanley Schneider, C.D. Holloway, Shanna Harper, Wanda Holloway, and Troy McKinney leave the Harris County Family Court Building in March of 1991 after Wanda's custody fight with ex-husband Tony Harper.

Amber, Jack, and Verna Heath leave the courthouse after a tense day of testimony at Wanda Holloway's trial for solicitation of Verna's murder.

Shanna Harper, always second best to Amber Heath, on her way to her mother's sentencing.

Michael Boddy/The Houston Post

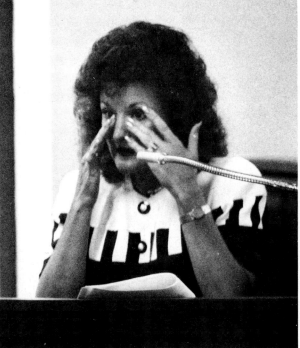

Michael Boddy/The Houston Post

Wanda Holloway, in tears on the stand.

Prosecutor Michael Anderson points the finger of justice at Wanda.

Gaylon Wampler/The Houston Post

Tony Harper, father of Wanda's children, was accused of plotting against his ex-wife. His brother, Terry, is visible behind him in the courthouse hallway.

Jane Howard

Terry and Marla Harper, during a happy phase at their Channelview trailer home. The scar on her right knee is from her self-inflicted oven-cleaner burn.

Wanda Holloway and Terry Harper met in the parking lot of this fast-food restaurant to plan Verna Heath's death.

Michael Boddy/ The Houston Post

Do handcuffs go with diamonds? A well-dressed but pensive Wanda Holloway being escorted to jail by sheriff's deputies after receiving a fifteen-year sentence for her crime.

ened to take the tape over to Amy Goodson's mother so that she could "see what kind of a daughter she had." Wanda, in fact, called Mrs. Goodson and mentioned the tape. Mrs. Goodson said she had no desire to hear such a private conversation between her daughter and Shane.

Shanna was, in Harrison's estimation, still deeply involved in symbiosis with her mother. "Her mother is her best friend," Harrison said. "She is still very defensive about her."

In these types of relationships, says Harrison, there usually comes a time when the child does make an attempt at separation and individuation from the clinging parent. But all too often that process itself can lead to more problems. "It is not at all unusual," he says, "for girls to end up in teenage pregnancies or in relationships with older, substance-abusing boyfriends. The pregnancies are an attempt to finally have someone to love them for themselves," Harrison explains. "Which of course can lead to disastrous results, since babies do not exist to love their parents."

It sometimes happens, according to Harrison, that a teenage mother will "sacrifice" her baby to her mother, just to get free herself. Then the grandmother becomes overly involved with the new baby, and the whole cycle repeats itself. When a child does manage to break free from the overly clinging mother, Harrison says, the mother in turn rejects the child. For example, as Shane Harper became more separate and independent from Wanda, Wanda responded by withdrawing from his activities to devote more time to Shanna. She also reneged on a promise to buy him a car at high-school graduation.

In his judicial assessment, however, Harrison had to determine only one thing—whether the children were in serious, immediate danger if they stayed with Wanda. He concluded that they were not, and that forcing them out of their home might, in fact, be worse for their emotional health than staying, especially for Shanna, who had not yet reached the stage of wanting to break free from her overly involved mother.

On the morning of March 6, thirty-seven-year-old Wanda Holloway and thirteen-year-old Shanna Harper, along with their young undertaker friend, Patrick Gobert, and Wanda's attorney, Stanley Schneider, met Tony Harper and his attorneys at the Harris County Family Court for a hearing regarding the custody of Wanda's children. Patrick came along to help fend off the waiting media and to provide moral support for his good friend Wanda. Besides, he said later, "I am real good at keeping people away. I don't take anything off anybody." He had also volunteered to testify, if needed, that Wanda was an excellent mother.

Shane Harper was conspicuously absent from the proceedings, but then his custody was not really at issue. Texas law provides that any child fourteen years of age or older can make his own decision about which parent he lives with. Shane was nearly eighteen and getting ready to go off to college. It really didn't matter to him.

The two sides met in the judge's closed chambers for about three hours that morning. Shanna sat on a bench with Patrick Gobert outside the chambers, although she was asked to come in for questioning once or twice. Tony's lawyer, Paula Asher, explained her client's position: Tony wanted to be able to take his children for desperately needed counseling, and since Wanda had refused to allow this, he was forced to seek this modification of the original custody order granted in the court. Besides, Asher added, if Wanda ended up incarcerated, the children would be left without a managing conservator. Appointment of their father, at least as joint managing conservator, would eliminate that eventuality. Wanda was not really in much of a position to argue. After all, family courts tend to frown on felonous parents, even though not yet convicted.

After reading Dr. Kit Harrison's recommendation that the children still be allowed frequent access to their mother, Judge Schuble suggested that the parents settle by agreeing that the children be jointly awarded to Wanda and Tony. Tony's visitation rights would be increased from every first, third, and fifth weekend of each month to every other week from Wednesday night to Sunday afternoon. This arrangement would allow Harper ample time during business hours to take the children to Dr. Harrison's office for therapy.

When the parties left the courthouse, they were all smiles. Both sides considered themselves victorious. Wanda smiled broadly for the waiting camera crews, and held Shanna's hand as they walked across the courthouse plaza. Tony talked briefly with reporters, and explained his motivation in seeking the change in custody arrangements. "I think this is causing a lot of emotional trauma to my kids," he said. "They are a lot more tense."

On other legal fronts, Wanda's case was making its way through the bureaucratic maze of the Harris County District Attorney's Office. Although Assistant D.A. Joe Magliolo had initially handled the case, and was eager to follow it through to trial, the powers that be recommended instead that the case be handled by the D.A.'s Division of Organized Crime.

Alice Brown was then assistant chief of the division, and drew what seemed to her the unenviable task of taking the case to the grand jury and later to a trial court. Brown, thirty-five, had been with the D.A.'s office since 1983 and had quickly established a reputation as a hot-shot trial lawyer. A native of the Dallas area, Brown had come to Houston to attend the University of Houston Law Center and had stayed on after graduation, first working for well-known criminal lawyer David Berg and then going over to the state's side. Her courtroom skills were such that she was even teaching a class in trial advocacy at her alma mater.

Alice Brown was known as a smart, tough, and tenacious advocate. She was quick to grasp the true issues in almost any case and could explain the facts to a jury in plain, unvarnished language. A petite brunette, she was always totally prepared for the courtroom and impressed her colleagues with her willingness to work hard. Although she was the mother of two young children, Alice was completely dedicated to her career as well. After the birth of her second child, she spent only two weeks at home before resuming her responsibilities as a prosecutor and a law school teacher.

Over the years Brown had handled almost every variety of case. Before her transfer to the Organized Crime division, she had been the chief trial lawyer in Judge Ted Poe's state criminal court. There she'd seen everything from babies whose skulls had been bashed in by their parents to victims of knifings, gunshots, and barroom brawls. Harris County had had its share of bizarre criminal cases in the past.

There was Dr. John Hill, the plastic surgeon from River Oaks, who allegedly fed his young oil-heiress wife a poisoned danish and then watched dispassionately as she lay for hours in the throes of death. There had been the serial killer Dean Corll, who had lured young boys into his van, sexually tortured them to death, and then stashed their bodies in a boatshed under sacks of lime. Before his years of such activity were discovered and ended, more than thirty boys had died.

And there had been the "Candy Man," Ronald Clark O'Bryan, who one Halloween night slipped a Pixie Stick sugar straw laced with cyanide into his own son's trick-or-treat bag. Although he pretended to police that his son had been the victim of a sinister unknown neighbor, and shed appropriate amounts of crocodile tears for the television news cameras, it was later discovered that the week before his child's death O'Bryan had taken out a large life insurance policy on the boy. He had also purchased cyanide from a chemical company. The practice of trick-or-treating ended in Houston after this incident.

But there had never been a cheerleader murder plot before. And Alice Brown dreaded the relentless glare of the media that she knew would haunt the case from start to finish. "I never wanted anything to do with this case from the very beginning," she later said. "And once I got into it, I really wished I'd never heard of it."

Before taking the case before a grand jury, Brown had to investigate the facts. All she knew at the outset was that a young mother had been arrested for hiring the murder of her neighbor and rival. But after several investigatory trips to Channelview and interviews with Terry Harper and the officers who worked the case, Alice Brown realized the case was going to be a little more complicated that she'd first thought.

As she wryly said later, "Here was this absolute carnival of characters—Wanda, the brother-in-law with the record, the undertaker guy, the lady with the oven cleaner....It was just all so ridiculous." She shook her head in wonder at the recollection.

Some attorneys relish publicity and eagerly look for chances to get their names in the newspaper or sound bites on TV. Not Alice Brown; she took the law very seriously and did not believe the judicial process should be turned into a media circus. With the cast of players in this case, though, she knew that could not be avoided. But still, she wished she didn't have to be the ringmaster.

Nevertheless, she and her appointed investigator, Larry Winkleman, went about the task of interviewing dozens of people who were in some way important to the case. They talked to school officials, pastors, friends, neighbors, teachers, and relatives, asking about Wanda's character and any previous incidents from her past that might reveal her motive more clearly. Alice Brown even interviewed Shane Harper about anything he may have heard his mother talk about relating to wanting people done away with.

They learned all about the earlier cheerleader competitions, and how Wanda had reacted to Shanna's losses. It began to seem clear that Wanda had, in fact, wanted Verna Heath dead because of them. Brown quickly learned just how quickly news about newcomers travels in Channelview. After her first visit to the community, she said, she was instantly recognized on subsequent trips, even by people she had never interviewed.

By February 19, Alice Brown was ready to go before a grand jury to seek an indictment against Wanda Ann Holloway. Because she wanted the jury members fully aware of all the peculiarities of the case, she didn't spare any of the details. She explained about Terry Harper's checkered past and even had Marla Harper testify about her suspicions of a plot between Terry and Tony. But she also played the tape recordings of Wanda's conversations with Terry. And she read them the charge against the woman—that Mrs. Holloway tried to hire a hit man in a bizarre scheme to improve her daughter's chances of becoming a high-school cheerleader, and that the would-be victim in the case was the mother of Wanda's daughter's chief cheerleading rival.

The members of the grand jury listened intently to the state's presentation of evidence. They had some doubt about some of the details in the case, but the tapes were impossible to ignore. Later that afternoon, after short deliberation, they returned an indictment. It stated:

IN THE NAME AND AUTHORITY OF THE STATE OF TEXAS

The duly organized Grand Jury of Harris County, Texas presents in the District Court of Harris County, Texas, that in Harris County, Texas, WANDA A. HOLLOWAY AKA WANDA WEBB HOLLOWAY, hereafter styled the defendant, heretofore on or about January 28, 1991, did then and there unlawfully with the intent that capital murder be committed, request, command and attempt to induce Terry Lynn Harper to become a party to the commission of the offense of capital murder by requesting Terry Lynn Harper to employ another to intentionally and knowingly cause the death of Verna Heath for remuneration and promise of remuneration, AGAINST THE PEACE AND DIGNITY OF THE STATE.

The language may have been stilted, but the meaning was clear: The grand jury thought she'd done it.

It was another blow to Wanda. She and her attorneys had hoped this whole unpleasant business could be done away with. If the grand jury had failed to return an indictment, the charge against Wanda would have been dismissed. Now, however, she would be forced to go to trial to try to establish her innocence. A trial date of June 6, 1991, was set by the courts.

During the next three months as she waited to be judged by a jury of her peers, Wanda attempted to retreat into relative obscurity in Channelview. Shane and Shanna returned to their classes on a regular basis (immediately following their mother's arrest they had missed a lot of school), and Wanda went on with her housewifely duties of cooking and shopping. Patrick Gobert continued to visit her daily, and says that the case was never discussed. Although members of the press still came around from time to time, there was no longer a twenty-four-hour-day contingent waiting at the front stoop of the Holloway home, and Wanda was able to grocery shop and run errands in Channelview without drawing much more than curious stares from her neighbors and furtive whispers from fellow customers in the stores.

Shane was busy preparing for his high-school graduation in May— Wanda and Patrick were coordinating the details and the decorations for the church hall where a party would be held in his honor. Shanna continued to do well in school. That spring she was inducted into the school's honor society. Even though she and Amber Heath stood next to each other in line (Heath was next alphabetically after Harper in the list of new members), the other kids at school did not gossip or jeer. Every other week both Shane and Shanna met with Dr. Harrison during their stay with their father.

Terry Harper and his wife, Marla, returned to normalcy also. Although the ink was barely dry on the divorce Marla had been granted only weeks before, she remarried Terry in March. She thus became Terry's sixth and seventh wife simultaneously. Even so, the couple continued to play out their pattern of frequent arguments and separations throughout that season.

As the time for Wanda's trial drew nearer, their arguments intensified. Terry still didn't want Marla to testify on Wanda's behalf, but Marla was still insistent that she was going to. More was at stake now than just Terry's reputation as a hero. Movie producers had begun sniffing around Tony and Terry, looking to sign them to a story-rights contract for a considerable amount of money. Tony and Terry had already discussed how they would split the money—25 percent each for the brothers, 25 percent each for Tony's children. But if Marla later successfully discredited Terry and helped win Wanda's acquittal, his story would not arouse as much interest, since he would be cast in the light of a bad guy. Once again, Terry felt as if Marla was trying to screw him around, and it really pissed him off.

Discord was developing on other fronts, too. Patrick Gobert, Wanda's close friend and confidant, noticed a distinct chill in the

Holloway home toward late spring. He became aware of the same kind of withdrawal on the part of the Denman family. They were the Holloway's close friends and also had a teenage son, Blake, who Patrick extensively counseled in the previous two years, ever since Blake's friend, and Wanda's nephew, Jerry Webb, had been tragically killed.

Patrick had once been so close to the Denmans that they asked him along on their summer vacation. He, in turn, had surprised them by having their lawn professionally landscaped while they were out of town. He spent large amounts of money on dirt-biking equipment and other incidental gifts for Blake. Patrick had wanted to give Blake a dirt bike, in fact, but his parents, Roy and Teresa Denman, bought the gift before he was able to. Patrick says that instead he "spent thousands of dollars on protective equipment for Blake." Similar extravagant gifts were bestowed on Shane Harper, including some gold and diamond jewelry.

For some reason, though, Patrick began to get the impression that his visits were not as welcome as they had once been at both households. Since the time of their initial meeting, Patrick felt as if he had almost become a member of the Holloway household. It was a routine thing to go out to eat with C. D. and Wanda after church on Sundays, and he frequently dined with the family during the week as well. But the invitations became few and far between during that spring while Wanda awaited her trial date.

Privately, Wanda and the Denmans had been talking about Patrick Gobert and about some reservations they had about the young man. They wondered, for instance, how he managed to have so much money to lavish on Blake and Shane when he was still just a student at the morticians' school. They also thought it was a little unseemly for a young man seven years older than the boys to spend all his time with the teenagers.

Early in May of that year Patrick went to see Wanda with a burning question. He had just found out that a week or so earlier Elwyn Denman's father had passed away and no one had even notified Patrick, much less contacted him for help in arranging the services. He wanted to know why, after all he'd done for the family, they had not let him know of their troubles. He had been helping Wanda plan Shane's graduation party for several weeks, getting the decorations together, choosing the linens and silver for the tables, but had been troubled by the growing coolness in Wanda and the Denman family.

Wanda, busy working in her kitchen at the time of Patrick's visit, finally confronted him with some questions of her own. He later said that she asked him about "some lies she thought I had told. She seemed to think I was not being honest about myself and the kind of life I was leading."

Wanda accused Patrick of promising Blake Denman that he would buy him a new car for his high-school graduation. She wanted to know why he would say such a thing if he couldn't actually deliver. And she wanted to know, if he could manage to buy the boy a car, why he would do so. Something about Patrick's interest in Blake and Shane had finally begun to seem a little strange to the boys' parents.

Patrick reacted indignantly to Wanda's probing. "I don't have to prove anything to you or anybody else," he told her angrily, and then he left the Holloway house for the last time. He did not contact her or the Denmans ever again. He even started going to a different church.

Wanda never asked Patrick if he was still planning to testify for her at her upcoming trial. As things turned out later, he did, in fact, take the stand. But it was not for the defense.

8

Under the Big Top

The case of the *State of Texas v. Wanda Holloway* did not go to trial on the scheduled date of June 6, 1991. As things turned out, Troy McKinney, Wanda's lead attorney, had to ask for a continuance because of a family medical emergency. His wife needed immediate surgery. Because the request was legitimate, Judge George H. Godwin granted the delay. A new trial date was set for late August in the 174th District Criminal Court where Judge Godwin presided.

Shortly after the continuance was granted, a change in assignments at the district attorney's office resulted in Assistant D.A. Alice Brown finally getting rid of the case she detested. She and her division chief, Ted Wilson, were transferred from the Organized Crime division into Special Crimes. In turn, Casey O'Brien and Mike Anderson, who formerly headed the Major Offenders division, landed in Organized

Crime and were handed the bizarre case of Wanda Holloway just six short weeks before trial.

Mike Anderson recalls his first reaction on hearing he and Casey O'Brien would be trying the case: "Why me?" Like Alice Brown before him, Anderson was reluctant to become embroiled in such a high-profile case, especially one with such a strange cast of characters and an off-the-wall motive. But Anderson also had another reason to be wary. Unlike Alice Brown, he had grown up not far from Channelview and knew exactly what kind of people he would be dealing with. During his high-school summers Anderson had worked as a dockhand and seen the lifestyle of the industrial workers close up. "I've been around that type all my life," he later explained. "They've definitely got their own style about them."

As a team of litigators, Mike Anderson and Casey O'Brien were everything that Wanda's pair of attorneys was not. Both were articulate, good-looking, and sharply dressed. In contrast, Troy McKinney and Stanley Schneider leaned toward disheveled, mismatched clothing and stammering delivery of their arguments. Both prosecutors were career members of the D.A.'s staff. O'Brien, a dapper forty-three-year-old pipe smoker with a blond mustache and thinning blond hair, had been with the office since 1980. Anderson had joined the staff while still a student at Houston's South Texas School of Law, which granted him a degree in 1982. "The D.A.'s office was the only place I ever wanted to work," says the dark-haired, mustachioed, thirty-five-year-old Anderson now. Like most members of the district attorney's office, these men were idealists who truly believed they could make a difference.

Neither man had originally considered a career in law. O'Brien, who grew up in the Washington, DC, area, started out as a teacher in a junior college before deciding to attend law school. Mike Anderson had studied communications at a small Texas Lutheran college and worked for a year in that industry before moving to Houston for legal studies. Both had shown immediate aptitude for the field, however, after enrolling at the South Texas School of Law.

After being given their assignment, the first order of business for Anderson and O'Brien was to familiarize themselves with all the state's evidence and witnesses. As soon as they got to the material on Terry Harper both men suspected they might run into some problems. They read about his record of petty offenses and drunk and disorderly behavior over the years and saw right away what a field day Wanda's defense could have with it. In a trial court, establishing a witness's credibility with the jury is of paramount importance. It is a whole lot better to have a priest for a witness than a jailbird, for example, but Anderson and O'Brien were stuck with Terry Harper.

After their initial meeting with Harper, both men *knew* they'd have some problems. Mike Anderson later explained, "The first time I met him I got pissed off at him because he got drunk. And after that there were lots of altercations."

Terry would frequently call one or the other of the prosecutors during one of his and Marla's constant drunken brawls. They would try to talk sense to him and calm him down while he raved on drunkenly. After just a little taste of this behavior, both Anderson and O'Brien were concerned about reaching the date of trial without some new disaster occurring, like Terry getting arrested again.

In addition to that burden, the prosecutors had to immerse themselves in all the little details of the cheerleading competitions that had led up to Wanda wanting Verna Heath done away with. Minutiae and trivia about contest rules and regulations soon crowded their minds.

But Terry Harper remained their chief worry. Early on in the preparations for trial, Mike Anderson talked to Terry Harper in the prosecutors' office downtown near the Harris County Criminal Courts Building. Anderson didn't pull any punches with the state's star witness. "Terry," the attorney said forcefully, "they are gonna make you out to be a turd in this deal."

Terry Harper didn't bat an eye. In fact, he grinned like a possum as he responded, "Hell, I am a turd. So what?" As the two discussed the details of what had happened between Terry and Wanda Holloway, Anderson began to feel more confident. As he got to know the Channelview native better, Anderson started to see that Harper seemed sincere about trying to do the right thing for once in his life. He may have had a string of petty offenses to his name, but he was not a bona fide bad guy. As Casey O'Brien put it, "Drunk and rowdy, yes. But a criminal, no."

Besides, both attorneys knew from listening to the tape-recorded conversations between Terry and Wanda Holloway just how damaging that evidence would be to the defense. There was virtually no way the defense could get around the way Wanda had been talking to Terry with such venom in her voice. Terry Harper may have been a turd, but on the tapes it sounded like Wanda was one too.

Just to be on the safe side, though, three weeks before the new trial date of August 23, the prosecutors decided to add another count to Wanda's indictment. In addition to the first count of solicitation of capital murder, they went before a new grand jury and asked for an indictment against her for solicitation of aggravated kidnapping. In her conversations with Terry Harper, Wanda had, after all, suggested that Verna Heath could be carted off to Cuba for fifteen years. If a jury failed to find her guilty of the first count, the attorneys reasoned, maybe they could win a conviction on the lesser charge.

In addition to meeting with their own witnesses, the two prosecutors naturally had to interview Marla Harper as well, since she would be one of the chief witnesses for the defense. Neither man took long to make up his mind about her. Anderson later put it bluntly, "Now there's a real nut." But in spite of all the couple's brawling and backstabbing, Anderson said, "I think they really love each other."

He probably didn't think that on August 22, the night before jury selection in *Texas v. Wanda Holloway* was set to begin. In the few weeks they had had to prepare leading up to that day, both Anderson and O'Brien felt they had things under control and all their witnesses carefully lined up. They knew that Terry and Marla were currently on the outs, what with the trial nearing and all, but that was par for their course. Marla had left Terry a few weeks earlier after hearing a rumor about Terry cavorting with a prostitute in front of Marla's son. The team of prosecutors became aware of the falling out, but didn't let it worry them much. Then all hell broke loose at the last minute.

Mike Anderson was at his home going over his trial notes when the phone rang the first time. Last minute pretrial jitters plague most attorneys, and Anderson was no exception. The insistent ringing of the telephone was an unwelcome intrusion. He answered it with a brusque, "Hello." On the other end he could hear a woman shrieking. It was Marla Harper, drunkenly going on about something she said Terry was trying to do to her at a motel in Channelview. She was calling 911, she said, and was going to have Terry Lynn arrested.

"Shit," thought Anderson. "That's all we need." He eventually managed to coax the near-hysterical Marla into telling him where she was and what phone number she was calling from. Then he promptly hung up and called Casey to alert him to the trouble brewing in Channelview.

As they later heard the story from both Marla and Terry, the prosecutors learned that the couple had bumped into each other by chance at a friend's snow-cone stand on Market Street the evening of August 22. Because they had been estranged for several weeks, they decided to spend a little time together. They went to a nearby restaurant—in separate vehicles—and had some drinks. Several strong drinks, as it turned out. They left the restaurant and weaved their way over to sit underneath a nearby bridge over the San Jacinto River to continue their talk.

From there on, Terry's and Marla's stories diverge wildly. They both agree they ended up at a motel on Interstate 10 in Channelview. She claims he began to harass her about her upcoming testimony against him, and urged her to head for Conroe, a town north of Houston in a different county, to avoid being subpoenaed as a witness. He tried to get her to call the prosecutors to tell them she had made up her whole story, the one about Terry and Tony Harper plotting against innocent Wanda Holloway. He dialed Mike Anderson's number, she later said, and became incensed when she refused to recant to the prosecutor. Marla claims Terry then started roughing her up, and she grabbed the phone and began to shriek that she was being attacked.

Finally Terry was persuaded by either Anderson or O'Brien or both to get the hell out of there. Marla spent the night alone in the motel room after summoning some patrol officers, who advised her to go back to her room and stay there.

Mike Anderson and Casey O'Brien, meanwhile, passed a restless night waiting for their nine o'clock docket call the next morning. As if they didn't have enough on their minds already, they now had to worry that the chief witnesses for both the state and the defense would kill each other before the trial even started. But when the two seasoned prosecutors showed up in court the next morning, there was no trace on their faces of any anxiety they might have been feeling.

The first order of business in any jury trial is selecting the members of the panel who will sit in judgment after the evidence is presented. In a case such as Wanda's, which had received extensive, nationwide publicity, one of the main concerns of both sides is whether the potential jurors have been tainted by their exposure to media coverage of the case. If a case has already more or less been tried in the newspapers and on TV, it is much harder to find impartial jurors who will listen with open minds to the evidence set before them in the court, while ignoring anything they may have heard or read in the press.

In *Texas v. Wanda Holloway*, Judge Ted Poe, who presided that day over all jury selections, knew it would be harder than usual to find twelve jurors plus one alternate who met the proper standards of impartiality. It was not necessary to find people who had never heard of the case, only some who had not completely made up their minds about the defendant's guilt or innocence. Nevertheless, Judge Poe thought it prudent to choose a venire, or pool of prospective jurors, much larger than would be sent ordinarily. In an average criminal case, a pool of thirty or forty potential jurors is sent to the trial court for the prosecutors and defense attorneys to choose their jury from. In Wanda's case, Poe sent 125 potential jurors.

Many successful trial attorneys have said the crucial part of any trial is selecting the jury carefully. A whole science has developed around the process, in which hired experts in psychology and human behavior assist attorneys in deciding which jurors are telling the truth, which might be pro-state or pro-defense, and which might be most sympathetic to the particular facts of a given case.

Wanda's defense team had not hired such a jury consultant to sit with them during the voir dire process, but they had commissioned one to help them prepare a detailed questionnaire for all the veniremen to fill out. They ended up with a nine-page document containing seventy-nine questions that would supposedly help them choose the best panel members. The questions covered general information topics such as type of employment, number of children, and marital status, but also asked things like, "How often do you attend church?" and "What magazines do you routinely read?"

The questions numbered 20 and 30 would later prove to be of great significance. Number 20 asked jurors, "Have you ever been involved in a criminal case, either as a victim, defendant, witness or attended court for any reason?" Number 30 asked, "Are you currently involved in any community service projects?"

After the 125 venireman had been sent to Judge George H. Godwin's 174th District Court, where Wanda's trial would be held, each was asked to fill out the questionnaire. That in itself took some time, and the attorneys for both sides took even longer to study each response before meeting face to face with the venire for individual questions. The selection process alone took all Friday and part of the following Monday, August 26.

By late Monday morning, both sides had agreed to seat a panel of four women and eight men, plus an alternate, that included representatives from various age ranges and ethnicity.

The procedure had gone smoothly, both sides agreed, although later Casey O'Brien would recall thinking it odd that Troy McKinney and Stanley Schneider seemed eager to have venireman number 48, Daniel Enriquez, thirty, who had answered on his questionnaire that he was already "leaning toward guilty" in the case of Wanda Holloway.

During the voir dire process, Casey had leaned over and whispered to Mike Anderson, "Wonder why they'd want somebody so obviously pro-state?" It would be many weeks later before the answer became clear.

Judge Godwin, a serious, no-nonsense member of the state judiciary, announced all present were ready for trial, set to begin immediately that morning. He admonished the jurors to refrain from watching or reading the news about the case or discussing it with anyone outside the courtroom, and also issued a gag order forbidding the attorneys or any of the witnesses from discussing the case with the press until after its conclusion. The wise judge already knew of the media sensation the case had caused, but he was determined to limit the trial coverage to events and statements that actually occurred in his courtroom, not those that might arise in the courthouse halls.

The small courtroom of the 174th court was already jammed with spectators. Most were media representatives, some from as far away as England and Australia. All of the Houston newspapers and television stations were on hand, as were correspondents from such out-of-town papers as the *New York Times* and the *Los Angeles Times*. There was even an independent filmmaker in the crowd, who had driven in from Austin just to see Wanda Holloway in person.

Judge Godwin's courtroom was unfortunately located on the third floor of a cramped old building that served as a courthouse annex. The hallway leading from the elevators was already almost impassable because of radio and television sound and video equipment. Wires and cables snaked in every direction across the floor, and the glare of the television camera lights shone on every principal in the case as each would try to make his or her way to the courtroom.

Once inside, jockeying for position became intensely competitive.

More than one heated argument arose between spectators about who had which seat first. In addition to the media, Wanda Holloway and Verna Heath each had sizable contingents of supporters present from Channelview. They were easily recognizable: The women all wore big hairdos, permed and frizzed out around their heads, and the men wore either polyester suits or western wear replete with jeans and boots. Peggy and R. E. Harper were there to offer support for their sons, both of whom were scheduled to testify during the trial.

Wanda herself looked more like she was a participant in a ladies' fashion luncheon than a defendant in a criminal trial. She wore a stylish, expensive bright-red suit with braid trim and gold buttons, and she had matching nail polish and lipstick. Her hair was coiffed to its usual massive perfection, forming a brown corona around her head. She smiled broadly at the cameras as if she were a movie star as she walked to her seat at the defense table. C. D. Holloway was conspicuously absent, but Wanda's parents, Clyde and Verna Webb, sat close behind their daughter.

Verna Heath was dressed equally well, although her demeanor was much more reserved. She and her husband, Jack, stayed away from the press and did not smile.

Judge Godwin immediately lectured the assembled eclectic multitude about how he expected them to behave. His court would not become a circus, his attitude made clear. He addressed the audience after giving his admonishments to the jury and the attorneys. "For everyone else remaining in the courtroom," he said with a commanding air, "I realize there is widespread interest in this case. I apologize for the physical facilities. They are, to everyone's obvious pain, severely limited." Indeed, the air inside the courtroom on that hot August afternoon was already close. The air-conditioning system was no match for the volume of spectators.

The judge then set forth his rules. "There will not be any getting up and going in and out of the courtroom. If you want to stay, you may stay. If you want to leave, you may leave. We will probably take about an hour and a half's worth of testimony and then take a break. We will try to remain on that schedule."

Godwin's next order caused several groans from the audience. "There will be no standing up in this courtroom. If you have a seat, you may stay. If you do not have a seat, you may not stay."

Many reporters standing at the rear of the crowded room and along the side aisles, who desperately needed to be in the room to cover the case for their news outlets, let out audible moans as they realized they would have to leave. Nevertheless, the court bailiff politely but firmly ushered the SRO crowd out the door, where many remained to peer through the small rectangular window into the courtroom.

Roughly 150 people remained behind, tightly packed cheek-to-cheek into the ten or so wooden pews that served as seating. A few folding chairs were allowed to be set up in the remaining empty space at the rear. More than one eager reporter was chided by the judge for trying to sit on a small wooden table in a back corner.

"That is not a seat," Godwin said firmly to those who tried to perch there. "You will have to leave."

No one dared to argue; it was clear from Godwin's manner that anyone who crossed him would be permanently evicted, or worse.

Finally, Judge Godwin put a further damper on media efforts to cover the event about to unfold by announcing, "There will be no cameras or tape recorders allowed in the courtroom. I apologize. We have to do this because of the facilities. The county father's office is over at the administration building. If you want to complain, I am sure they will be delighted to hear from you."

With that business out of the way, the judge, brow furrowed to show he meant business, turned to his bailiff. "Let's bring them in, Mr. Bernard," he said formally, asking that the jury be seated on its platform in front of the witness stand. The judge and all the attorneys stood in respect as the jury filed in somberly and took their seats.

"Good morning, members of the jury," Godwin said. "Mr. Anderson, present the indictment to the jury, please."

The case of Wanda Holloway may have been the subject of jokes and gossip for months, but Judge Godwin was going to make sure the woman's trial proceeded with all the pomp and circumstance and respect for the judicial process that he felt it deserved. It was not a laughing matter to him.

After Mike Anderson read the indictment, the judge asked him to give the state's opening statement. All criminal trials are carried out in a set order. First both sides give an opening statement, usually limited to a set time of approximately thirty minutes. The prosecution always goes first, since it has the burden of proving the defendant's guilt beyond a reasonable doubt. After the defense concludes its opening remarks, the state presents its evidence and rests its case. The defense is then allowed to put its witnesses, if any, on the stand, although there is theoretically no necessity that it do so. If the state has not shown convincing proof of all the elements of the crime of which the defendant is accused, the defense could choose to remain silent, although this rarely happens in practice.

At the close of all the evidence from both sides, each side makes a final statement in which the attorneys summarize the evidence that was presented during the trial and attempt to persuade the jury to analyze it from their point of view. In both the opening and closing statements the defense and prosecution are permitted considerable leeway to advance their positions, much as a debate team would.

Mike Anderson strode confidently to the center of the courtroom, stopped in front of the jury panel, and began his opening address in the time-honored way, first thanking the judge, and then turning to the jury.

"Ladies and gentlemen," he said, "I'd like to, first of all, congratulate you for being selected to this jury. You may have mixed emotions about being here, but you are doing your civic duty and I hope that you'll be as attentive during trial as you have been during the voir dire process."

Anderson was obviously at home in the courtroom. His posture, his voice, his lack of notes, all pointed to careful preparation and previous experience. His strong Texas drawl identified him as a native, always a plus with a local jury. He next began to outline what the state would be presenting as evidence. "I anticipate that we will bring you Verna Heath. Verna Heath will no longer be just a name. You'll be able to put a face to that name. She's no longer some innocuous individual or some innocuous word that floats around out there. She's a human being, and you'll get to meet her.

"You'll find out about how she and Wanda Webb Holloway became acquainted, how that acquaintance became sour when Miz Heath's daughter, first of all, won a seventh-grade cheerleading contest and Miz Holloway's daughter did not."

Anderson became more forceful in his delivery as he got further into the story. "Then you'll find things continue to sour the next year when Miz Holloway's daughter is disqualified for disobeying the school rules in campaigning for cheerleader. There are other cheerleading contestants, as well, but somehow, since Amber Heath was elected to cheerleading, somehow that became Verna Heath's fault. All of this became Verna Heath's fault," he said, and paused dramatically for a split second. "Everything that happened bad to Wanda Holloway became Verna Heath's fault."

The jury stared in rapt attention as the young attorney paced in front of the jury box. He was getting almost as worked up as a hard-shell Baptist preacher at a tent revival meeting. Then he stopped, and said in a much lower tone, "And then Wanda Holloway began to talk about having her done away with. First she wanted to have the thirteen-year-old daughter done away with. She talked to several people about doing this. They said, 'You're crazy. That's absolutely ridiculous.'" She talked about how she wanted her killed, to other people. 'That's crazy.'

"She then found Terry Harper," Anderson continued, and described his witness bluntly. "And you'll find that Terry is no hero. Terry is not the kind of guy you want to take to dinner. But he is the kind of guy you want to hire to find a hit man for you."

Anderson then explained about Terry's troubled past, and included the fact that at the time Terry was on probation for driving while intoxicated, or DWI. He explained how Terry reacted, how his first thought was of himself and how he might get implicated in whatever Wanda was cooking up. He related how Terry then went to the police and, with their assistance, later taped several conversations with Wanda Holloway that showed her true desires.

"You'll hear her on the tape," Anderson promised, "where they exchange earrings. She says, 'Tell him to go for it.' In the tape I anticipate you will hear her talk about the death of Verna Heath and Amber Heath, and then talk about having Verna Heath kidnapped and sold into slavery. And at the end, she basically says, 'I don't care what you do with them. I don't ever want to see her showing up in Channelview again.' Then she tells him to go for it." Mike shook his head sadly as if in wonder of it all before he concluded:

"Ladies and gentleman, the first few witnesses that you'll hear will be setting up the basis for the relationship between Wanda Holloway and Verna Heath. And after that we will bring you evidence of the actual negotiations between Miz Holloway, mention that she makes of this to other people, and then the other negotiations between Miz Holloway and Terry Harper."

After politely thanking the jury for their attention and urging that they continue to listen as the trial wore on, Anderson was through with his opening remarks.

Judge Godwin turned to the defense table. "Mr. McKinney, do you wish to respond?" he inquired. The tall, lanky McKinney unfurled himself from his chair and stood up with a sheaf of papers in his hand. "Yes, I do, your honor," he said. He ambled over to a podium placed in front of the judge's bench and stood behind it with his notes before him. In stark contrast to Mike Anderson's easy, fluid delivery, McKinney seemed nervous and ill at ease addressing the jury. Nevertheless, he began to read his remarks.

"Ladies and gentlemen, I wish this case were half as simple as Mr. Anderson suggests to you that it is," he started. "But I suggest there is going to be a whole lot more to this than Mr. Anderson just told you about. There's a whole lot more to this than a relationship of two mothers who have daughters running for cheerleaders. There's a whole lot more to this than what's on the tapes."

McKinney went on for a few minutes about how, in several places on the tapes, Wanda seemed to be equivocating about whether she in fact wanted the deed done or not. "You will hear Wanda Holloway constantly saying, 'I don't know if I want to do this,'" McKinney insisted. "Constantly questioning and saying, 'I don't know.' Trying to back out, trying to find ways not to do it. In the next to last conversation, you'll hear Wanda say, 'Blow it off, I'm not interested, I don't want to do it.'" McKinney paused for a moment before adding with emphasis, "And then you'll hear Terry Harper say, 'But wait a minute, have I got a deal for you!'" He uttered Terry's name with a contemptuous sneer and began to outline the defense view of the conversations between Terry and Wanda.

"What the evidence will show you," he insisted, "is that back in January of this year, Terry and Tony Harper got on the telephone together. Terry called his brother and said, 'Brother, Wanda came to talk to me and this is what she talked about.' I expect you'll hear from Terry and Tony in this case and you'll hear their versions of who said what to who on that occasion are different. They can't keep the stories straight today and that's what the evidence on the witness stand will show you." McKinney was obviously referring to the information he and Schneider had received from Marla Harper about the "plot" between Terry and Tony to "burn" Wanda Holloway.

The tall, thin attorney continued to cling to the podium as he tried to clarify the evidence about the plot. He said, "What's important here is why Terry did that. Terry did that because for a long time he has been an outcast in his family, a black sheep, if you will, and this is his way to get back in good with his family. But I'm jumping ahead of myself because y'all don't know all the players in this case." The attorney's deep, gravelly voice paused as he looked through his notes. He attempted to briefly explain the tangled web of characters.

"Tony Harper is Wanda Holloway's ex-husband. They were divorced in 1980," he explained. "Wanda has custody of the children and always has. Tony has paid child support since day one and the evidence will show you he's fought it tooth and nail and always hated to do it."

By his choice of which facts to accent from the long history of these people, McKinney artfully attempted to cast the action in a new light, one more favorable to Wanda.

"Wanda and Tony have had a less than pleasant divorce," he said. "Tony has always resented everything that Wanda has done with the children, so when Terry picks up the phone and calls him, his brother, and says, 'I've got a way for you to get your kids back,' Tony says, 'Alright.'"

McKinney skimmed over the police involvement and the tapes the state had arrayed against Wanda. Instead of relying on the tapes alone, he suggested, the jury should listen to the defense's star witness, Marla Harper. "You won't have to just judge Terry Harper's credibility because you'll hear it from another witness in this case—you'll hear it from Terry Harper's own wife, Terry Harper's sixth and seventh wife."

McKinney's opening remarks rambled on and took several various turns in an attempt to make sure the jury bought at least one of the scatter-shot excuses tossed out to explain Wanda's behavior. After describing how Marla would testify about her husband's plot against Wanda, McKinney tried explanation number two, that Wanda was just kidding.

"When you listen to the tapes, you'll hear things that will suggest to you that Wanda Holloway wasn't serious. You'll hear a bunch of laughing and joking and playing around, not the kinds of things you would expect to hear from someone that seriously wanted somebody killed," he said.

Further evidence of Wanda's lack of intent, McKinney explained, came from the section of the tapes where Wanda explains to Terry she has no money to pay for the deed. "The evidence is going to show you that she and her husband are worth two million dollars," he intoned. "The evidence will show you they keep five thousand to seven thousand dollars cash sitting around the house. The evidence is going to show you that twenty-five hundred dollars, for that family, is no problem. The evidence is going to show you that if she has the kind of malice the state suggests to you she does, twenty-five hundred dollars would not have stood in her way."

As if those explanations might not suffice, McKinney added still more. Terry lured Wanda into the plot, he said. He was the first to mention murder as a solution. Or else there were more conversations that the two alone were privy to that were not taped by police. And last but not least, McKinney suggested that Wanda went along with Terry Harper because she was afraid of him and didn't trust him. "Now if she wanted to do this," said McKinney, "she wouldn't have gone to somebody she didn't trust; she would have gone to someone she trusted. The evidence in this case is going to show one thing and one thing only conclusively. It's going to show Wanda Holloway is innocent and the only two real guilty people in this case are Terry and Tony Harper."

Slamming down his notes for emphasis, anger at the two brothers in his voice, McKinney strode away from the lectern and back to the defense table.

"Call your first," Judge Godwin said to the prosecution. With the verbal jousting by the attorneys out of the way, along with its customary selective display of the events, actual presentation of the facts in Wanda's case could begin. The jurors all leaned forward eagerly to watch the drama unfold.

9

Laying the Foundation

Mike Anderson stood and said, "The state would call Ida Gilbert, Your Honor."

Ida Gilbert, a well-dressed middle-aged black woman who was the assistant principal at Alice Johnson Junior High, was the first of a series of state witnesses put on the stand to lay the foundation for the state's contention that Wanda Ann Holloway had slowly, over a period of two years, developed an intense hatred for Verna Heath. This point was key to the prosecution, since it established a motive for Wanda's later hit contract against Verna. In any criminal trial, the prosecutors must prove not only that certain key acts occurred that constituted a crime, but also that the defendant had the mens rea, or guilty mind, that showed an intent to commit those acts.

Painstakingly, Anderson led Gilbert through a detailed accounting of the cheerleader competitions at Alice Johnson Junior High during the previous two years. It was essential to show the jury just how serious these competitions had been for Wanda and many of the other would-be cheerleaders' moms. Anderson had to demonstrate that cheerleading, in Channelview, was not just another school activity. Indeed, he had to show that in Channelview cheerleading was matter of life or death.

As the jurors listened intently, Gilbert described Shanna's last attempt to make cheerleader, and her subsequent disqualification for using banned campaign materials. When Shanna and her mother were told that Shanna would be barred from the competition, Gilbert testified, Shanna reacted "real well." Wanda's response, the official added, was quite different.

"She was, I would say, upset," Gilbert stated. "She cried. Shanna did not."

Gilbert was followed on the stand by Donna Jackson, the junior-high cheerleading sponsor, and Ann Goodson, a secretary at Channelview High. Both women described Wanda's intense involvement in Shanna's two failed cheerleading campaigns. Jackson related how Wanda had angrily accused her of prematurely leaking the results of the first competition, where Shanna had placed third behind Amber Heath and Summer Rutledge.

Ann Goodson, who had helped Wanda get her one-day temporary job at the Channelview High School, knew Wanda personally because Wanda's son Shane had dated Goodson's daughter. Prompted by Mike Anderson, Goodson said that when Wanda worked with her at the school, she often talked about Shanna's cheerleading and specifically cited Verna Heath as the reason for Shanna's failures.

In early January of 1991, just weeks before Wanda's arrest, Goodson said, Wanda had given her a blow-by-blow account of the history of Shanna's cheerleading experiences. According to Goodson, Wanda said then that Verna Heath had caused Shanna to be "blackballed" from cheerleading.

"She thought there was a person, perhaps in the junior high, who was giving information to Verna Heath," Goodson told the jury. "She felt as if that person was really watching Shanna, at all times, and reporting back to Verna." Like many of the people in Channelview, Wanda saw plots and manipulations in every setting. When Mike Anderson asked Goodson what she thought of Wanda's behavior, the woman summed her opinion up in one word. "Obsessed," she said bluntly.

After the school employees' direct examinations, each was rather ineptly cross-examined by Troy McKinney, who attempted to elicit testimony that Wanda had, in fact, reacted as any other involved, interested parent would. During Ann Goodson's cross, McKinney asked her if Verna Heath had been visiting the high-school campus to lobby on her daughter's behalf, nine months before Amber would even be enrolled in the school.

"Right," Goodson answered. "Also, Verna went to Mr. Pantoja and talked to him about allowing Amber to become a twirler the first year." Goodson described how the band director had always had a rule that students had to have a year of high school behind them before they could try out for twirler. Verna, she said, attempted to persuade him to alter his rule for Amber, but Mr. P refused to budge.

"Then Verna said, 'Oh well, I guess she'll just have to be cheerleader,'" Goodson related. "Wanda overheard the conversation and that last remark really upset her."

McKinney had successfully drawn out the fact that Verna Heath was certainly as much a stage mother as Wanda Holloway.

After several hours of this rather monotonous testimony, the jurors as well as the spectators in the courtroom were sleepy and bored.

But the state's next witness perked everyone right up. Verna Heath was called to the stand. Members of the media, especially, leaned forward eagerly to see the woman Wanda Holloway had wanted shipped to Cuba or killed. Verna kept her eyes modestly downcast as she walked sedately to the witness box. It was obvious she had dressed for her dramatic role in this little drama—her hair was softly curled around her heavily made-up face and she wore her Sunday best. Her hands were demurely folded in her lap around a lace-edged hand-kerchief. Wanda Holloway just stared at her, her face impossible to read.

Mike Anderson gently questioned the would-be victim of the case, beginning by asking her the routine questions about who she was and how she lived. She explained that she had four children, aged three to thirteen, and that her oldest children were twins, Aaron and Amber. Mike asked her if she worked outside the home, and she said softly, "Yes, I teach dancing and twirling, and have done that for twenty-five years."

Mike then asked Verna if she knew a person named Wanda Holloway, and, if so, if that woman was in the courtroom that day. "Yes, I know her, and yes, that is her over there," Verna said, pointing at the woman who "wanted her gone." "That's her in the red suit with the gold buttons." Wanda's face barely twitched as her nemesis stared her down. It was easy to see how a rivalry had developed between these two—they were so much alike.

Anderson asked Verna about her relationship with Wanda. Verna described in a quiet voice how she had met Wanda years earlier at Channelview Christian School, and how for a time they had been close friends. She told the court that the friendship had cooled when Amber and Shanna had taken gymnastics together at the school and Amber had demonstrated greater skills at some of the maneuvers. After Amber won the 1989 cheerleading position at Alice Johnson Junior High, Verna explained, the friendship had virtually come to an end.

Once more, in mind-numbing detail, Anderson lead Verna Heath through an account of both cheerleading competitions that Amber and Shanna had participated in. As a dance and twirling instructor herself, Verna went into even greater detail than the previous witnesses about how the practice sessions were conducted and what maneuvers the girls were expected to know.

She smugly added that Amber could do many things that the other girls were unable to perform. As a result, said Verna proudly, Amber had won cheerleader in both 1989 and 1990, and Shanna Harper had not. After that, Verna explained, things turned icy between the two women. They didn't speak to each other, or even wave if they passed each other in their cars.

"What about in January of 1991?" Anderson inquired. "Did you notice any further change then?"

"Yes," said Verna. "Amber and Shanna had been in gymnastics class together, but she took Shanna out of Amber's class and we didn't speak anymore. She came in the door and went straight down to the floor, she had no eye contact with me and we just didn't speak anymore."

In conclusion, Mike Anderson asked the court's permission to have Amber Heath brought in for identification. What he really wanted was for the jury to see the sweet little thirteen-year-old that Wanda so hated and had wanted killed. Amber was brought in by a deputy. Like her mother, she appeared as she might for a tea party, in a lace-trimmed pastel dress with white stockings. Her long, dark-brown hair was teased and curled and artfully clipped back on top with a big blue bow, to match her big blue eyes. Wanda Holloway's eyes visibly narrowed as she saw her daughter's rival.

After excusing Amber, Anderson passed Verna Heath to the defense for cross-examination. Once more, Troy McKinney began his drawling questions in an attempt to discredit the state's witness.

"When did you first hire a lawyer?" he snapped at Verna.

Verna looked stunned but tried to stammer a reply. Before she could finish McKinney interrupted sharply.

"Didn't you hire Bob Shults at one point? And didn't he hire someone else and eventually you had an agent?" McKinney pressed the blushing housewife on the stand. Verna finally stammered that she and her husband had consulted with Shults and had eventually sold their life-story rights to someone in Hollywood. The lanky defense attorney had scored a minor point by showing that the state's "innocent victim" was, in fact, going to profit from her traumatic experience.

"Have you been on any talk shows yet?" McKinney asked sarcastically, but did not wait for Verna's reply.

McKinney jumped backward in time to January of 1991, when Wanda had complained about Verna hanging out at Channelview High to watch the cheerleading practice at a school where none of her children were even enrolled. "Did you ever have occasion or occasions to go up to the high school, which the girls weren't enrolled in at the time, as I understand it, and speak to the cheerleading sponsor and observe and watch the practices of the current high-school cheerleaders at that time?" he asked Verna.

His motive was obvious; he wanted to show that Verna was a pushy, ambitious mother.

Verna looked defensive as she answered, "I'm sure there were some occasions that I went over there because the junior-high cheerleaders would go over and practice on the track at the high school because they didn't really have a place to practice at the junior high, and that's also where the high-school cheerleaders practice. So, we were all sitting in the stands."

McKinney quickly asked, "Apart from those occasions, were there other occasions when you went?"

Verna was evasive, and only said, "Possibly."

Again, McKinney had just dropped a seed of doubt about just how perfect this sweet little lady was, and went on to another topic. He asked about the day that Verna learned that Wanda was arrested. "Do you recall what your initial reaction was?" he queried.

Verna Heath looked on the verge of tears as she said, "I was very upset. I was very hurt."

That was not the point McKinney wanted to drive home, and he asked another question to clarify it. "In your wildest dreams," he drawled, "no matter how cold you thought the relationship was, had you ever imagined or thought that Wanda was capable of what the officers had told you she had done?"

Verna had to admit it had never occurred to her. "I would not have thought that she could do something, or even want to," she said. "But whenever they told me, you know, when they told me her name, I said, 'Does this have anything to do with...over cheerleading,' because it all sort of fell into place."

That was not exactly what the attorney had expected her to say, so he abruptly changed tactics. He adopted a look of mock astonishment as he asked sarcastically, "You're not down here today telling the jury she's guilty, are you?"

Verna seemed flustered as she stammered, "I'm just testifying. I'm just telling the truth."

McKinney ended by asking Verna about her attempt to win Amber permission from the high-school band director to try out as school twirler as a freshman.

"Isn't it true that when you went in and talked to him, you knew that freshmen weren't allowed to be twirlers, right?" he asked, to demonstrate her blatant ambition on her daughter's behalf. It would make anybody sick to hear about it, not just Wanda, he thought; he was half right, at least.

Verna looked tense but smug as she tried to explain, "Well, they didn't have any twirlers at the time, and..."

"So you went in and talked to him about having Amber as a twirler?" he interrupted.

"Right," Verna snapped. "I wanted to know what her options were. She had hoped some day to try to get a scholarship on her twirling, to be a feature twirler somewhere and there was no twirling in junior high. So, she tried out for cheerleader and I wanted to know what her options were in high school, as far as was she...could she be allowed to try out at some point, possibly as a freshman or, you know, I just wanted to find out those questions." It was not really clear just who wanted Amber to be a twirling star. Perhaps Verna was hoping to relive her own glory days as the National Strutting Champion through Amber.

With one last parting shot, McKinney asked Wanda's supposed victim, "Have you ever seen Wanda say anything or do anything that indicated hatred or anger toward Amber?"

"No," Verna admitted. "I can't say that I have."

McKinney passed the witness, and the court recessed for lunch. Verna left the witness box with an exhausted sigh and was immediately hugged by Jack Heath as she exited the courtroom. Her friends and family crowded around her and congratulated her on a job well done.

The prosecution next put up brief testimony from several more witnesses. After Verna Heath, Pete Reyes, Shane's friend, took the stand. The primary purpose of the twenty-three-year-old's testimony was to relate how he had visited the Holloway home near Christmas of 1990 and found Wanda talking with Shane and Amy Goodson about "people she hated." "Can you tell the ladies and gentlemen of the jury what that conversation was about, Mr. Reyes?" Mike Anderson asked the Venezuelan native.

"We were discussing people in the band and Ms. Verna Heath," Pete said. "And Wanda asked me if I would or I could kill Verna Heath." The jury looked at Wanda with shocked expressions. How could the woman talk to a young man like this about such terrible deeds?

Under further questioning, Reyes related how he had heard Wanda talk about the Heaths and the cheerleading on several occasions during that time period, even though he had only known the family for about three months. He told about how Wanda had asked him to go talk to the Channelview High band director to see if there was anything that could be done to help Shanna get elected cheerleader. And he also told the jury about how Wanda had reacted after her arrest. While she was out on bond immediately following the revelation of her "plot" against Verna, Reyes said that Wanda had told him and another of Shane's friends "that she had made a mistake and she had to live with it, but she couldn't discuss it any further."

Next up was Marcel Dionne, the detective with the Harris County Sheriff's Department who had first taken Terry Harper's call back on New Year's Eve. He was questioned by Casey O'Brien, who was taking his turn at doing some of the direct examinations of the state's witnesses. Dionne told the court about how he had interviewed Terry Harper in the presence of Marla Harper, and that Marla Harper had not acted afraid or taken any steps to speak privately with the officer.

Stanley Schneider asked Dionne under cross-examination if he had taken any steps to check Terry Harper's criminal record or reputation for truth and veracity in the community. The officer admitted he had not. "Did you investigate Wanda Holloway?" Schneider asked. "No, I did not," Dionne answered truthfully. The implication was clear; if the police had just made reasonable inquiry into these people, they would have never bothered to investigate further. At least that's what Schneider wanted the jury to think, so he passed the witness before any more could be said.

Casey O'Brien next led Detective George Helton through a step-by-step description of how the undercover investigation of Wanda Holloway was conducted. He told of the six recorded conversations, and how either he or Sergeant Blackwell was present at each. He described the equipment used to record the conversations and the chain of custody for each tape at the conclusion of the conversations. He told of the conversations on January 10 and January 14, and the meeting at Grandy's on the fourteenth.

Like most law enforcement officers, Helton was an experienced witness. He impassively described watching Wanda Holloway drive into the parking lot and Terry Harper getting into her car. His testimony continued until he had related all the details of all the meetings between himself and Terry Harper and between Terry Harper and Wanda Holloway, concluding with the fateful meeting on January 28 when Wanda handed Terry Harper the diamond earrings as a down payment on the planned hit of Verna Heath.

Helton described how the earrings were stored in the police evidence room at the Organized Crime field office. He was then asked to identify, one by one, the tape cassettes of the conversations so that they could be entered into evidence. Likewise, he identified a pair of diamond stud earrings, which were then proffered by O'Brien to the court.

"And what was the next thing you did in the case after the twenty-eighth?" O'Brien asked Helton.

"An arrest-warrant affidavit was drawn and signed by a judge and we executed the arrest of Ms. Holloway," he said bluntly.

"Pass the witness," O'Brien said.

Stanley Schneider began his cross-examination of the officer politely. "We've met on several occasions before, haven't we?" he asked Helton.

"Yes, we have," agreed the seventeen-year veteran officer.

Abruptly Schneider switched his questioning. "You use informants a lot in your work, isn't that correct?" he asked.

"Yes, that's true," agreed Helton again.

"What kind of informants do you use?" the attorney inquired.

"Normally, we use narcotics informants," said Helton.

"You mean criminals??" Schneider said with mock surprise. Standard defense practice is to discredit police informants by implying they are all low-life criminals who would say anything to save their own skins.

"Objection!" shouted Casey O'Brien, jumping to his feet. "Judge, I don't see any relevance in that!"

From there, Schneider continued to imply through his questions that the police couldn't trust Terry Harper because of his record, and also that the police didn't properly supervise Terry Harper at all times during the investigation of Wanda Holloway. After establishing that the officers had instructed Terry not to act alone, Schneider asked about the phone call that Terry was allowed to place to Wanda unsupervised on the day of his first scheduled meeting with Wanda at Grandy's.

"So you decided to violate your own normal practice not to lose control over a case by having your informant make a telephone call without you being present, is that correct?" Schneider repeatedly asked.

"No, that is incorrect," Helton said testily.

"But you weren't present, were you?" Schneider wouldn't let it drop. Finding and going after any weak spot was his only hope. His next questions all implied that perhaps during that unrecorded conversation more had been said than Terry reported. He also implied that Terry could have called Tony Harper, also, as well as any number of other people, without the officers ever knowing.

He then hammered at Helton about the fact that the officer had failed to check Terry Harper's criminal record or Wanda Holloway's, even though he had access to county computers that could call up that information in a split second.

After Schneider concluded his cross-examination, Casey O'Brien rehabilitated his witness. "Can you tell us why you didn't investigate Wanda Holloway's background?" he asked the officer.

"Because there would have been no investigation," the officer said laconically, glaring at Stanley Schneider as he spoke. His meaning was clear: If he had made a few calls about Wanda, she would have found out and would have been scared off, at least for this time. A few more questions clarified that, as far as Detective Helton was concerned, Terry Harper had acted in accordance with police instructions throughout the investigation into Wanda Holloway. Once more O'Brien asked about each and every meeting and phone call between Harper and Holloway, concluding with the meeting on January 28. "What was the purpose of that meeting?" he asked the detective.

"That meeting was to get the diamond earrings and payment for the murder," Helton said.

Stanley Schneider jumped to his feet in outrage. "Objection," he shouted. The judge sustained him. "Ask the jury to disregard," Schneider continued. "Ask for a mistrial."

Judge Godwin looked sternly at Stanley Schneider before answering, "The jury shall disregard, request for mistrial is denied."

George Helton was excused from the witness stand, and the state called Terry Lynn Harper.

Terry looked pleased as punch with himself as he clomped up to the witness box in jeans and cowboy boots. He grinned out at his parents and smiled at the jury. He seemed to relish his moment on stage. He even smiled over at Wanda, who responded with a stony stare.

Casey O'Brien began his direct examination. It was late in the afternoon and he knew he would not finish before the judge announced a recess for the rest of the day. Nevertheless, he began his long series of questions of the state's main witness.

He began by asking Terry who he was and where he worked. Terry explained he was out of a job at that very moment, but had a job lined up to start the next week as a pipe fitter for the refineries. Next, the attorney asked about the various members of the Harper clan, how they were related and how old they were. Then he asked, "Do you know Wanda Holloway?"

"Yes, sir, I do," said Terry proudly. "She's my ex-sister-in-law, was married at one time to my brother, Tony Harper." Next O'Brien established through Terry that Wanda had had two children with Tony—Shane, who was away at Baylor University as a freshman that fall, and Shanna, who was then starting the ninth grade at Channelview High.

The jury, of course, was still completely in the dark about all the details of the family relations, as well as about what had happened between Wanda and Terry, so the whole story had to be told once more from the witness stand. Terry loved telling it, fortunately, and eagerly rose to the task.

O'Brien lead him through standard question-and-answer format. "Do you know who has custody of these children?" he asked Terry.

"I believe Shane is at Baylor, and he resides with his father, Tony, and I believe Shanna still lives with her mother, Wanda," he said.

"Now I want to direct your attention to the fall of 1990," O'Brien said to Terry. "Did you have occasion to meet with Wanda Holloway at some point during that period of time?"

Terry related how Wanda had dropped by his trailer one afternoon, and told about the conversation that later ensued down at Bo's Super Stop about getting rid of Verna and Amber Heath.

"Was that an unusual incident?" asked O'Brien. "Did you have occasion to talk to her very much?"

"No sir, I sure didn't," Terry laughed. "I hadn't talked to Wanda in, mercy, I don't know. It's been quite a while. We're talking a year, two, maybe three. I can't remember exactly when I had talked to Wanda prior to that, besides maybe at my father's convenience store, where we crossed each other in the pathway and said hi. That's about the extent of it."

"Did you ever see her at family gatherings?" Casey asked.

"She don't come to our family gatherings," Terry said, as if the idea itself were absurd.

"But you saw the children at family gatherings?" O'Brien clarified.

"Sure," Terry said, "because they were there with their father and Mickie."

"So this was unusual for her to stop by," O'Brien repeated.

"Yeah, it kind of shocked me," Terry admitted. He said he was also shocked by Wanda's vehement anger at the Heaths.

He told the jury that when they met at Bo's that fall afternoon in 1990 "Every so often she'd say, 'You know, I just hate them two. I just can't stand them.'" Terry said that it was also at this meeting that he told Wanda it would be difficult, if not impossible, to find anyone who would make a hit on a thirteen-year-old girl, and that it would be very expensive if such a hit man could be found. "I told her, five, ten, fifteen, maybe even twenty thousand," he said somewhat proudly.

Next O'Brien asked Terry about the message he received from Shanna on Christmas Eve to get in touch with her mother.

"Did you know what she meant by that?" O'Brien inquired.

"I had an ideal [sic]," Terry confessed. "It was one of two things. It was either that Wanda had decided to forget about it, or else she was wanting to get serious and see if I had found somebody for her."

Terry was then questioned about his call to Tony Harper about this on New Year's Eve, and his subsequent visit to the sheriff's office that same afternoon. He included the fact that he had told his wife, Marla, the whole story, and that she had accompanied him down to the station house.

O'Brien asked an important question. "What was your motive in going to the police?"

"It's just like I told the police in my report," said Terry confidently. "If something happened to this woman or little girl, I wanted them to hear it from me first. I didn't want it to come back on me and say, you know, 'I heard Terry Harper say this one time, that he loved his niece and his nephew more than life.' That's my motive right there. I didn't know if she was serious or not, okay? But I'm not going to take a chance with someone's life. If it was a joke, fine, it wasn't no big deal. It would be hearsay." Once more, Terry Harper was demonstrating his extensive knowledge of the law and the world of criminal justice.

O'Brien began asking a series of questions designed to elicit the same details previously heard from Detective Helton about how the meetings and conversations between Terry and Wanda were arranged and tape recorded. Once again, each step in the process was covered. Finally, O'Brien got around to discussing the first tape recording that was made on January 10. "Did you have occasion to listen to that tape recording after it was made?" he asked Terry.

"Yes, sir," Terry said.

"Was that a true and accurate recording of the conversation you had just had with Wanda Holloway?" O'Brien asked. For purposes of identification and laying a predicate, or foundation, for introduction of the tape into evidence, all these tedious steps had to be taken in order to satisfy the rules of evidence.

At that point, Judge Godwin interrupted the proceedings. It was getting late in the day, and he announced that the court would recess until the next morning at nine o'clock Terry Harper would resume the stand at that time.

Everyone seemed relieved that the first day of testimony had drawn to a close. It had been a long, tense day for all. But the trial was far from over.

—————————————————————————————— **10**

The Venomous Voice

The first order of business when the trial of Wanda Holloway resumed the next morning was to introduce the tape-recorded conversations into evidence for the jury to hear. But before beginning to play the tapes for the jury, O'Brien had some more questions for Terry. Once again, the young Channelview pipe fitter was outfitted in western wear for his appearance on the stand. Once again, he seemed to be enjoying his star turn.

O'Brien began simply enough. "Mr. Harper, are you the same Terry Harper who was testifying as we broke yesterday?" As if that fact weren't obvious—Terry Harper was an original, one-of-a-kind individual. After seeing him testify the day before, no one in the court would ever mistake him for anyone else. But such formalities were necessary in court.

Immediately, O'Brien resumed discussion of the tapes. He asked the judge to have typed transcripts of the conversations circulated to the jury. Judge Godwin consented, but admonished the jury accordingly.

"Members of the jury," he said. "I will instruct you that you will only be permitted to use these transcripts as you listen to the tapes to aid you, if it does aid you, in understanding the contents of the tape. This is a transcript prepared by the state of Texas for your use at this time and you will remember that they caused it to be prepared. If there should be, in your mind, any variance between what you hear on the tape and what you see on the transcript, you are to remember what is on the tape and not what is on the transcript."

This was yet another formality designed to meet fairness guidelines. After the transcripts were distributed, O'Brien asked that the court play the first tape of the phone conversation on January 10 between Terry and Wanda. A court deputy turned on a small tape recorder, and the voices of Terry Harper and Wanda Holloway began to fill the air. The jurors, as well as all the spectators, listened in rapt attention as they heard Terry ask Wanda, "You still interested in taking care of that problem?" There was no mistaking her answer: "Uh-huh," she said without hesitation.

Next they heard the conversation that took place in the Grandy's parking lot on January 14. They listened as Wanda worried about whether she had been followed, and heard her tell Terry about how mad she was that Verna Heath was already "down there at the school kissing ass so bad it's unreal." The unadulterated hatred in the woman's voice was unmistakable, and hard to reconcile with the primly dressed lady at the defense table.

This day Wanda had chosen a more demure outfit, a conservative black-and-white print dress with a silky black handkerchief in its breast pocket. Perhaps her attorneys had warned her that bright red suits might give the wrong impression and make her seem like a scarlet lady. Wanda did not move, even to so much as blink, it seemed, while her taped voice caused the jurors to glare at her fixedly.

Their eyes nearly bugged out of their heads as they heard Wanda say of Amber Heath, "But Terry, you don't know this little girl. Ooooooh, I can't stand her. I mean, she's a bitch, makes me sick. I mean, I could knock her in the face, you know?"

The image of pretty little Amber, who had been brought in for identification purposes while her mother was on the stand, was still fresh in their minds. Who could want to hit that sweet child? Much less have her killed? The jurors, especially some of the women, narrowed their eyes and watched Wanda closely. Still she showed no emotion.

And on it went, through all six tapes. This was very damaging evidence. Why did Wanda sound so full of venom if she hadn't meant it, the jury wondered. Why had she passed the diamond earrings to Terry Harper if she was just kidding around? How could a daughter making cheerleader be that important to anyone? It just didn't make any sense.

At the conclusion of the last tape, O'Brien asked Terry Harper some questions to clarify some of the statements on the tapes. "On that conversation on the twenty-eighth," he started, "You mentioned something about 'pictures.' What did you mean by that?" he asked Terry.

Terry did his best to explain. "Well, it just popped into my head, just for one reason, why I would be calling Wanda. Because Wanda and I don't speak."

That was the conversation where Wanda obviously had other people in the room, because she immediately started using the "pictures" excuse as well. "She kept using the word *pictures*," Terry said. "She told me, 'I'll get you your pictures. I just picked them up today.'"

"At some point did this word *picture* change in meaning from 'We got to deceive Shanna' to 'We got the goods'?" O'Brien asked.

"Evidently she was referring to the earrings," Terry answered.

By this time the courtroom was abuzz with whispered speculation from the audience. Some reporters had already leapt up to rush in the news about the taped conversations to make the next edition of the newspaper or the six o'clock television news. This was hot stuff, all this talk about bitches and bashing people's faces in and Cuba and white slavery. No one had ever heard anything like it before, especially from the mouth of a Missionary Baptist organ player.

After having Terry Harper identify the diamond earrings in police custody as the same ones he had been handed by Wanda, O'Brien went one step further. He made sure that he, and not Wanda's defense attorneys, told the jury the whole unpleasant truth about Terry Harper.

First he asked Terry about calling Tony Harper regarding Wanda's solicitation. He asked who else had heard anything about Terry's work with the police investigation. Although Terry had been asked by the investigators to keep the information to himself, he had told not only Marla and Tony, but also a friend from work, Bob Wilburs, who Terry described as his "spiritual advisor." And last but not least, Casey O'Brien asked, "If you would, listen to this question carefully. What, sir, have you been convicted of in the past, what crimes?"

Terry didn't bat an eye as he responded. In fact, he smiled. "I have been convicted of PI, public intoxication, disturbing the peace. I was arrested on a drug charge. I was arrested on a misdemeanor possession of marijuana. I have two DWIs. I'm currently on probation now for my second DWI. And several traffic tickets. To the best of my knowledge, that pretty well covers it."

"Pass the witness," was O'Brien's only response. The jury was excused for lunch before the defense could begin its cross-examination.

Before the attorneys and the defendant were excused for lunch, another little matter had to be taken care of out of the presence of the jury. The state had intended to call one Patrick Gobert to the stand after Terry Harper, but the defense was objecting that Patrick had already violated the rule imposed on all witnesses not to discuss the case with anyone outside the courtroom. The very night before, they told Judge Godwin, Patrick Gobert had been caught bragging down at the Channelview YMCA, where he was then working as a fitness counselor.

They knew about it, Stanley Schneider told Judge Godwin, because a private investigator who just happened to know Wanda Holloway had just happened to go down to the Y the night before. The private eye, Kevin Pipkins, claimed to have heard Gobert boasting to friends that he was going to be a star witness for the state. This had happened, said Pipkins, when a television at the gym had broadcast on the ten o'clock news that the trial was underway downtown.

Patrick Gobert, looking miffed at this insult to his integrity, was put on the stand for questioning about this supposed incident so that the judge could determine if indeed any rules had been violated.

McKinney asked the former undertaker, "Did you ever tell anyone last night that Terry Harper was your buddy and that you helped him tape the conversations and you're going to have to come down here today and stick up for your buddy?" The very idea of Patrick and Terry being "buddies" inflamed the Christian young man.

"I certainly did not," he said indignantly, refuting Kevin Pipkins' earlier testimony.

Patrick said of his first ordeal on the witness stand, "I am not and never was Terry Harper's runnin' buddy, like they tried to say in court. That is preposterous!"

Indeed, the very idea of these two men teaming up was so ridiculous as to be absurd. But this would not be the last time a witness would take the stand in this case and testify to outrageous fabrications.

The state next put up a routine witness, Ben Gordon, who was a jewelry appraiser called to testify as to the approximate value of the diamond earrings Wanda had given Terry Harper. As an independent appraiser and graduate gemologist, Gordon told the court, he thought the diamonds were worth around $1995 retail.

Stanley Schneider used his cross-examination of the gemologist as an opportunity to show the jury just how well-heeled his client was. He asked Gordon several general questions about the wholesale diamond market and then produced several large, sparkling diamond rings he said belonged to Wanda Holloway. He asked the expert's opinion of their worth. When Gordon estimated that one ring, taken right off Wanda's finger in court, would cost about sixty-five hundred dollars, and another in the twenty-five-hundred-dollars range, Schneider looked jubilant. He hoped this exercise would show the jury that Wanda could easily have given Terry Harper jewelry worth the amount the "hit man" needed to proceed, twenty-five hundred dollars.

Wanda herself looked proud, and smiled as the jeweler described the value of her baubles.

The remainder of that afternoon was filled with other routine courtroom housekeeping matters, and the second day of testimony came to a close. Judge Godwin announced that, although he was not happy about Patrick Gobert talking out of turn at the YMCA, he did not feel the young man had been in serious violation of the witness rule, and his testimony would be allowed the following day. After all the palaver, the court recessed for yet another day. It was only two days into the trial, and both sides were predicting it could last through the next ten days.

The next day, August 28, spectators began arriving at the courtroom as early as 7:00 A.M. for the 9:00 A.M. starting time because of the competition for seats. As the news of the trial had spread, many more curiosity seekers joined the ranks of the reporters and supporters of the participants.

Some were semiprofessional trial watchers, courthouse junkies, who thrived on the real-life dramas that unfolded daily in the downtown forum. One woman had been through her own trial—she sued her doctor for malpractice—and won so much money that all she did anymore was watch other people's trials. Another was a drama coach who was there to observe the spectacle of the Cheerleader Mom, with her painted face and permed big hair. Still others were retired couples who came armed with videocams to film their favorite television reporters in the hallway outside the courtroom.

There was an air of festivity, almost gaiety, among all the spectators, except for the families and friends of the Holloways and the Heaths. Even Peggy and R. E. Harper seemed to be having a good time, although both their sons, Tony and Terry, would have to testify.

Once again, Wanda wore black and white, but of course it was a different dress. Her husband C. D. was still strangely absent—taking care of business, presumably. Shanna was kept away from the courtroom, too, to spare her the strain of the gawking media.

This week Shanna had just begun her first classes at Channelview High School as a freshman. Although some of the other students snickered behind her back as the pretty blond ambled through the cavernous hallways, most of her classmates were especially nice to her. Many felt sorry for Shanna because of the embarrassment her mother's actions had caused her.

"It's not her fault," said one classmate defensively. The students believed what the junior-high principal had lectured them about the previous winter, when Wanda had been arrested: Children are not responsible for the actions of their parents.

The proceedings that third day of the trial began with Terry Harper resuming the stand. This time, Mike Anderson continued the direct examination. "What kind of relationship did you and Wanda Holloway have?" he asked Terry.

Terry giggled, "I can't say there's been any kind of relationship with Wanda Holloway and myself. I don't have any feelings for her and I'm sure she don't have any for me," he said with another laugh. He glanced over at Wanda and grinned, but she ignored him.

"Can you describe Wanda's demeanor, how she looked and so forth, during that first meeting, sir?" Anderson asked.

"Well, like I say," Terry began. He had a tendency to run on in his answers, he liked testifying so much. This was in stark contrast to the nervous school officials who had lead the state's witnesses. "I hadn't seen Wanda in a long while. But just in the tone of her voice, she sounded desperate, that she had to have this done by a certain period of time."

The prosecutor asked, "Do you recall what this period of time was?"

"I believe she said she had to get it done by March," Terry said, "because cheerleader tryouts were, I believe, at the end of March or the first of April."

Again the room was abuzz. People in the audience were still having trouble understanding the to-do about cheerleading. At the start of the trial, many didn't quite believe this could have happened, but after hearing the witnesses, and especially the tapes, the doubts were fading and the realization that Wanda Holloway might in fact have planned someone's murder over cheerleading began to set in.

As O'Brien had done the day before, Mike Anderson began to question Terry about his motivation for getting involved in this case. Terry launched into a long, involved answer designed to make himself look heroic.

Before he could finish, Troy McKinney stood and asked Judge Godwin if he could approach the bench. At a bench conference, McKinney asked Judge Godwin to strike that last "self-serving" remark of Terry Harper's. Godwin refused, but asked Mike Anderson to stay in question/answer format, and then lectured Terry himself, saying, "Mr. Harper, once again, please, sir, there's no reason for this to get out of hand. I want you to listen to the question. Answer just that question that is asked of you. They are smart enough to think of the next question, okay?"

The judge had adopted the patronizing air of one talking to a child. "Yes, sir," Terry said, somewhat chastened.

Anderson asked several more questions about who Terry had told of his involvement with Wanda. He especially wanted to draw out the extent of Tony Harper's knowledge of the case, since he already knew, from Troy McKinney's opening statement, that the defense was planning to allege a plot between the two brothers as the explanation for Wanda's current legal troubles. Terry forthrightly admitted he had told Tony, "I hope we burn the bitch," just as Marla had reported to Wanda's lawyers.

Next Anderson asked about Marla herself, and whether she had been privy to this conversation. Terry said she had. The state's attorney then asked, "Can you describe your wife, Marla, for the ladies and gentlemen of the jury?"

Terry began, "She's about thirty-eight years old. She's got a little over shoulder-length reddish-colored hair. She got, kind of like, green eyes, weighs 125 pounds, is about five foot five."

Anderson asked, "How long have you been married to her?"

Terry shot back with a grin, "Which time?" and laughed. Later he reported proudly, "That judge nearly fell over in his chair when I said that!"

"Well, how many times have you been married to her?" Anderson asked, trying unsuccessfully to suppress a smile himself.

"Twicet," Terry said. Several jurors exchanged glances at the witness's country pronunciation of the word. Terry then went on to say that all together, counting both periods of married life with Marla, he had been married to her for a little over two years.

Anderson then moved on to another area. "I wanted to clear something up about something you said yesterday," he explained to Terry, "about your criminal history."

"Yes, sir," Terry agreed.

"You talked about that you'd been arrested for drugs," Anderson began. "What was the result of that?"

"I received five years deferred adjudication," Terry said.

"Was that a felony?" asked the lawyer.

"My understanding is that I was not convicted of a felony," Terry said.

Troy McKinney objected that the answer was nonresponsive, and asked Judge Godwin to instruct Terry to give a simple yes or no answer. Mike repeated the question, and Terry had to admit, "I have no idea if it's a felony or not."

Anderson continued to draw out the details of the offense. "Was that charge possession with intent to deliver methaqualone?" he asked Terry, who agreed it was.

"Have you ever had a carrying-a-weapon case?" asked Anderson.

Terry answered, "Yes, sir, on one of my DWIs, was a possession of a firearm."

With that, Anderson concluded the direct examination of Terry Harper and passed the witness.

Troy McKinney began, in his gruff, monotone voice, by asking Terry why he hadn't told the whole story of his criminal record the first time he was asked during the previous day's direct examination. "How is it that you came to recall it differently this morning, without having anybody point it out to you, but you didn't recall it yesterday?"

McKinney was attempting to imply that the state's attorneys had somehow gotten wind of McKinney's planned questions for cross-examination and realized that Terry hadn't mentioned all his arrests. The prosecutors wanted to make sure their side, and not the defense's, mentioned all the damaging information about Terry first. It looks bad to the jury if they have to hear about bad things from hostile attorneys' questioning. It appears the witness has tried to hide something.

McKinney, however, as was typical of his style, continued to pursue this relatively unimportant side issue to the point of monotony. It really wasn't that big a deal that Terry had left out a minor charge. It was a simple enough mistake given that he had so many convictions to keep track of.

McKinney then passed the witness, subject to recalling him during the main presentation of the defense.

Young Patrick Gobert was the next to take the stand for the state. Dressed in his church-best suit, his black hair carefully slicked down, Patrick, too, seemed unfazed by having to testify and appeared to rather enjoy the drama in which he was about to play a part.

Patrick, once one of Wanda's best friends, told Mike Anderson how he had met Wanda at the San Jacinto Funeral Home, and had later become close to the family.

The prosecutor asked, "Can you describe the efforts that you saw Miz Holloway make in enhancing her daughter's chances for being elected cheerleader?"

Patrick smiled and said somewhat sarcastically, "She made a lot of efforts."

"Well, let's take them one at a time," Anderson suggested, and then asked, "Did she make her daughter practice cheerleading?"

"Yes, sir," Patrick said vigorously. "Her daughter practiced several nights a week, going to different areas, hiring professional cheerleaders to teach her."

Next Patrick was asked if there was any space in the Holloway home dedicated to cheerleading practice, and Patrick described the area in Wanda's garage that had a springboard, a trampoline, a little platform, and a mirror.

"Was Shanna required to have these sessions even if she was ill?" Anderson asked. The jury stirred in its seats to hear the answer.

"If she was truly ill, she was not required to go," Patrick explained. "Like if she had a temperature or was vomiting. But if she just didn't feel very well, she still had to go."

"Did she ever complain about going?" the prosecutor asked.

"Yes, on numerous occasions," Gobert said. His testimony worked to the state's advantage. Through his words, the state managed to portray Wanda Holloway as a relentless stage mother who constantly drove her daughter toward her desired goal of having a cheerleader for a daughter, whether the daughter was interested or not.

"Were you ever asked to do any projects for Shanna so that she could continue her cheerleading practice, meaning school projects?" Anderson inquired.

"Yes," Patrick admitted. "I remember I was asked to help with a project for a class in school, and I think what I did was a Stephen F. Austin village on miniature scale."

He seemed proud as he described his artistic endeavor. A few spectators in the courtroom tittered at the absurdity of it all. What a trial so far—ambitious mom, deadbeat uncle as informant, cheerleading as a motive for murder, and now miniature Texas-pioneer villages!

"And that was turned in as her work?" Anderson asked. Patrick said that it was. The implication was clear: A mother who would cheat on her child's schoolwork, to help her have more time to practice her cheering, would do most anything, even plan a murder.

Anderson, having successfully portrayed Wanda's mindset regarding cheerleading, and just how seriously she took it, moved on to the heart of his direct examination.

"Were you around Miz Holloway, Wanda Holloway, during the time of the disqualification?" Anderson asked.

Patrick admitted he was. "What was her mood at that point?" asked the prosecutor.

"She was very upset," Patrick said. Asked to elaborate, he added, "I could tell by the tone of her voice, the way she conducted herself. Her voice, I'm not going to say it was hostile, exactly, but she was very upset."

"Did she say anything about why Shanna had been disqualified?" the prosecutor asked.

Patrick answered readily. "She said that the other ladies had plotted against her to get Shanna disqualified. And when I say the other ladies, I'm talking about the other mothers of the children who were trying out for the cheerleading squad, and also some rulers were involved."

"Did Wanda ever say anything about Amber Heath or Verna Heath?" Anderson asked.

"Not at that point," Gobert said. "Later in the conversation she did, though," he added. Anderson asked Patrick more details about this conversation the day of Shanna's disqualification. Patrick described it as "mostly one-sided," because Wanda was doing all the talking. Or ranting, from the sound of things. "It was not a pleasant conversation," Patrick said understatedly.

"Did you say anything?" Anderson asked.

"After a while, maybe an hour, I had listened to it and heard enough of it, and I told her, 'Why don't you just have her killed?'" Patrick said, explaining he was referring to Verna Heath.

"Why did you say that?" asked the state's attorney.

"Because she continued to say it was Verna Heath who had instigated the other women into plotting against her. She felt at that time that Verna Heath was the head of the plot," Patrick explained.

"What did Wanda Holloway respond to your suggestion to have her killed?" Anderson asked.

"She laughed, at first," Patrick said, "and then she just kind of looked at me for a moment, with a really blank face. She just looked at me."

"What makes that look stand out?" Mike Anderson asked. "How does that look contrast to any other look that makes you feel it's worth talking about in front of this jury?"

Patrick thought a moment and then responded, "The look was one of... one that I felt like that she wanted to know more. I said one more thing after that," he continued. "After she just kind of looked at me, I told her that I had a number she could call, if she wanted it done. But I was not serious, because I really didn't think that she was serious."

By asking several more questions, Anderson got Gobert to discuss several more conversations with Wanda in the weeks immediately after that first discussion in which the subject of hiring a killer arose. Patrick told the court that about two weeks after the disqualification, Wanda asked him for the phone number he had mentioned that first day. He described the frequency with which Wanda made reference to the cheerleading fiasco. "For the first week following the disqualification," he said, "it was the first priority of conversation in her home. It was discussed quite often."

And on several subsequent occasions, he told the court, Wanda had repeated her request for the hit man's phone number.

"She kept stating that the ladies at the school had plotted against her," he said. "Her statement was that she would have her killed, and from that point on I knew she was talking about Verna Heath." Patrick looked over sheepishly at his former best friend as he finished. Wanda refused to meet his eyes and kept her face turned downward.

Anderson passed the witness to the defense.

Stanley Schneider shuffled some papers on the table in front of him as if looking for something before beginning his cross-examination of Patrick Gobert. He pushed his glasses up higher on his nose and rubbed his beard, and then launched an attempted character assassination on Gobert.

He implied through a long series of questions that Gobert had had an unhealthy interest in both Shane Harper and Shane's friend Blake Denman. He questioned Gobert at length about the presents he had given the teenage boys, and then implied that Gobert's testimony was given out of anger at Wanda Holloway's ultimate rejection of his friendship because of his behavior with the boys.

Patrick consistently denied any improprieties.

Schneider then shrugged his shoulders in exasperation and passed the witness.

Judge Godwin, having earlier been given a list of the state's witnesses, saw that Patrick Gobert had been the last on the list. "Is the state going to rest at this point?" he asked, peering over the top of his reading glasses.

Mike Anderson announced that the state rested. Troy McKinney stood and made the routine defense motion for an instructed verdict. He said, "There has not been any direct evidence that Wanda Holloway, in fact, solicited. The only evidence has been that, if anything, Terry Harper solicited her."

It is customary for defense attorneys to move at the close of the state's case that the state has failed to prove the elements of the crime. If each and every element of a crime has not been demonstrated by at least some evidence, such an instructed verdict may be granted. In this instance, however, the judge said the motion would be denied. He apparently felt the state had indeed met its burden of providing enough evidence of Wanda's involvement in the plot to continue the trial.

It was still early in the day of August 28, only midmorning. A brief recess was called by Judge Godwin, for the defense team to finalize its preparations for presenting the defense of Wanda Holloway to the jury.

At last the world would hear Wanda's explanation for what had happened.

11

When All Else Fails, Use a Shotgun

The defense attorneys spent the rest of that morning putting up a series of witnesses whose sole purpose was to discredit Gobert's testimony. Wanda was not even mentioned. The defense apparently wanted to distract the jury from what Gobert had sworn he had heard in Wanda's kitchen.

After a lunch break, the tempo got livelier. Marla Harper was called to the stand by the defense. Dressed in a royal-blue polyester dress, her hair streaming down her back, Marla was heavily made-up and, like her husband, seemed to enjoy having her picture taken by photographers and being the center of attention.

Stanley Schneider lead the direct examination of the defense's star witness. What irony: Terry Harper had been the state's star witness, and now his wife was the defense's. Never before had either Terry or Marla had such important jobs to do or received so much attention. Prior to this case, they had just been a lower-middle-class, drinking, brawling couple from Channelview, indistinguishable from hundreds just like them.

Marla was lead through a series of questions to show her connection to the case. She had never met Wanda Holloway prior to the previous day, she said, but had been married to Terry Harper on and off for the last two years. During that marriage she had made the acquaintance of Wanda's children, Shane and Shanna, at a couple of family gatherings.

She related her story of the previous Christmas Eve, when she had seen Shanna Harper approach Terry at the Harper Christmas gathering. She explained how Terry had told her later that night about Wanda's meeting with him earlier in the fall. Her story, so far, did not differ at all from Terry Harper's.

But then she began to talk about his behavior on New Year's Eve, the first time he had called his brother, Tony, about Wanda's plot. Marla said that Terry was bragging about his fall meeting with Wanda to Tony.

Stanley Schneider then asked Marla, "Did Terry tell you what he felt about Wanda Holloway?"

Marla nodded that he had. "Can I say it?" she inquired of Schneider. Having never been in court before, Marla didn't know if she could quote verbatim the obscenity Terry had allegedly used. The lawyer told her she could.

Marla said, "He told me he hated that bitch, because she had accused him of trying to sleep with her and she had told Tony when they were married and that Tony wouldn't speak to him for a long time, and also that she had turned him in for stealing from the railroad."

"Turned who in?" Schneider asked, surprised.

"Tony," Marla clarified. "Tony lost his job there after Wanda reported he was stealing." The courtroom buzzed again.

"Did Terry and Tony talk about setting Wanda up?" Schneider asked, again referring to the phone call on New Year's Eve.

"Yes," Marla said vigorously. "Terry told Tony he had a way for Tony to get his kids back. He told him they were going to burn her, that he was going to get her to say things with him wired."

Through more questioning, Marla revealed the whole story, once again, of Tony telling Terry to go to the police. She told of accompanying Terry to the police substation and meeting with Marcel Dionne, the homicide investigator on duty that day.

According to Marla, Terry was the one who first mentioned to the police that he should be wired. "He kept telling them he wanted them to wire him, that he could get her to say this, this and this," she reported.

"Did you tell the police about the phone conversation you had earlier heard at your home?" Schneider asked.

Marla smiled ironically and answered, "No, sir, I knew better, because I had to go home with my husband."

"Were you afraid of your husband?" Schneider asked.

"Very much so," Marla said. "Because of the abuse, physically and mentally that I had been through since before I married him." She then said that the abuse had continued throughout their life together.

"How many times were you separated from your husband from the time you first met him up until January of 1991?" Schneider inquired.

"I wouldn't be afraid to say more than twenty," the strawberry blonde said. When asked why she kept going back, she replied, "I thought I loved him. I felt there was a chance he might change, that he would quit drinking, and I..."

"Did you ever try to tell Detective Dionne what was going on?" Schneider asked.

Marla said she had tried to surreptitiously signal the detective while Terry was in the men's room, but failed to communicate her fears that her husband was trying to frame someone.

"What happened after you got home that day?" Schneider asked. "Did Terry tell you why he was doing this?"

Marla said he had. "He told me that he had always been the black sheep of his family and that he was cut out of his father's will when he was doing drugs and that Tony was executor and that if he was closest to Tony, that he would see that he was taken care of. He was also talking to Tony about a job, selling insurance, where he didn't have to use his hands and be real tired," she explained in her stream-of-consciousness style.

"Tony had already promised him a job?" Schneider asked. This was the first anyone had heard of that.

Marla related that Tony had promised to help Terry work something out in the insurance industry. She added that after the police investigation of Wanda began, Terry told her he had repeatedly threatened Wanda about what the hit man might do if Wanda backed out of the plot against Verna Heath. She implied that Terry wanted Wanda busted for his own personal reasons, and not because of any vague ideals about right and wrong.

"At some point in January of 1991 did you leave Tony?" asked Schneider. Even he had trouble keeping all these players straight.

"You mean Terry," Marla said. "Yes, I did." When asked why, she answered, "This whole situation was out of hand. This whole fabrication. And I was scared because of what I had been through, and I figured I'll do it as long as I can, until things got to be too much, and then I went over to my son's house."

"Why didn't you call the police then?" Schneider asked.

Marla related the terrible incident in which Terry had held a gun to her head for three hours. The police had shown up that night, she said, and Terry had threatened a shoot-out.

"He said he wasn't going to go alive," she told the courtroom, which was held rapt by this wild tale. "He said he would go to Honduras first. And the police ended up arresting him, handcuffing him, and then letting him go." It was clear that after that experience Marla felt calling the law would do no good.

During more questioning, Marla told the court what she had done after learning of Wanda's arrest. She described her meeting with Wanda's attorneys, and explained she told them everything she knew about Tony and Terry's plot against Wanda. And then she told about reconciling with Terry after that and telling him what she had done. She described his reaction, "He couldn't believe that I had done it and just hovered over me and just would scream and yell and get drunk and knock me around and make threats and..."

"What kind of threats did he make toward you?" Schneider asked.

Marla described how Terry accused her of trying to ruin his character and spoil his one chance to clear his name. She added that she had even gone to the D.A.'s office shortly after her meeting with Wanda's attorneys, to tell them what she knew about the case. Terry was constantly pressuring her to call both sides and withdraw her story, she said, but she consistently refused to do so.

"How many times did Terry Harper threaten you or try to force you to change or retract your statements?" Schneider repeated.

Marla answered, her voice quivering. "Sometimes ten times a day and then sometimes a week or two would pass and there would be nothing said about it."

"Did you ever tell a doctor that you were hallucinating and hearing voices?" asked Schneider in a surprising change of topic. Like the state had done during the presentation of its case, Stanley Schneider was going to bring out any negative information about his witness himself to attempt to defuse the state's cross-examination of Marla.

Marla conceded that she had, in fact, told a doctor about hearing voices. When asked why she said it, Marla explained, or tried to, although her statement did not make much sense. She said it had all been a ruse to get away from Terry, who had repeatedly told her she was mentally ill.

"Did Terry ever try to convince you that you were emotionally disturbed?" asked Schneider. Marla said that he had.

"Did he ever talk about being a hero?" Schneider asked, again changing the subject.

Again, Marla said he had. "He also talked about the money that he was going to get from a movie from this case," she said loudly. Hollywood reared its ugly head once more in the trial of Wanda Holloway. To hear the defense version of the story, everyone involved in this case, except for maybe Wanda Holloway, was a greedy opportunist intent on seeing himself or herself portrayed on the silver screen.

Marla then related how, in his numerous threats to her, Terry had mentioned that she was trying to "mess up" his chances for fame and fortune. He threatened her by saying, she claimed, "that he would mess me up so bad my own momma wouldn't recognize me."

"Why were you living with him, then?" Schneider asked.

Marla hesitated before answering, "I figured he would just finally accept the fact that I wasn't going to change my story, and I didn't have a job. I didn't have any place, really, to go, and I just thought maybe he's going to get some snap and do what's right."

"Did he ever tell you that he would change his story if you came back to him?" the lawyer asked Marla.

Marla said that several times Terry had promised her exactly that.

"Did he ever promise he'd stop drinking?" Schneider asked.

Marla said he had.

"Did he promise he'd stop doing drugs?" Schneider added, again to show the jury what sort of man the state had as its chief witness—a drunken, drug using, wife beater.

Marla said that she had heard all those promises. Schneider then asked her when she had last left Terry Harper.

Two weeks before the trial, Marla answered. She then related the strange meeting the two of them had on the eve of trial.

According to Marla, she had run into Terry by chance at a neighborhood snow-cone stand owned by a friend on Market Street. She was still very angry with him, she related to the court, about an incident that had occurred in her trailer with Terry, her son Scott, and another woman.

"I told him he was white trash and I didn't want anything to do with him," she said with anger in her voice.

Nevertheless, somehow Terry persuaded her to go with him to a nearby bar for a few drinks.

A few drinks turned into several, for before long Marla said she had accompanied Terry to the Western Motel on I-10 in Channelview.

As soon as they were comfortably ensconced in the room, she said, Terry began calling the prosecutors. She wasn't sure who was contacted in what order, but she knew Terry had three phone numbers he kept trying.

Stanley asked his shaken witness, "Did you want to talk to these people?"

Marla said, "No, not until the rough stuff started. He started knocking me around and choking me and pulling my hair and trying to keep me from getting out the door. He asked me if I had been subpoenaed, and I lied to him and told him I hadn't. Then he ordered me to go to Conroe...." Once again, Marla was getting so excited that it was hard for anyone in the courtroom to understand what she was talking about. Schneider interrupted to slow her down.

"Why did he order you to Conroe?" Stanley asked.

Marla explained, "That way I wouldn't have to testify, and he didn't want me to testify."

Marla had been subpoenaed as a witness in the case. Conroe was in a county north of Harris County. Terry thought erroneously that subpoenas were only effective in the county in which they had been ordered.

Marla related how Terry had eventually found the subpoena, which she had hidden, by grabbing her purse and rifling through it. "He also thought I was wired," she testified. "And then he started beating up on me."

Dramatically, Marla gestured to her neck and arms, and said she had several bruises that were already fading. She then related how the prosecutors had counseled Terry to leave the motel immediately, and that when he did, she made a run for it.

She headed out the room to her truck in the parking lot. Terry soon followed, however, she told the court, and resumed his attack. "As soon as I got to my truck," she related, "he came right in on top of me and was choking me, and I turned my head and then he started beating me in the back of my head with his fist and I grabbed ahold of him and bit him and he jumped off of me and then I went past him. He grabbed my purse off my arm and took everything out of it and scattered it on the parking lot and I went to the office to call the police."

The jury was staring at Marla with wide eyes. Marla may have been spinning out a wild story, but it all had the ring of truth to it. Many had never heard of such goings-on.

Schneider asked Marla again if Terry ever found the subpoena. "Yes," she said, "he took it out of my purse, and he told me I couldn't get in the courtroom without it." Marla said that when she got to the office of the motel she asked the clerk to call the police. In an instant, she said, Terry ran up there, too, and told the clerk to call 911 if Marla tried to leave. "He told them I'd been drinking," she said, "and that they shouldn't let me leave there. Then he jumped in his car and took off."

After Terry's hasty departure, Marla said she called the police herself. Eventually two patrolmen from the sheriff's department stopped by the Western Motel to check out her complaint. Marla said, "I was sitting there crying and I just told them that my husband had just beat me up. They asked me if I had been drinking, and I told them yes. Then they told me to go back to my room and lock the door and stay there."

Schneider then asked, "Have you ever heard of someone named Allen Step?"

Marla said she had.

"How does it relate to this case?" he asked Marla.

"Hollywood," was all she said, her voice spitting out the name. Allen Step, in fact, was a high-school acquaintance of Terry's who had since moved to Hollywood and become a production assistant. Since news of Terry's involvement in the case had appeared, Step was one of many agents and producers who had contacted various members of the Harper clan.

With that last flourish of innuendo against Terry Harper, Stanley

Schneider passed the exhausted witness to the state for cross-examination.

Mike Anderson began questioning Marla Harper slowly and politely—it was bad form for a male attorney to badger a female witness too aggressively. In the eyes of the jury, such behavior might be construed as bullying and ungentlemanly, traits that Texans despise. And if the jury dislikes an attorney's behavior, the verdict will often reflect that feeling.

Anderson gently told Marla that he needed to ask her a few questions about her statements to Stanley Schneider, and added, "If that's okay with you." She said it was. And then the prosecutor methodically picked her story to pieces.

He first attacked Marla's suspicions that Terry and Tony had hatched a plot against Wanda Holloway. The young prosecutor suggested that perhaps she had been mistaken.

"You haven't heard those tape recordings, have you?" Anderson asked. Marla said she had not. "So you're saying all this based on not having even heard the tape recordings of the conversations between Terry Harper and Wanda Holloway?" Mike Anderson asked, a little more forcefully, as if he could not believe it.

"Mr. Anderson," Marla started to say in an irritated way.

Anderson immediately stopped her. "Excuse me, ma'am," he instructed the witness, "but I guess that calls for just a yes or no answer."

She ignored him. "From living it," she said. "It's not just one thing, it's a number of things combined."

"That may be," the attorney said with a shrug. "But *my* question is, you haven't heard those tapes?"

Marla quietly conceded she had not.

Anderson's attack began to pick up momentum. "You mentioned at one point that you had gone somewhere because you had hurt yourself," he said softly. "Can you tell the ladies and gentlemen of the jury a little bit about that?" Anderson knew a lot of damaging things about Marla Harper from his own pretrial investigation and that conducted by Alice Brown before him.

"Terry had raped me and beat me up," Marla began, "and so I . . ."

"Ma'am, can I interject something here please?" Anderson politely stopped her. "Your stepfather had raped you, is that correct?" Marla said he had.

"And your brother had raped you?" he queried.

"My half-brother," Marla corrected.

"And several other people have tried to rape you, have they not?" Anderson asked. It was easy to see what he was doing—by recounting all of Marla's accusations against myriad people, he could show that she was just the sort of person who often made outrageous claims about the people in her life.

"True," was Marla's sole reply.

"What about your mother?" Anderson asked. "Did your mother sexually assault you as well?" Now that the topic had turned to sex, everyone in the courtroom was eagerly awaiting Marla's replies.

"No," she said, "but she knew about my stepfather."

"And Terry raped you before y'all were married, but you married him anyway?" he asked in disbelief.

"Yes," she said quietly.

Anderson shook his head in wonder. "Well, let's get back to where you hurt yourself," he said. "What did you do?"

"I sprayed oven cleaner on my leg," she said almost proudly.

"Why?" the prosecutor asked.

"Because I was under so much pressure from him and control from him to where I had to get away," Marla began, her words once again coming out in a rush. "I had to have time because I knew if I could get away from him I could get my thoughts together and if I really was as ill as he was saying I was…"

"How many times have you hurt yourself?" Anderson interrupted. He already knew the answer; he just wanted the jury to know what kind of witness the defense had.

"Four times since I've been with him," Marla said, referring to her relationship with Terry.

"But what about before him?" Mike asked. He didn't want anyone to think this was all Terry's fault. Marla denied that she had ever hurt herself before, although, in fact, she had on several occasions, beginning at age fourteen when she swallowed her mother's glycerine capsules.

Anderson began questioning Marla about her psychiatric treatments. He had access to the medical records from Ben Taub Hospital, and was fully briefed on the doctors' diagnoses.

"Didn't you tell the doctors that were treating you that you hurt yourself because of your stepfather?" he asked.

Marla admitted, "Some of the doctors, I told that to."

"And didn't you tell the doctors that you would see your stepfather come to you at night and talk to you and tell you to hurt yourself?" he asked. She was beginning to sound pretty far out. Spectators in the courtroom whispered to each other; some giggled and laughed, but hid their grins with their hands.

"Yes, I did say that," Marla openly admitted.

"And did you tell the doctors that you had been having violent outbursts toward your husband? When you're not having one of those outbursts, you feel really good, and when you have them, they're so violent that you want to kill him?" Anderson asked, looking at the medical records as he spoke.

Marla had to clarify that point. "I wanted to hurt him," she said. "I did say that, and I did feel that."

"Was it because of Terry that you told the doctors that you have trouble distinguishing between the truth and fiction?" Anderson asked, his voice soft. Again, he did not want to appear harsh toward this poor, obviously unstable woman.

"I told them between reality and my imagination, yes I sure did," she said with no shame.

"But didn't you write letters to people, talking about how Terry was the greatest thing that you had ever found and that he cared about you?" Anderson asked, producing a piece of writing paper in his left hand.

"You talking about the letter to his probation officer that he wanted me to write?" Marla replied.

"No, ma'am," Mike Anderson explained. "A hypothetical letter dated March 3, 1991."

"That's exactly what it was," Marla stated with conviction. "A hypothetical." How a hypothetical letter could be produced on paper she did not explain, however.

After he proffered the letter to the court's clerk to be marked as evidence, Anderson handed the papers to Marla.

"Is this the letter you wrote, ma'am?" he asked. Marla said she needed to make sure all the pages were intact, and then pronounced it her own handiwork.

"Would you read the first two pages in this letter to the ladies and gentlemen of the jury, please?" Anderson asked nicely.

Marla said she would, but first reiterated that this was just a hypothetical letter. "It was being proofread," she said. "So I was careful what I said, or at least I thought." She must have meant the letter would be read by others, not "proofread." She began to read slowly, "It's March eighteenth 1991: 'Dear Daddy: Why did you hurt me? Why did you make me feel like I was bad and trying to hurt you? Why did you use my momma and brother and sisters and family to shut me up? Why? How do you sleep at night now? How many granddaughters does Dotti,' which is his wife now, 'have? Did you feel it wasn't wrong, only illegal? Know what? I'm fixing to tell you something and I want you to really think about this before you act. You can call me a liar all you want but no one can fake the torment and depression I've suffered for twenty years. There's no way, Daddy dearest...'"

"Excuse me," interjected Mike Anderson. "May I ask you something? How long have you known Terry Harper?"

"Two and a half years," answered Marla. After having just told the jury shortly before that Terry Harper had caused all her problems, Marla was reading the evidence that she had been mixed up for the last twenty years. Anderson wanted to make sure the jury noticed the discrepancy, and after getting her answer, asked her to continue.

"'I was made to say I love you for so long, I thought I did, under my pain. I only said it for survival,'" she read. "'Buster Crosby, I hate you [Crosby was her stepfather].'" She spat out the words. "'You have ruined my life. And there are others in the family that's guilty. They will also be notified. I have a question. Would it surprise you to know that I have had fantasies and dreams about killing you? You should be thankful that I was able to have dreams.' I meant by that, instead of acting it out," Marla explained.

She seemed to actually enjoy the drama of her reading, and kept on. "'That's the only reason you still walk and breathe. In my dreams I would always come up behind you and start to kill you and at that last split second, you turned and looked at me and I froze and couldn't move. Then you would take the knife away from me and always cut me, and I would wake up or snap out of it. Isn't that a lovely way to live? Do you have any idea how many times since I was fourteen years old that I've tried to kill myself because I couldn't deal with the pain you caused me? And you have the balls to say I hurt you? Know who else I hurt for? My wonderful beloved husband. He pays on a daily basis for your sins. Hard for you, Buster? And Dotti,' which is his wife now, 'I tried not to like her but I couldn't. She is truly a child of God and I care about her. I have a suspicion about you and not that you would even admit to it, but I have to ask: Did you burn down Dotti's home like you did ours on Evanston?'"

This case was getting stranger with each passing witness. First cheerleading and ambitious mothers, then domestic violence, and now incest and arson.

After Marla finally finished reading to the stunned courtroom, she began to explain herself. "When I wrote this letter," she told Mike Anderson, "the reason I wrote hypothetical on it is simply because I was instructed by doctors to write down my feelings. And Terry proofread everything I wrote down, so he had a big impression on the things about him in this letter because I knew he was going to read it," she said, and added again, "But the whole thing is hypothetical."

"Okay, all right," Anderson assured her, "but the stuff about Terry is hypothetical, too?"

Marla said that part of it was true. "At that time, I did love him," she explained. "I thought he would quit drinking, I thought he would stay in church, I thought he would change. I thought he would quit beating up on me and I thought he would quit being sexually abusive, but he didn't."

"Well, ma'am, I don't mean to argue with you," Anderson began. "But you have told the doctors that you had uncontrollably violent outbursts toward Terry?"

After Marla explained that she had feelings like that, but didn't act on them, Mike asked, "What triggered those feelings?"

"His abuse, his control of me," Marla said plaintively. "I wasn't even allowed to walk around in my own house. He made me go to the bathroom with him when he went, you know, and if I didn't think the way he wanted me to think, I was in trouble."

"So how did you get away from him to hurt yourself, to pour the cleaning fluid on your legs?" Anderson inquired. If she had been under Terry's constant control, it is doubtful he would have allowed her to spray her leg with oven cleaner.

"Twice I did that when he wasn't home," she explained.

"And how was he controlling you when he went to work every day, wasn't he working about six-tens?" Anderson asked, referring in the local parlance to Terry's long workdays six days a week.

Marla looked angry and said, "Have you ever been abused?"

"No ma'am, I haven't," Anderson conceded. "But the bottom line is that you said he was hovering over you all the time."

"Not physically," Marla tried to clarify what she meant. "He had control of my actions, my thoughts, my feelings, all of it. He had threatened my family, and done other violent acts toward my family."

"Like your stepfather?" Anderson asked. The obvious implication was that this poor, confused woman kept mixing up her stepfather's past actions with her current husband's. Marla did not attempt to defuse the suggestion.

"Exactly," she answered. "Terry is a lot like my stepfather."

"Do you remember being diagnosed as having loose associations and flights of ideas?" the prosecutor asked Marla next. The woman's testimony so far indicated the diagnosis was accurate, but Marla qualified her answer. "I told them that because I wanted to get away from Terry," she repeated. There was nothing wrong with her, she clearly meant, but her wild stories indicated otherwise.

She continued her explanation. "He said all I had to do was say I didn't remember or tell them I'm seeing things or hearing things. He said, 'You've got sexual hangups. You need to go get it taken care of.'"

"That's really none of my business, ma'am," Anderson interjected. "All I'm trying to do here is ask you about certain things."

Stanley Schneider jumped up and objected. "I object to Mr. Anderson's sidebar remarks," he said. "Ask the court to instruct the jury to disregard his remarks. And I ask for a mistrial."

Almost every time Schneider objected, he also asked for a mistrial. It was apparent that these frequent requests irritated Judge Godwin, who this time merely looked at Schneider in disbelief. "The jury will disregard the last comments of the prosecutor," he said solemnly. "Request for a mistrial will be denied."

Mike Anderson then asked a series of questions of Marla taken straight from the medical records. One by one, he asked Marla if she had told the doctors she had feelings of unreality, suspicions about other people, and often felt persecuted. She admitted she had said all those things. She had also told her doctors that she was confused and that she had resisted Terry's efforts to obtain treatment for her to prevent her from hurting herself again. She was asked about the medications the doctors had prescribed, and admitted she had taken some but did not recall the names.

"Imipramine?" Anderson read from the charts. Marla said that was one. It is a commonly used antidepressant drug. "Why did you take that?" the prosecutor asked.

"Because I told them I was seeing things," Marla said.

"Didn't you tell a Dr. Cohn that you saw fur chasing you through the house? Wig fur?" the prosecutor asked. Wig fur? What was it, and how could it chase someone? Neither the jury nor anyone else in the room understood it.

Marla nodded her head yes.

"And didn't you say that dreams started when you were at the mailbox and you run to the door asking to be let in and people stand there and they won't let you in and there are snakes on the road, and two snakes in the driveway, and they talk to you? [sic]"

Anderson himself seemed about to laugh. Marla explained she had actually had that dream as a teenager, after her stepfather began sexually abusing her, but that she hadn't had it recently.

After that, the wig fur and the talking snakes, Anderson passed the witness.

On redirect examination, Stanley Schneider had Marla elaborate on Terry's violence to her. Marla related incidents in which Terry had fired his gun at their trailer, and also at her relatives' trailers. "He went straight over to my sister's house and shot up the house next door to my sister," she added. "And he told me, 'If you fuck up again, I'm going to show you what easy access I have to your family.'"

Finally, Schneider asked Marla about Terry's ability to control and manipulate her. "Did Terry ever talk to you about how he learned to control people?" the bearded attorney inquired.

Marla nodded her head vigorously up and down. "Oh yes," she said readily. "He said he got it from his mother, and from his brother. He said they were very good teachers. Plus, he had an obsession with Mafia books—read them all the time."

The defense's shotgun approach, in which it scattered out numerous explanations for the events of January 1991, had just added another new twist. Now Terry Harper was, in addition to being a black sheep wanting to go straight, and a money-grubbing opportunist with his eyes on Hollywood, a Mafioso-wannabe. The implication of this information was that Terry was merely playacting, trying to live out stories he had read in dime-store detective novels. Perhaps, in the face of the overwhelming taped evidence against their client, McKinney and Schneider were willing to try anything. Perhaps they thought that if they tossed out enough theories, the jury might snap at one and be hooked. They wouldn't know for sure until the verdict was rendered, and that was at least a few days off.

And even though they had already put forth several defenses to the charges against Wanda Holloway, more would follow before the jury retired for deliberations.

Even the sober Judge George Godwin was getting testy about the nature of the evidence and the bizarre twists and turns it had been taking all day, especially during Marla Harper's testimony. Since it was getting late in the afternoon, the judge announced that the court would recess for the day after Marla finished her tale. But he ended the day with a stern warning to both the prosecutors and the defense attorneys after he had excused the jury.

"For the record," he said, leaning down from his bench and eyeing all four attorneys in turn, "I have tried to give both sides leeway in developing their cases. But I think we are perilously close to getting into peripheral issues and sideshows here, and I am going to do what I have to do to tighten it up. I say that for guidance for both sides with regard to the forthcoming direct examinations and cross-examinations of either sides' witnesses. I want you to get your witnesses, get them prepped, and get them to the issues as we've outlined them, and stick to what the issues are."

It was a polite way of saying he was afraid that the trial of Wanda Holloway was becoming a three-ring circus.

12

Closing In for the Kill

By the next morning, newspaper headlines and television broadcasters around the nation were trumpeting news of Wanda's trial. WOMAN SAYS EX-BROTHER-IN-LAW HATCHED PLOT, screamed one headline; WITNESS ALLEGES A SETUP said another. Television reporters scoured the community of Channelview for anyone who would go on camera with comments, although most of the area residents were reluctant to talk because of their embarrassment over the way their neighbors were acting downtown.

"We're not all that way," many said to reporters. "Please don't paint us all out to be that kind of trash." It had been bad enough before, after Wanda had been arrested, what with all the commotion about the Cheerleader Mom. But now, with the introduction of the likes of Terry and Marla Harper into the case, the town was really looking bad.

Wanda Holloway's young daughter, the ultimate reason for all the furor, was safely tucked away in the community of Kingwood, north of Houston, where her father resided. Tony Harper's March 1991 custody agreement called for the child to spend Wednesday through Saturday with him every other week. This was a particularly good week for Shanna to be out of Channelview because of the swarming reporters.

Besides, it was time for her biweekly appointment with her psychologist, Dr. Kit Harrison. Wanda wouldn't take the girl there; her father had to.

When the trial resumed on the morning of August 29, 1991, the defense team was ready to pursue its odd course of firing salvos from every direction. First on its hit list was Terry Harper, who had yet to be fully cross-examined by the defense. Terry eagerly took the stand again, knowing full well, as he had said himself during his direct examination, that all of his skeletons would be dragged out of the closet. His own wife had just discussed most of them the day before, but defense attorney Troy McKinney was going to see what more damage could be done.

McKinney began by quizzing Terry about his marital track record. "Exactly how many times have you been married?" he asked right off the bat. Terry said he had gone through seven nuptials.

"For the record, can you give us a rundown of who they were and how long they lasted?" McKinney asked. Mike Anderson objected that the question was irrelevant, and Judge Godwin agreed. He had already indicated his impatience the previous day with the rabbit trails the two sides kept following. He had no intention of seeing this trial through weeks and weeks of extraneous, inconclusive evidence.

Instead, McKinney switched gears to cover Terry's employment history. "Mr. Harper, how many different jobs have you held in the last three years?" he queried.

Terry thought a moment and forthrightly answered, "Let's see now, close to fifteen."

"Fifteen?" asked McKinney incredulously. "Fifteen different jobs? In the past three years?" Terry acknowledged that was true. Later, he explained that the nature of a pipe fitter's work is to move from location to location fixing pipe as needed. Others in the business confirmed that frequent moves are the norm, not the exception, and had no real reflection on Terry's character or abilities.

McKinney shuffled awkwardly through a ream of papers on his table for his next ploy. He attacked every previous statement Terry Harper had made and added several bits of innuendo introduced by Marla.

McKinney tried to suggest that everything Terry Harper had done was an attempt to win his older brother's favor. He touched on all aspects of Terry's life. He seemed especially interested in Terry's deals with Hollywood agents.

"You've talked with your brother Tony since January several times about the movie rights to this case, haven't you?" McKinney asked harshly. "Isn't it a fact that you wanted a greater share, a greater percentage of what he was trying to get in money. Isn't that true?"

The jury looked at Terry with suspicious eyes. What sort of people were these Harper boys, anyway? Talking about movie rights and such just days after the shocking news of Wanda's arrest?

After that, McKinney literally spent hours going over the taped conversations and their transcripts with Terry Harper in mind-numbing detail. He questioned Terry about every instance in which Terry, and not Wanda, had mentioned killing, maiming, burning houses down, and car wrecks. He highlighted especially the portions in the conversations where Terry had made veiled threats about what the hit man might do if Wanda didn't come through with the money. "Isn't it true that you told Wanda that this person doesn't play games and that if she backed out you would turn him on to her?" he asked Terry.

Terry squirmed a little and answered, "That's not exactly what I said, I don't believe." In fact, he had made several hints in the six taped conversations about the kind of trouble the both of them could get in for "inconveniencing" the hit man.

Although Troy McKinney obviously tried to imply that Wanda had been entrapped and coerced, the defense was careful not to maintain this argument as an official part of its case. In the eyes of the law, technically, it doesn't really matter who was the first person to suggest someone be murdered. If a second party hears the suggestion and goes along with it, for whatever reason, they are equally as guilty as the individual who thought it up.

McKinney asked Terry about his fascination with Mafia-type novels. "Have you ever read the book *Mob Star*?" McKinney asked. Terry said he had read parts of it.

"Isn't it true that part of the book you read had to do with manipulation and coercion of witnesses against people?" asked McKinney. Judge Godwin frowned at the stooped attorney with the gapped teeth. This was exactly the sort of tangential issue he had told them to avoid the previous day. It was silly, and lacked dignity, he thought, to drag in all this nonsense. But he kept quiet for the time being.

Terry just grinned at the lawyer. He loved this game of matching wits. "Just about every mob book I ever read has that in it," he said with a hearty chortle. Several other spectators and jurors laughed out loud as well.

"Did you ever tell Marla that you were running drugs in New Orleans and that those people wouldn't be happy with you if your wife testified against you here?" McKinney queried.

Terry again laughed out loud. "No, sir!" he said when he stopped. McKinney didn't smile at all. "It's not all that funny for you to run drugs, is it?" he asked the witness. At that point, Casey O'Brien objected that the question was collateral, in fact the whole line of questioning was collateral. Judge Godwin agreed. He had been hoping the prosecution would object a long time ago, and put a stop to all the foolishness.

Terry Harper was excused as a witness, but not before Judge Godwin had delivered his opinion of the proceedings.

"Ladies and gentlemen of the audience," he said with a frown. "I tended to notice we had several reactions to the testimony today. I'm not trying to stifle anybody, but I do not want any shaking of heads, any smiles, or any kind of editorial comment with regard to the credibility of what any of these witnesses might say. You may sit there, but I am asking you to remember that we have a fact-finder [a jury] in this courtroom and the integrity of that process will be upheld. If you cannot control yourselves, you will be asked to leave this courtroom."

He still wasn't through with his lecture. "I have also been advised that there have been some incidents among the gallery itself." Here he was referring to the frequent verbal battles over seats. "That is," he clarified, "that certain members of the gallery are making things uncomfortable for their fellow members of the gallery. I will, once again, apologize. I did not build this courtroom, and they didn't ask me how to design it or ask me if we were going to be trying lawsuits in here. But I will remind you that if you cannot be cognizant and considerate of your fellow gallery members' positions in here and their right to hear and see these proceedings, you will be asked to leave."

Next up was Marla's son, Scott Anthony Whited, twenty, who was called to the stand outside the presence of the jury for what is known as a Bill of Exception. Scott swore that Terry Harper had promised him expert legal help for his drunk-driving accident case if Scott would help persuade his mom to forego her testimony against Terry.

McKinney's next question caused raised eyebrows and shocked expressions throughout the courtroom.

"A couple of weeks ago, was there some incident involving a prostitute?" he asked the young man.

Scott said there was, and McKinney asked him to describe what had happened. "But you don't need to go into graphic detail," he assured Scott.

Scott explained that one morning Terry had come over to his apartment and picked him up. "We went riding," he said. "Should I say exactly the words he used? Profanity involved," he explained.

"Let's just skip to the end of this," McKinney urged. "How did it happen that you two were looking for a prostitute?"

"He said he was horny," Scott explained, looking slightly embarrassed. "And my mother, he said, since my mother wasn't there and wouldn't do it, he was going to go find somebody that—excuse me—that will swallow, is what he told me."

"Did he offer that prostitute to you?" McKinney asked. Scott said he had. "Did he tell you why he was offering her to you?" McKinney pressed.

Scott began to answer, "Well, I figured..."

Mike Anderson objected before he could say another word. "I object to what he 'figured' about anything," he told Judge Godwin. Godwin sustained the objection, and Scott Whited was excused.

After that salacious testimony, planned to make Terry Harper appear to be someone who would bribe a young man with a whore, McKinney brought in several more witnesses for more bills of exception. All of these witnesses had been discussed with Judge Godwin prior to the start of trial. The judge had ruled at that time that these witnesses would not be allowed to testify before the jury for various reasons. So the defense was including what they would have testified to in bills of exception for purposes of appeal.

They included a brother-in-law of Marla's, who swore that Terry Harper had irreparably changed Marla's demeanor for the worse, and two women who offered testimony that both Terry and Tony Harper had previously offered to help them get rid of undesirables in their lives.

The two women told Judge Godwin that on different occasions Terry or Tony Harper had promised to hire a hit man to get rid of their estranged husbands, since the husbands were causing the women problems.

Judge Godwin refused to allow any of the testimony before the jury.

He told the defense, "Under your theory we would be here a month of Sundays because every impeachment would then get a further response, and we'd have impeachment of impeachment of impeachment, and we would end up calling the entire population of Channelview, which this court does not intend to do." After the sampling he'd seen so far, no judge in his right mind would consider having any more of those strange citizens in his courtroom.

After the lunch break, the defense called none other than Wanda's ex-husband Tony Harper. He was being called as an "adverse witness," allowable under the Texas Rules of Evidence.

Unlike his younger brother, Tony was appropriately dressed in a suit for his courtroom appearance. In the ten years he had been away from Channelview, the older brother had managed to pick up a little polish and sophistication—traits Terry sorely lacked. Then too, he worked in the insurance industry and had learned to dress like a businessman instead of a laborer.

Stanley Schneider asked Tony not once but some twenty-odd times, in different ways, if he had tried over the last ten years to get his children back from Wanda's custody. "In the years after the divorce, didn't you want custody?" he asked, and "Didn't you talk about remarrying Wanda so you could be with your kids?" Over and over again, Tony Harper denied it all.

Next Schneider questioned Tony about his relationship with his brother. He attempted to imply that Tony and Terry were best friends, and that Terry would have done anything possible to help Tony out.

Tony refuted these charges, saying, "I see him maybe once or twice a year, usually when I go to see my parents."

When Schneider tried to implicate Tony in a plot to avoid paying child support, Tony said calmly, "I've always paid what the court told me to pay."

Court then recessed for the day.

The next day, August 30, the courtroom was once again packed. It was the day Wanda Holloway was supposed to take the stand on her own behalf, and the media and the merely curious alike were all eager to see what the woman had to say for herself. Throughout the trial so far, she had continued to maintain her stony, albeit impeccably groomed, exterior. Everyone was anxious to see how she would act on the stand.

But they had to wait. Wanda Ann's own mother, Verna Webb, was

called next. Mrs. Webb explained to the court that she and her husband
had lived in Channelview for forty-five years and had always been close
to Wanda and her children. The next question revealed that Mrs. Webb
was serving as a character witness for her daughter.

Troy McKinney asked her, "How would you describe your daughter's relationship with Shanna?"

Verna Webb, looking shaken and nervous, said, "Well, pretty much
like Wanda and I was. Very close, very stable in their relationship.
Respectful for each other. And Shanna is a very smart, very courageous
young fourteen-year-old girl. She admires her mother and loves her
very much. And..."

Casey O'Brien objected to the run-on answer. But it had been a
telling one. Just as Dr. Kit Harrison had testified in his deposition for
the family court about the symbiotic relationship that existed between
Wanda and Shanna, the disorder was usually multigenerational, passed
from one generation to another. Verna Webb had just uttered the words
that seemed to prove it by saying Wanda and Shanna were just like she
and Wanda had been—enmeshed and overly attached.

Verna Webb was then asked about Shanna's cheerleading activities
and Wanda's reaction to the same. Mrs. Webb acknowledged that she
had been kept apprised of all the events, and had even gone with
Wanda Ann to the school board to complain after the first competition.
She explained, "I wanted to find out why they had allowed a
nonstudent, Amber Heath, to participate in a school function. And also
we just wanted to feel them out and see, you know, what the deal was
on it and to also ask them could they add another cheerleader to that
particular..."

McKinney interrupted with another question, but not before the
jury had noticed Mrs. Webb's confusion between her "I's" and "We's."
It was another telling sign of the confusion of egos among these
women.

Troy McKinney asked why they had wanted another cheerleader
added to the squad, and Verna explained, "I felt like they hadn't
followed their own rules."

McKinney jumped forward in time to ask, "What was your reaction
when you heard Wanda was arrested?"

The sixty-ish matron answered, "I was in shock."

"Had you ever seen anything in the relationship between Wanda and
Shanna that would cause you to think that Wanda's behavior was
excessive?" McKinney asked.

Verna naturally said she had not.

On cross-examination, Mike Anderson's first question was, "Ma'am, are you familiar with the findings of Dr. Kit Harrison in regards to your daughter's relationship with Shanna?"

Before Mrs. Webb could answer, Troy McKinney's objection was sustained. The jury was told to disregard the prosecutor's question. Up to that point, no psychiatric diagnosis had been mentioned before the jury, and so could not properly be discussed on cross-examination. But the implication was still clear, and even though the jury was told to disregard the question, the panel no doubt absorbed the innuendo that this was a very sick family.

Finally the drama the crowd had been waiting for began to unfold. After Mrs. Webb was excused, her daughter, Wanda Ann Holloway, was called to the stand. As she had been throughout the trial, Wanda was primly attired, this time in a black-and-white print dress with a little lace collar. Her nails and lips were painted bright red, her pancake makeup was visibly thick, and her hair was frizzed out in a curly halo around her head. She seemed composed and steady as she took her place in the witness box and repeated the solemn oath to tell the truth.

The audience and the jury sat still and quiet, eager to hear every word the notorious woman said. They had all heard the various people up until this point tell conflicting stories about the defendant. Now they would hear her own story.

McKinney began by leading her through her life story. She had been born and raised in Channelview, she said. She married Tony Harper right after high-school graduation and bore him two children during their eight-year marriage. Their divorce in 1980 was bitter, she said. She then married Gordon Inglehart and moved to Beaumont for a year and a half, but was back in Channelview by 1983. Then she described her marriage to C. D. Holloway on March 7, 1986.

Wanda's voice, despite her outward composure, was quavery. McKinney stopped the narrative questions and asked, "Are you a little scared and nervous up there?"

Wanda smiled a little weakly, and said, "Yes, I am very nervous."

McKinney then turned to the main topic of the trial—cheerleading, and what it had meant to Wanda. He asked her about her relationship to Verna Heath.

"We were friends," Wanda said in her nasal twang. Like Verna Heath had before her, during the state's case, Wanda described how the two women car-pooled and took turns caring for each other's children.

"Did there come a time when you and Verna began to drift apart from each other?" McKinney asked.

Wanda said yes. "It was after the first cheerleading incident," she said. So far, her story was just like everyone else's. She told about how she had approached the school board when Amber, and not Shanna, had been elected cheerleader in 1989, and complained about the rules not being followed. "I did not ask for Amber to be removed, though," she turned and told the jury. "I just asked that another spot be added."

"If you thought the rules had been violated," asked Troy McKinney of his client, "Why didn't you ask that she be removed?"

Wanda answered, "Because if that had been my child, I would not have wanted someone coming down there and trying to remove her. It was not the child's fault that the rules had been violated, and I didn't think it would be fair to have Amber kicked off."

Wanda was demonstrating what a nice lady she was.

"What was your impression of what was going on with Verna and y'all's relationship at that time?" McKinney asked.

Wanda made out like any acrimony was all one-sided on the part of Verna. "I thought she was mad at me," she said, sticking out her jaw defiantly. She was tired of being the villainess, when Verna Heath was no saint either. "Right after the school board meeting, when I would pass her in the street, driving by or something, she would just kind of look at me, and before we had waved and, you know, had kind of a friendlier situation. But after that, it got kind of cold."

"Did there come a time when your feelings toward Verna become pretty strong?" Troy asked. No sense in denying Wanda's anger, so evident on the tapes made with Terry.

"Well, I had anger, yes," Wanda conceded. "I did have anger toward Verna." Then she explained why. "During all these cheerleading incidents, I felt like Verna was manipulating the school system to her advantage, and I didn't feel it was fair to my daughter or any of the other contestants that were in the cheerleading campaigns."

"How angry did you get," her attorney asked.

"Just angry," explained Wanda. "I mean, you know."

"Did there ever come a time that you were mad at Amber?" McKinney asked. Wanda didn't answer, but stared stonily down at her folded hands.

"That is just a yes or no answer, Miz Holloway," her lawyer prompted her.

"Yes," she said quietly.

"What was it that caused you to become mad at Amber?" Troy asked solicitously.

Wanda lifted her head and became more animated. The courtroom could hear the growing intensity of anger in her voice even now as she described events from the year before. "During the second campaign," she began, obviously accustomed to telling and retelling this story, "When Shanna was disqualified for using the rulers, and after we had had a meeting with the principal and the assistant superintendent, they called Shanna in and they explained to my daughter that she was going to be disqualified because I had told her she could use these rulers."

Wanda spoke in a rush of words that was hard to understand, she was so excited.

"Then they dismissed Shanna," she continued. "And told her if she wanted to go home, they would give her an excused absence that day or she could stay at school. Later as Shanna was walking down the hall, probably an hour or two after she had been disqualified, and they were changing classes, she said that Amber walked past her and laughed at her."

Wanda spat out the last three words. It was bad enough to lose to that Amber, but to have to endure her scorn as well was obviously too much for Shanna. Or, more accurately, for Wanda.

"How did Shanna react to that?" McKinney inquired.

"It hurt her feelings," Wanda said.

"And how did Shanna react to being disqualified?" McKinney asked.

"Well, she took it better than I did," Wanda admitted. That much was obvious by now, and many were surprised that even Wanda admitted her extreme reaction. "She handled it much better than I did."

"Why do you think that was?" Troy McKinney asked Wanda softly.

Wanda wiped away a tear with a lacy handkerchief as she said, "I felt like I had caused my daughter to be disqualified. It was a bad judgment call and it was my fault." Wanda apparently had had a lot of bad judgment calls.

"Had Shanna done anything wrong in the competition?" McKinney asked.

"No," Wanda said staunchly. "I had made, like, a little picket sign in the shape of a megaphone out of poster board and we glittered them up and I had gotten some pointy sticks from Winn's (dime store) and I had attached those to the little megaphone to make like a sign to hold up, and, you know, banter around, and I needed about fifteen more sticks, because I had twenty-three of the little megaphones. And when C. D. came home from work, I asked him if he would go by and get me some more."

McKinney interrupted, "Did you already have the rulers at the house?"

"Yes," Wanda said eagerly. "Tony and I had bought five hundred pencils and rulers with her name and VOTE SHANNA on them."

McKinney asked Wanda if she had been aware of the campaign rules, and Wanda admitted she knew of them.

"Did you initially want to use those rulers on the megaphones?" asked the lawyer.

"No," Wanda said firmly. "C. D. suggested it, but I told him we couldn't, because of the rules. But then I looked at the rules again and it said the only things not allowed was candy and gum, cookies, food-type things, and there was nothing on there that said we couldn't use the rulers."

Wanda conveniently ignored the fact that she had checked with a school official just the previous day and been told the rulers could not be used.

"So you put the ruler on the megaphones and let Shanna take them to school?" McKinney asked.

Wanda began to weep and nodded her head yes.

"Why does thinking about that incident make you so upset?" he asked gently.

Wanda dabbed at her eyes and managed to stammer, "Because I feel like I was the one that caused her to be disqualified. It was nothing she had done. She had practiced, and she was ready to go, and here I go, and C. D. and I had caused this to happen."

"Was there ever a point in time when you were so mad at Verna and Amber that you wanted either one of them killed or kidnapped or anything harmful to happen to them?" McKinney asked.

Wanda shook her head vehemently. "No," she said, still wiping away tears. "I have never wanted Verna or Amber Heath killed, never."

"But some of the things you were saying on those tapes are pretty strong comments, aren't they?" McKinney asked.

"Yes, those are terrible comments," Wanda agreed.

"Explain to the jury just basically why you were saying those kinds of things about them, " McKinney suggested.

"I'm sure when people get angry they say things and I have a tendency to run my mouth too much and I was angry. I was scared. I said things I shouldn't have said, but I never realized that Terry was serious. I really never figured that this was going to happen. I didn't. I never believed it," Wanda answered, turning to the jury to plead for understanding as she spoke. In response the twelve jurors only offered blank stares.

Her lawyer next quizzed her about her children's numerous activities, as if to show that cheerleading, alone, could never have been so important that Wanda would want someone killed because of it.

Wanda described how Shanna and Shane had both taken music lessons; how Shanna sang at the church, which they attended regularly; how Shane had been the assistant band major at his high school; and how Wanda had done volunteer work at the schools on and off throughout the children's school careers. Just your average housewife and mother.

After having his client describe how wholesome and normal her activities were, Troy McKinney asked, "You heard Terry Harper testify that sometime in the fall of last year you drove by his house, honked your horn, and asked him to meet you. Did you ever drive by his house?"

"No, sir, I did not," Wanda said emphatically. She had just finished describing what a good woman she was. Why on earth would she have ever consorted with the likes of Terry Harper? Instead, Wanda described a chance meeting with Terry at Bo's convenience store.

According to her, she had merely been running errands in the vicinity of Terry's home when she stopped for a cold drink at Bo's.

Wanda claimed she hadn't seen Terry in a long while, so the two started discussing Shane and Shanna's activities. As always, Wanda told Terry all about Shanna's cheerleading woes.

"Did you make comments to him about Verna Heath that have some of the flavor of the stuff in the tapes?" Wanda's lawyer inquired.

"Yes, unfortunately, I did," Wanda admitted sheepishly. "And when I mentioned that Amber had laughed at Shanna, he acted angry, like he was mad, and he said there wasn't any sense in that, and that he could take care of people who did things like that."

Fast forward to Christmas of 1990. McKinney asked Wanda about Shanna's visit to the Harper family gathering. "What did Shanna give everyone for Christmas that year?" he asked.

"Shanna had given an eight-by-ten picture of herself with a frame to all of my side of the family and Tony's side of the family for Christmas gifts," Wanda said, looking pleased with herself. "Shane was going to do the same thing—he had had a freelance shot in his drum-major outfit taken on the field, and I had ordered some prints but they hadn't come in yet."

McKinney then asked, "You heard Terry testify that at Christmas Shanna pulled him off to the side and told him, 'Mom wants you to call her.' Why was that?"

"Because I had told him I would give him some pictures, but I forgot until I saw Shanna in there wrapping hers, so I told Shanna, 'Tell your Uncle Terry to call me, I need to talk to him,'" Wanda explained. Again, a perfectly innocent reason for everything the state's witnesses had testified to.

Wanda then related her version of the events of that previous January, the events which had led to her being the defendant in this trial. Terry had called, as asked, and they had talked about pictures. Then Terry had reminded her of their discussion earlier in the fall. "He said he had got in contact with someone who could take care of my problem," Wanda said. "I just kind of laughed and I told him, 'Really? Are you serious?'"

"Did you think at this point that he was seriously thinking about hiring somebody to kill anybody?" McKinney asked. Wanda said no.

"So why did you ask questions about it?" inquired the defense attorney. He had to get in an explanation for everything.

"I didn't think he was serious," Wanda said. "Plus, I was curious, you know, I've never known anybody that knew anybody that went out and killed people."

Line by line, McKinney went through the transcript of the first recorded phone call, asking Wanda what she meant or why she had said the things she did. Each time, she replied that she was not serious, that she did not think Terry really meant what he was saying.

"So why did you agree to meet him at Grandy's?" McKinney asked, which was a good question.

"Because I didn't want to be talking over the phone with him, with my children around," she explained. But she added quickly, "I called him the next day to tell him I was not really serious about that."

This call was obviously not recorded, and probably never occurred. But Wanda's version of events indicated Terry had turned threatening after she told him she wanted no part of his suggestion. "He said, 'Wanda, you don't understand,'" she explained. "'I've already contacted this guy, and you just don't go to these people on a whim. If you waste people's time, they don't like it, and you're going to make me look stupid. When he gets mad at me, I'm going to turn him on to you. I'm going to tell him where you live.'"

"What was your reaction to that?" asked her lawyer.

"I was scared!" she said, widening her eyes.

So why, McKinney asked, when they finally met at Grandy's, did Wanda say to Terry, "Okay, what's the deal? Give me the scoop."

Again Wanda had a ready answer. "Because he had already indicated that he had already contacted this guy, and I felt like I needed to go ahead and talk about it, act like I was interested. I was afraid he might do something. I didn't know," she rambled on.

So it went, through the rest of the long conversations. For every damaging remark she had made on the tapes, Wanda had an explanation. She had been scared. She had been joking. She had not known what to do and had gone along with Terry all the way. But she never thought any of it was really going to happen.

Certain elements required more explanation, however. McKinney asked about the detailed information Wanda provided Terry about Verna Heath: address, daily schedule, car make and color and license number. "Did you have to make any effort to get that information?" he asked his client.

"No," Wanda insisted. "I already knew her address. She just lived around the corner. I knew what kind of car she drove, and I knew the license-plate number because a lot of times I'd park behind her at school and I could see it through the windshield."

And memorize it? How many people know their own license number by heart, let alone a neighbor's?

Wanda's attorney next focused on the subject of money, and the numerous times on the tapes where Wanda tells Terry she's having trouble coming up with the cash. "Has money ever been a problem around your house?" he asked Wanda.

She shook her head vigorously from side to side. "No," she said. "Not at all."

"Can you give us an idea what you and C. D. are worth?" he asked her.

"My husband is worth approximately two million dollars," Wanda Ann said proudly.

"If you needed twenty-five hundred dollars or you just wanted twenty-five hundred dollars," McKinney asked. "Tell the jury what places you could have gotten it from."

Wanda began to tick off the various ways she had of getting cash. "I have credit cards with I think up to four thousand dollars credit, and I could have went to the bank probably on a signature loan. Could have gone up to Channelview Bank, my husband used to be on the board of directors."

Again she looked out smugly at the courtroom. Wanda always was proud of her rich husbands.

"Where else could you have gotten the money from?" McKinney prompted. His client had forgotten one of the sources they had discussed before trial.

"Oh!" she said, seeming to snap out of her reverie. "C. D. keeps anywhere from five to seven thousand cash on hand at all times. In the pipeline construction business, they work seven days a week, and the trucks run back and forth through Louisiana, and several times they've gotten caught for being overloaded, and they have to pay fines, and the banks are closed on Saturdays." It all came out in a rush.

Next she added that C. D. regularly gave her a household allowance of two thousand dollars a month, which was more than sufficient to pay her bills. She could easily have skimmed from that to come up with the money Terry kept asking for, if she had really been serious, she explained.

Led by McKinney, Wanda further described how, before giving Terry the diamond earrings, she had even gone to see Terry's dad, R. E. Harper, at his convenience store, and asked him if he could loan her twenty-five hundred dollars. "I thought if Terry was trying to rip me off," she explained to the court, "That if I got the money from Mr. Harper, then nobody would get ripped off and I can tell Mr. Harper what happened and he could get his money back from Terry and this whole thing would be over."

Unfortunately, R. E. Harper told his former daughter-in-law he didn't have the money to loan out, so Wanda ended up giving Terry some jewelry.

"Why did you do that?" McKinney inquired.

"I was afraid not to," she said. "I figured he was trying to rip me off, but I was still afraid he might get this guy after me if I didn't give him something."

Finally McKinney got to the most damaging part of Wanda's taped conversations. "You said to Terry, 'I don't want her, two weeks later, coming up and pointing the finger at me,'" her lawyer quoted.

"You said, 'I just want her out of here. I don't care if you ship her off to Cuba for fifteen years.' Why were you saying those things?" he asked.

Wanda blushed and answered, "I was just reinstating [sic] the fact that, with all these cheerleading problems, that if they were out of my life or if they moved or something, that would be fine with me."

"Did you really think he was going to take her to Cuba for fifteen years?" asked McKinney.

"No, I did not," said Wanda firmly.

"Do you regret that you got involved in this?" McKinney asked.

"Yes, yes, I do," Wanda said, starting to sniffle again.

With that last tear shed, McKinney passed the witness.

After a brief lunch break, Mike Anderson was ready to tear Wanda's testimony to shreds during his cross-examination. Always polite in his demeanor, Anderson nevertheless did not hesitate to point out the holes in the defendant's story.

He went straight to the heart of the matter. "Mr. McKinney asked you several questions from a transcript and you heard some tapes played earlier, along with the ladies and gentlemen of the jury, did you not?" he began.

"Yes, sir, I did," Wanda said, jutting out her chin.

"Is that your voice on the tapes?" Anderson asked.

Wanda had to agree that it was.

Anderson next went after her explanations about the money—that she obviously wasn't serious because she could have gotten the twenty-five hundred dollars needed to pay Terry at any time.

Anderson pointed out, in a series of questions, that if Wanda had gotten money from any of the sources she had described during her testimony, her husband, C. D., surely would have found out about it through bank statements and the like. "C. D. didn't think this cheerleading stuff was all that important, did he?" Anderson inquired.

Wanda said, "No, he did not."

"And he wouldn't have gone along with this kind of business, would he?" Anderson asked. Wanda again agreed, and said, "Absolutely not."

Next, the prosecutor turned to Wanda's feelings about Verna Heath. Once more, the courtroom was treated to a recitation of the facts surrounding the cheerleading competitions. "You said that it was the first cheerleading election that you really started disliking Verna," he began. "What was it about that election, if she didn't have anything to do with it, that makes you dislike her?"

Wanda squirmed a little, and tried to explain. "I think she and I both had a misunderstanding of the situation," she said. "I think Verna thought I was out to get Amber disqualified and pulled off the squad. When actually, I was only trying to get another child added, according to the rules. And I think she felt I had it in for her, and we just got our wires crossed."

"Okay," Anderson said. "For whatever reason, your wires were crossed. In fact, from what you say on those tapes, your wires were crossed pretty well." Sarcasm dripped from the young attorney's voice.

Wanda looked chagrined. She attempted to wriggle out of this trap lamely. "People say things in anger that normally..." she trailed off and began again. "People pop off in anger all the time and say things they don't mean, and when you're scared, that compounds the problem."

"Uh-huh," Mike Anderson said, with a knowing air. "And then things rocked on and the next cheerleading tryouts came."

"And did you feel like Verna Heath had something to do with your daughter being disqualified?" he continued.

Wanda began another run-on answer. She gave a quick summary of her standard version of how Shanna had been robbed of cheerleading by jealous, ambitious mothers. According to her, all the other girls' mothers, but most especially Amber Heath's had plotted to rob Shanna of any chance of ever being a cheerleader.

Anderson asked her if that explained her subsequent actions. Wanda sought to explain. "Being disqualified, not following the regulations that the school sets out, even the regulations that I felt they had put out for the rulers was not adequate. Amber laughing at Shanna..."

Mike Anderson stopped her. Now they were getting somewhere. "Amber laughing at Shanna," he repeated slowly, turning toward the jury dramatically. Of course! That explained everything. Anyone would get murderously mad about something like that.

"Anything else that could be remotely tied to Verna Heath?" the prosecutor asked quickly.

"At this time, I don't know," Wanda said weakly.

"Amber won," stated Anderson for confirmation.

"Yes, that's correct," said Wanda grudgingly.

"And Shanna lost," Mike Anderson went on.

"Yes, well, she was disqualified on that one," Wanda hastened to add. It was obvious she did not like her daughter characterized as a loser.

"And here," Anderson went on, pointing to the March 1989 date he had written on chart paper. "Amber won, and Shanna lost."

"That's correct," Wanda said through clenched teeth.

"And those are the only instances we're talking about that caused your wires to cross, that caused things to fester, that caused you to say the things you said about Verna Heath and her daughter on those tapes?" he turned and stared open mouthed at Wanda dramatically. His courtroom skills were far and away superior to the monotone droning of Troy McKinney and the befuddled stammering of Stanley Schneider.

Wanda again reddened. "It was—yeah, cheerleading. Mostly cheerleading, that I can recall right now. Just cheerleading."

"Cheerleading would make you sick at your stomach about some little girl?" the prosecutor asked, stepping closer to Wanda.

Wanda was cornered, and she knew it. "I said...I have said some very stupid, very..."

Anderson stopped her. "Excuse me, Judge. I ask that she be instructed to answer the question."

Judge Godwin complied and told Wanda to answer a simple yes or no.

But Wanda had forgotten the question. Anderson asked again, "Are *these* the things that caused you to say what you said about that little girl and her mother? Specifically, 'The little girl makes me sick at my stomach?'"

Wanda again tried to explain, "When I said that about being sick at my stomach, it really had nothing to do with that. It was just..."

"Well, what was it?" Mike Anderson thundered. "Why did she make you sick at your stomach?"

Wanda was at a loss to explain. She tried weakly, "That was just something I said to Terry. I was angry and I just said that."

Anderson kept on, going over every horrid statement Wanda had made to Terry about her rival. "At some point, you had Terry sitting in the car with you and he said that this guy was going to want some information about Verna Heath and her daughter, right?" asked the prosecutor. Wanda nodded affirmatively.

"At that point, you didn't tell him, 'Whoa, time out, I don't have any information,' did you?" he asked Wanda.

"I don't believe I did," she said softly. Anderson then produced the sheet of paper on which Terry had written down Verna Heath's address, the description of her car, and her license-plate numbers. "I could find Verna Heath if I had never seen her in my life by using this, couldn't I?" Anderson asked the defendant.

"Yes," was her only response.

"You told us earlier you were terrified," Anderson went on, switching to cover one of Wanda's other excuses, that she had been too scared to back out of the talks with Terry.

"But you never called Verna Heath and told her about the fact that you had given a hit man information on her, so you could stop all this, did you?" he queried.

"I never called Verna, sir," Wanda said simply.

"Did you call the police after this meeting at Bo's?" he asked in mock wonder.

"No, sir, I didn't," Wanda said.

"Did you call the police after the first phone call after Christmas?" Anderson continued.

"No, sir, I never attempted to call the police, never," admitted Wanda.

"Even though you were so scared," Mike reemphasized, wanting to make sure the jury realized the lack of logic in Wanda's claim of being afraid. "Or maybe you thought Terry was being scared, but you never called the police?"

Wanda said she had not. Her cheeks were flushed with color.

Anderson began questioning her about some of her remarks on the tapes. "You talked to Terry about Verna Heath," he said, picking up the typed transcript. He began to read, "'Hell, it ain't even started yet, Terry, and they're already down there kissing ass so bad it's unreal.' Do you remember saying that?" he pressed Wanda. Wanda merely nodded her head.

"You were angry at that time, weren't you, ma'am?" Anderson asked her.

"I was aggravated, yes," Wanda admitted.

"Terry even tries to talk you out of it, saying, 'Why don't you just— Shanna can make cheerleader on her own.' And you say, 'No, this is a critical year, she don't make it this year, she ain't ever going to make it. Her little ego just can't take it no more,'" read the prosecutor.

Wanda said, "Yes."

"Basically, Terry was trying to tell you that Shanna was good enough to make it on her own, to let her try out, let her be a cheerleader on her own," said Anderson.

Wanda began to explain, "I knew Shanna was good enough to make it on her own. I knew she had the ability and the talent to do it. It wasn't that Shanna didn't have the talent!" she said heatedly. "It was all the other political things that were going on."

"Those angered you?" asked Anderson. Obviously they had. Wanda was getting worked up just thinking about it.

"I didn't feel like all the other people, Shanna included, were getting a fair shake, no I did not," said Wanda forcefully.

"And isn't it true that every time there's any mention made to stall in this transcript, in the tapes, Terry says, 'Hey, if you don't want to go through with this, we can stop,' and every time he says that, you call him off, 'No, no, no, no, I want to do it, I want to do it.' He tries four times, doesn't he, ma'am, he says, 'If you don't want to do it, we can stop.'"

How was she going to get around that?

She tried lamely. "But he also threatened me, sir," she began. "And you don't always hear that on the tape, you don't know how afraid of him I was."

"So you called the police, right?" the prosecutor asked. That's what normal people would do, if they were "so afraid."

"I've already told you I never called the police," Wanda said with irritation.

"Why is it that you don't sound afraid on these tapes, ma'am?" Anderson asked, highlighting the way Wanda had cackled with glee throughout the recordings.

"Because I thought the whole thing was a joke, Mr. Anderson," Wanda said. "I did not take him for real."

"Well, if it was a joke, how could you have been so afraid?" Mike had her caught in her own trap.

"Because he had threatened me, and I didn't really know. I know how Terry is," she explained, "and I didn't know what he was going to do, whether he was serious or not."

"Well, if you didn't know if he was really serious, why didn't you call the police? So that an innocent woman sitting out there somewhere not privy to this conversation wouldn't end up blown up or killed or have her kid's legs screwed up?" the prosecutor pressed. His cross-examination was working, and he knew it.

Wanda still struggled to explain herself. "I never felt like Verna Heath was ever going to get hurt, ever," she said to the jury.

Mike Anderson began to read from the transcripts again. Let her own words sink her. "Wanda: 'Now, if all the sudden her legs just happen to come up screwed up.' Do you remember saying that, ma'am?" he questioned politely.

"Yes," Wanda admitted.

"Who were you talking about?" Anderson asked.

"We were talking about Amber," Wanda said, looking down at her hands.

"And your concern was that that would be too obvious, wasn't it?" the prosecutor reminded her, and the jury.

"I was just feeling Terry out," Wanda said. "That's why I said that. Before, at that first meeting, he had kept saying we should do this, this, and this."

"And did you say," Anderson began, again reading Wanda's quotes, "'I think if the car got wrecked, or the car blew up or something where both of them died, it might be different, you know, like a car wreck or something. Impact, or explosion or something, then it wouldn't be so obvious'?" The courtroom was completely silent, the hate-filled words echoing in the air.

"Once again…" Wanda started, but Anderson interrupted her.

"That's part of the joke, too?" he asked sarcastically, and began to read again.

"Terry asked you, 'Do you want to meet the guy?' And you go, 'Hell, no, I don't want no contact. No way, Jose, I ain't getting my face in nothin,'" Mike hissed out the words just as Wanda had on the tapes.

"That's exactly right," Wanda admitted.

"You could have called the police and met the guy and had an undercover officer there to arrest him, couldn't you, ma'am?" he asked softly.

"I never even thought about that, sir," Wanda said weakly.

"There were plenty of times when Terry wasn't around you, and you could have called anybody in the world, couldn't you?" he asked.

Again Wanda tried to make him see it her way. "I could have called anybody, but how do I know who was watching me? I don't know if there wasn't somebody out there watching me," she said, again using her fear as an excuse.

"Did you say, 'Maybe I should go with the mother. And the kid, she can just be screwed with the mother, maybe it would mess up her mind'?" Mike asked.

"Sure, yeah, I said that," Wanda had to admit.

"That was part of the joke, too?" Mike inquired.

"The whole time we're talking on that tape, I'm laughing, Terry's laughing, we're laughing. I never was serious about that," she said.

"You were laughing a lot to be in the company of a man you were so deathly afraid of," Anderson pointed out.

"Sir," Wanda said angrily, "I had already told him I did not want to do this, that I was not serious and he told me that once we had contacted that guy, that we didn't waste their time. I did not know how these men work, I don't know what goes on."

"But three times after that conversation, ma'am, he told you, 'If you don't want to go through with it, that's fine,' and you said, 'Oh, no, no, no, no, no, I want to do it,' correct?" Anderson pointed out.

"Yes, sir," Wanda said quietly.

"Did you say, 'I've been talking about this for two years?'" asked the state's lead attorney.

"Yes, I did," Wanda admitted.

"Killing the kid," Anderson said bluntly.

"Yeah, I said that," Wanda conceded.

"And in the end, you gave Terry those earrings and said, 'Tell him to go for it!' Do you recall saying that?" the attorney asked.

"Yes, I did," Wanda said, leaning forward in her chair to explain. "Because I felt if I gave Terry the earrings, he would just go away, this whole situation would be over and I wouldn't have to worry about him anymore. I felt he was just wanting money," she concluded, again looking toward the jury for understanding. They continued to stare at her in wonder, their eyes widened as if they were seeing a being from another planet.

"If you didn't take it seriously," continued Anderson, "Why did you spend so much time talking about what was going to happen to them? Why didn't you just say, 'Here are the earrings,' and go on?"

"I was doing as I thought Terry wanted me to do," Wanda said senselessly.

"Was Terry Harper playing mind control on you, ma'am?" Mike Anderson asked facetiously.

Wanda was eager for the out. "Yes, yes, I think he was, sir," she said. Even she hadn't thought up that excuse, the only one she hadn't already tried.

"Did he control your mind when you said, 'Well, you said if he didn't kill her, he would take her to Cuba or something but she wouldn't be around, finally. Well, I don't want to know what he's going to do. Less I know, better off I am. This guy, bad ass, or what? Yeah, he's cold-blooded, he's got to be,'" Mike read, facing the jury. "'This is the only way I could ever do it, is to pay someone. I mean, you get mad at things and I think I could just shoot you, you know. You think about it, and you want to do it, but I could never do it. This is the only way I could do it, is to pay somebody,'" the lawyer stopped and turned to Wanda for her explanation of that. It sure didn't sound like someone who was just joking around. It sounded serious, deadly serious.

"Yes, sir, I have said those things," Wanda declared, again beginning to cry. She swiveled in her chair to look at the members of the jury and added, "I am sorry I said all those things. They're bad, I've already told y'all they're bad."

Anderson paused a moment to let her compose herself, but then hammered on, "Ma'am, there is nothing, absolutely nothing that in any way gave you any indication that after you handed those earrings to Terry Harper that Verna Heath was not going to die. Every statement, every bit of evidence, everything that's been said indicated to you that when you give these earrings to Terry Harper, he's going to the man and that woman who has had no idea what is going on is going to die," he stated plainly.

"No, I never felt that way, sir," Wanda insisted.

"Did you call Verna?" Anderson asked again.

"No," Wanda repeated, "I never called anyone, sir. But you just don't understand, you just don't understand...."

Anderson turned from the witness and ignored her pleas. No, he did not understand, and neither did anyone else in the courtroom.

With that last blow, Mike Anderson passed the witness. He looked almost jubilant.

Troy McKinney asked only one question in an attempt to repair the damage that had just been inflicted on his client.

"Miz Holloway, tell the jury whether or not you intended, you wanted, you desired Verna Heath to be killed or kidnapped?"

Wanda Ann turned in her seat, tears streaming down her face, streaking her pancake makeup, and begged her judges for mercy. "I never wanted Verna Heath killed," she wept. "Or Amber. Never. I never wanted anything to happen to them. And I'm sorry I said all that stuff, I know it sounds awful, but..."

Anderson stood up and objected to Wanda's nonresponsive and narrative answer. Judge Godwin looked down at the defendant icily and said, "That will be all, Mrs. Holloway. You may step down."

The defense announced its case was closed.

Casey O'Brien rose and said, "We close, your honor." Judge Godwin tapped his gavel and said, "Both sides rest and close. We will reconvene in this room after the long weekend for final arguments."

The jury was excused for the Labor Day holiday weekend, and the participants in the trial withdrew to begin crafting their last statements to the jury. It had been an exhausting five days for everyone, but soon it would all be over.

13

Send Her to Cuba

Throughout the long, hot Labor Day weekend that brought a break for the beleaguered trial participants, talk of Wanda Holloway and the Cheerleader Murder for Hire case was heard across the nation. Most of it was in a jocular vein—people were having a hard time taking the case seriously because of the bizarre motive that elicited the charges against Wanda combined with the strange testimony that had been heard from other witnesses, most notably from Terry and Marla Harper. What a bunch of weirdos, most people thought.

And, of course, there were the inevitable jokes. Even Johnny Carson mentioned the case on the *Tonight Show*, saying, "You know how to find this Wanda Holloway, the Cheerleader Mom, down in Channelview, don't you? She's the one standing out in the street with a pompon saying, 'Gimme a G, Gimme a U, Gimme a G-U-N.'" Lynn

Ashby, editor of the *Houston Post*, quipped from his column that Channelview High School had a new cheer: "2–4–6–8, who do we assassinate?"

The Texas connection in the case caused numerous commentaries about how that state has always been known for its preoccupation with football and its female counterpart, cheerleading. The television tabloid show *Inside Edition*, cited the fact that the Holloway case was unfolding "in the very backyard" of the infamous Dallas Cowboys cheerleading squad, already notorious for its bouncing buxom blond bimbos who comprised the nation's first professional sports-team cheerleaders. A reporter on TV's *Current Affair* said that most girls in America at sometime dream of being a cheerleader, but added, "That is especially true in Texas, where pompons are a major part of the Lone Star legend."

Even the Texas newspapers railed against the way football and cheering had assumed such importance in Texas society. The *Dallas Morning News* solemnly criticized the phenomenon, saying, "Cheerleading is a big deal to some in Texas. To them, the ideal boy plays football and his girlfriend spins a baton on the field or waves a pompon on the sidelines. And it is seen that way in Channelview."

Other pundits, both local and national, discussed from their print pulpits the issue of parental overinvolvement with their children, and how damaging such behavior can be for all concerned. Cases of Little League coaches being beat up by irate dads and cheerleading sponsors being bribed by overeager moms were cited as examples of the phenomenon that Wanda Holloway epitomized. In short, the case of *Texas v. Wanda Ann Holloway* was on everybody's lips.

Wanda herself spent the long weekend in seclusion with her family and her attorneys. She could no longer move about freely in Channelview, or Houston, either, for that matter, without instantly becoming the object of excited stares, whispers, and outright comments from strangers who recognized her from the papers and television. Shane had fortunately already gone off to Baylor University in Waco to begin his freshman year of pre-med studies, and Shanna was with her father in Kingwood for the weekend. Since she had thus far not attended the trial and had not had her photo widely published (most papers were printing old school yearbook photos that no longer even resembled the growing girl), she was still able to go about her usual activities without undue attention.

When Tuesday morning rolled around, after Labor Day Monday, folks began arriving at the courthouse annex on Preston Street in downtown Houston at seven o'clock. Those who had been in attendance since the trial's commencement knew that closing arguments were scheduled for Tuesday morning at ten; others had heard the news over the weekend and decided to check out the final hours of the by-then notorious trial.

Again, a festival air dominated the hallways. Reporters chatted lightheartedly about their weekends and gossiped about the audience members from Channeview. Media representatives from as far away as Australia and Great Britain were on hand, and even the venerable *New York Times* was providing coverage. The merely curious spectators eagerly approached many reporters for their professional assessments of the goings-on so far. The narrow hallways were once again jammed with myriad electronic equipment—microphones, cameras, video cameras. A large contingent of photographers had already staked out the elevators, waiting for the newsworthy to begin arriving.

Judge George Godwin, who banned the use of cameras and tape recorders in his courtroom at the start of the trial, had agreed to a concession after numerous pleas from the city's major media editors. He relented enough to allow one pool video camera and one pool microphone to be in the courtroom for the closing arguments in the case. All media would have equal access to the results. But the technical aspects of hooking up the equipment still caused a delay in the morning's proceedings, since the judge was adamant that the devices remain unobtrusive and he carefully supervised their location in the courtroom. Although judges all over the United States had begun to allow extensive live-television coverage of trials, most in Harris County were still reluctant to relax the traditional prohibition against electronic media intrusion into the courthouse.

Finally, the details were worked out and the proceedings were ready to begin. Wanda Holloway had again been escorted by her attorneys through a side door into the crowded chamber. She appeared more tense than she had previously, but, as usual, was groomed to perfection, again wearing a conservative, Sunday-go-to-church style dress in solid black with a single row of gold buttons down the front.

For the first time, she was accompanied by her husband, C. D. He cut an imposing figure with his large, husky frame and wavy steel-gray hair. He looked grim as he took a seat behind his wife on the front bench reserved for members of the bar to view the trial.

Wanda's parents, Clyde and Verna Webb, were also in attendance, as was the entire Heath family, with the exception of Verna's youngest boys. It was obvious from the faces of Jack and Verna Heath that they, at least, saw no humor in this situation; but for Terry Harper, they reasoned, Verna and Amber might at this very moment be dead.

The prosecutors, O'Brien and Anderson, had obviously taken extra pains with their appearances for their closing arguments. It is commonly suggested to lawyers in their training that they should always wear their best, most conservative suits for opening and closing arguments because such outfits will lend them an air of power and authority that can help give their remarks more weight with the members of the jury. Defense attorneys Troy McKinney and Stanley Schneider were likewise duded up more than they had been on less dramatic days of the trial.

Judge Godwin began the proceedings by admonishing the assembled crowd once more, before he had the jury brought in. "Ladies and gentlemen, these are very trying circumstances for everyone, no pun intended," he began. "We are very crowded in here, and we have tried, within the range of the physical facilities, to accommodate everyone. We have made some concessions," he went on, obviously referring to the presence of the media camera and microphone, "and perhaps prudence would dictate that we not make those concessions. However, we will do the best we can with what we've got."

After warning the crowd against any outbursts or other unseemly behavior, he suggested to the gallery, "If you cannot control yourself, you may leave now before you are forcibly removed."

Thus duly chastised, the animated audience members noticeably toned down their whispering and settled in to listen to the final moments of the trial.

First Casey O'Brien would give his summation of the evidence presented, since the state always goes first. The defense attorneys would then take turns providing their views, followed by prosecutor Mike Anderson, who would be allowed the last word before the jury was sent to the deliberation room.

Casey O'Brien, looking dapper in a three-piece suit, began by discussing the legal issues in the case. One of the hardest tasks a trial lawyer has is explaining the intricacies of the laws that apply to each case in layman's terms. The jury had already been handed five pages of jury instructions, prepared with the cooperation of all the attorneys and approved by the judge, which outlined the statutory elements of each crime with which Wanda was charged. It did its best to explain to the jury what all of the different terms of the law meant, for example, what "solicitation to commit capital murder" entailed, but for all practical purposes the document was still incomprehensible to the average person.

Thus it was up to the lawyers to try to explain it all to the members of the jury before they ended up hopelessly lost during deliberations. Nine times out of ten, jurors remained that way after the wordy lectures by the attorneys in any given case. Nevertheless, closing arguments were still viewed as an invaluable tool for influencing final opinions.

O'Brien, low-key as ever, strutted in front of the jury with his hands in his pockets as the audience leaned forward to catch his every word.

As is customary, O'Brien started by thanking the jury for their attention. "I know it's been an arduous eleven days since we began this case. We appreciate that," he said. "Now I want to take a few minutes to go through that legal mumbo-jumbo document and give you my impression of what it means."

He began by discussing the defenses that Troy McKinney and Stanley Schneider had outlined in the jury charge: entrapment and duress. O'Brien explained what duress meant. "This is an affirmative defense, which means the burden of proof rests upon the defense. Do you believe, that's what the charge asks you, that the defense has shown by a preponderance of the evidence that Terry Lynn Harper threatened imminent death or serious bodily injury to the defendant?" he asked the jury, squarely facing them.

He turned to a discussion of that evidence. "We had," he pronounced gravely, "a defense of extraordinary magnitude trying Terry Harper. For two days they tried Terry Harper, and we heard Marla Harper, and her fear of Terry and her mind control by him." He paused to let the jury consider that whole wild tale that Marla had spun.

Then he attacked that witness's credibility. "Now, I don't know if you believe that Marla was telling the truth," he said. "You heard evidence that she has extensive psychiatric problems, told doctors, more than one, about bugs crawling on the walls, snakes on the driveway..."

Troy McKinney leapt to his feet, shouting "Objection, judge. She never said anything like that, it's outside the record."

Judge Godwin just gave his usual frown and said to the jury, "The jury will remember the evidence as they heard it. What the lawyers say here is not evidence."

O'Brien continued, unrattled by McKinney's interruption. "But does any of that make any difference?" he inquired of the jury. "Is this case about Terry Harper? Is it about Marla? I don't think so," he added, shaking his head. He turned and pointed at Wanda Holloway.

"That lady, right there, is on trial," his face was deadpan as he spoke. "You heard her testify, and you heard the tapes, and I'm asking you, ladies and gentlemen, when you go back to begin your deliberations, that you listen to those tape recordings. That's the crime, as it happened."

For further emphasis of his point, Casey O'Brien halted his argument to ask that certain portions of the tapes be replayed at this point. "As you listen to these tapes," O'Brien instructed, "listen for the fear in her voice, and that will answer the theory of duress." The jury soon heard once again the laughing voice of Wanda Holloway, spewing her venom to Terry Harper about Verna Heath. She was obviously not the least bit afraid.

C. D. Holloway, on the front row of the courtroom behind his young wife, heard the tapes for the first time. He noticeably stiffened as he listened to his wife laugh as she mentioned his name and say, "Shit, C. D.'s so straight up it makes you sick."

Up to this point, the faithful husband had not been involved in his wife's defense except to foot the considerable bill. He must have wondered what his little wife was doing with this other man in the first place, laughing it up and impugning his name. His face had a hard look to it as he heard the rest of the portions O'Brien had earmarked for replay.

"Every question you have about this case can be answered by the tapes," Casey O'Brien pointed out when the recording finished. "That passage you just heard sets up the motive and explains why: She hates and she's frustrated and she finds no solution to her problem but the ultimate solution of taking life."

O'Brien then reviewed the whole story of how Wanda had first started her plan in her own kitchen with Patrick Gobert in March of 1990, recalling for the jury how Wanda asked Patrick for a hit man's phone number. Then how she asked Pete Reyes the following Christmas for the same information, and finally lit on Terry Harper. O'Brien had the bailiff play some more of a tape.

"Listen to that," he asked the jury. "She tells you on that tape, 'I've been thinking about this for two years.'" He also pointed out the portions of the tape where Wanda says she's afraid of being discovered. O'Brien suggested, "Did she fear Terry Harper? Does she tell you who she fears on the tape? She does. She's afraid of the hit man if she doesn't pay her bill."

O'Brien then turned to the defense's proposition that Wanda Holloway thought Terry Harper was just stealing from her. "Consider this," he suggested, "If Terry Harper was stealing from her, why not go for the seventy-five hundred dollars he first mentioned to her? Why drop down to the twenty-five hundred dollars for the mother, the 'crap,' as she's described on the recording? It makes absolutely no sense."

He then briefly reviewed all the defense arguments. "So those are the defenses. 'He was stealing from me; I was afraid of him; I didn't mean it; he's exercising mind control over me; and I thought he was joking.'"

"Just listen to the tapes," O'Brien insisted. "Listen. How many times does she tell Terry Harper, 'You don't understand, you don't understand the hatred I feel for these women, this little girl and her mother.' That's what she says repeatedly on those tapes, 'You don't understand.'"

"Folks," the senior prosecutor concluded, "I think we understand all too well what this case is about. This case is about her hatred. As ludicrous and stupid as it might sound, that's why we're here. And I think you do understand. Thank you," he finished and solemnly sat back down at the prosecutor's table.

It was Stanley Schneider's turn to attempt to persuade the jury to agree his client was innocent, not guilty.

Standing stiffly behind the podium, Schneider proceeded to rifle through the lengthy jury charge that had already been distributed to the jurors. In an overly legalistic plea, he ran through the various elements of the charged offenses, and begged the jury to find that the state had not proved those items needed to return a guilty verdict.

"This is the most difficult time for a lawyer," he began somewhat nervously, "to get up here and try to put some sense to the evidence." It was especially difficult in this case, since the defense had muddied the waters with so many varied explanations for what had transpired between Terry Harper and Wanda Holloway.

As he had throughout the defense portion of the trial, Stanley Schneider jumped quickly from theory to theory in his closing argument. First he suggested that Wanda had been unfairly tried in the media. "On January 30, 1991," he began, citing the day of Wanda's arrest, "The state, Terry Harper, and the media all tried Wanda Holloway."

He quickly moved on to one of his side's defenses, that Wanda had been entrapped. "All the evidence that you heard today or in this trial is that Terry Harper solicited Wanda Holloway." Then he referred directly to the jury charge. "The first sentence here regarding solicitation says that you must look to the circumstances surrounding her conduct as she believed them to be. That's only talking about Wanda Holloway, and what she believes, not what Terry Harper wants you to believe, but what she believes." Schneider was never regarded by his peers as much of a courtroom speaker, and his closing argument in this case clearly demonstrated why.

He rambled on, "The other thing is Wanda Holloway's intent must be corroborated by other evidence besides Terry Harper. The state may say that Pete Reyes and Patrick Gobert corroborate her intent, but both people say they were joking. And Patrick Gobert, four people say he is lying." Schneider was referring back to the Denmans he had put on the stand to say that they did not think Patrick was a truthful person.

Stanley Schneider then attacked the state's chief witness, Terry Harper, who sat in the second row from the front. For closing arguments, all the trial witnesses were allowed back in the courtroom, although they had been banned during the presentation of other testimony. Terry looked annoyed by Schneider's remarks.

"Terry Harper is unbelievable," the lawyer stated flatly. "He's a liar." He recalled for the jury how Terry himself had sat on the stand and told the court how the police had instructed him not to tell anyone about the investigation, but that Terry had gone ahead and told Marla, Tony Harper, and Bob Wilburs, "his spiritual advisor," Schneider pointed out sarcastically.

"Then there are the unrecorded phone calls," Schneider said, referring to the claims of Wanda Holloway that she and Terry had had several conversations to which the police were not privy. "And then you have Terry Harper's criminal record. He had six convictions. You have the evidence about the jewelry and the pawn shops. His six or seven marriages. Eleven jobs in the last three years. His stability—where is it?" Schneider queried. "These are all things to use to judge his credibility."

He turned and pointed to Wanda, sitting implacably at the defense table, hands discreetly folded in front of her. "The state has agreed that she has a reputation for honesty and being truthful. What does it come down to? She's been a sterling, substantial person in the community, and she is today." The jurors exchanged glances.

For the next several minutes, Stanley Schneider launched into an almost unintelligible analysis of the jury instructions, which is almost always a mistake. He should have kept it simple and kept it direct. After urging the jury that all the evidence was favorable to his client, he added, "Based on the evidence, Terry Harper is a liar, and based on his evidence, there is no evidence that can convict Wanda Holloway. You must return a verdict of not guilty." With that, he pushed up his tortoise-shell framed eyeglasses, ran his hand through his brown hair, and sat back down.

Troy McKinney was next up. Like his partner, he was not possessed of extraordinary courtroom demeanor. Like Schneider, he hid his large frame behind the podium, and lectured sternly to the jury. But instead of having a New York inflection, Troy's voice came out in a country twang, and he used plain language that his fellow Texans could easily understand. As the lead attorney on the defense, McKinney's argument lasted many minutes longer than Schneider's and covered more ground.

He began by assailing the state's main witness again. "This case is not about our defenses," he started out, "because before you ever get to the defenses, you have to first find two things: that Wanda solicited Terry, and that she intended for Verna Heath to die or be kidnapped."

He glanced into the courtroom audience at the Harper brothers before going on, "Why do I tell you these things? It's no big secret. I'm not going to make a big secret out of it here." McKinney continued, "Our contention is that Terry and Tony set her up. They set her up," he repeated, pointing at the two brothers again. "They framed her. It was their plan and their scheme from the beginning."

He went on to explain his theories about the Harper boys' motives. Terry, as black sheep of the family, wanted to get back in his family's good graces. Tony wanted his kids back. Terry saw a way to help his older brother accomplish that end, and the two conspired to frame Wanda Holloway to achieve their goals. The fact that Wanda seemed to willingly go along with Terry was never mentioned, nor were her hateful words about Verna. The fact that, on tape, Terry offered her several occasions to back out was omitted from his argument as well. Instead, the lawyer focused only on the Harpers, especially Terry and his ill repute.

"Think about it," McKinney suggested to the jury. "The man is thirty-six, thirty-seven years old; he's had seven marriages. Just over the past three years he said he'd had fifteen jobs, not eleven," the lawyer explained, correcting a statement made by his partner. "He's been arrested several times for other than traffic offenses. It's no wonder he's the black sheep of the family."

Troy McKinney started picking on Terry Harper for waiting almost a week to call Tony after hearing on Christmas Eve that Wanda wanted to talk to him. "He said he didn't have any idea who to call," McKinney jeered. "Little old innocent me. But keep in mind, this is the same guy who's been prosecuted by the same district attorney's office and is the same guy who's been arrested numerous times by various police agencies. He's on probation today. And he wants you to believe he didn't know who to call?"

McKinney waved his hand toward Terry in disgust. "That's the most ludicrous thing in this case today."

Then the young attorney got around to Wanda's role in the case. After all, her voice was on tape and had to be explained away. "Wanda was curious," he said forcefully, "and she wanted to know how things like this worked. My God, who of us haven't been curious about something like that? Who of us haven't asked questions? How much do things like that cost? Do people really do that? How do they do it?"

McKinney's list of hypothetical questions that the average person would want to know the answers to went on and on. There was just one problem: Most of the people on the jury, and in the audience, had never been curious about things like that, and had never asked anyone those questions.

McKinney wisely left that area of argument and instead zeroed in on the money. Again pointing out that C. D. Holloway was Mr. BigBucks incarnate, he explained in a lengthy discussion that Wanda was just trying to get rid of Terry Harper, and that's why she gave him the earrings. "She told you that first she went and talked to Terry's father, tried to borrow the money from him," the lawyer said in his abbreviated monotone speech. "Why does she do that?" he asked hypothetically, and then gave his own answer. "Because she figures Terry is ripping her off, and if Terry is ripping her off, she's going to let him rip off his own dad, and let him explain to his father what happened to the money. Why didn't the state put up R. E. Harper on the stand to tell you that wasn't true?"

It all came down to the money, McKinney insisted. That, and the question of who solicited whom. Wanda didn't even know where Terry Harper lived, argued McKinney, proving that Terry had lied about the day when Wanda supposedly drove by his trailer and honked him out for a meeting. "They ran into each other by accident, by coincidence only," McKinney said, "Down at Bo's. Nothing more, nothing less, and they started off doing the same thing they'd done before, exchanging pleasantries and some chitchat."

Then, said the lawyer, Terry brought up the subject of taking care of Wanda's problem, after she related the cheerleading fiascos for the umpteenth time that year. "Terry told you two very important things on the witness stand," McKinney repeated. "He told you the first idea to kill Verna Heath came out of his mouth the first time. His words were something to the effect of, 'Well, why don't you just do this mother and then the daughter will be too distraught to do anything else?'"

McKinney let that sink into the jury's minds while he looked over his notes again briefly. "But this is the same man the state wants you to think was appalled and shocked that anybody would even be talking about anything like this," he continued. "He's so appalled and shocked, he suggests killing and kidnapping her," he added, his voice rising in emphasis and outrage. "It was Terry doing it, not Wanda. Terry is the one who brought it up."

"And one other thing," he added, throwing everything possible into his soup of an argument. "Terry admitted on the witness stand to reading and studying about one particular book on John Gotti, and writing a high-school paper on manipulation of witnesses and control of witnesses," as if it were self-evident Terry was a would-be gangster just out to gratify his desire for Mafioso thrills.

He finally neared his conclusion. "I want you all to keep something in mind here," he advised the panel. "The state wants you to believe that Wanda Holloway was a malicious person, that she was so malicious that she wanted Verna Heath killed or kidnapped. But this is the same lady that the uncontroverted evidence shows you that she did not want Amber Heath kicked off the cheerleading squad in 1989. And that was because she did not want to hurt the little girl," McKinney said, looking in sympathy at Wanda as if she were a saint. It was quite a stretch for the jury, after all they'd already heard from the lady. But McKinney continued, "This is the same lady the state wants you to believe would go kill her mother? The lady has so little malice she wouldn't even have asked to have the girl kicked off the squad, but she would go kill her mother? I suggest to you it simply isn't reasonable," he finished, shaking his head at the insanity of the very idea.

After McKinney completed his defense summation Michael Anderson had a turn to speak, to conclude the state's argument. And he was ready. Unlike the hesitant, stammering defense counsel, Anderson paced about the courtroom completely at ease and in control. Instead of hiding behind the podium he walked easily up and down in front of the jury as he explained his views of the case. This would be the last voice they heard before they retired to decide Wanda's fate, and he wanted to make sure they listened to him.

After praising the opposing counsel, which made Mike Anderson look like a fair-minded fellow, the prosecutor briefly denigrated their case and then began his attack on the defendant.

He turned and looked straight at Wanda Ann. "Wanda Holloway is worth two million dollars, and she's a lovely lady, and she cried on the stand." He turned back to the jury. "And Terry Harper is a blue-collar guy who works on the ship channel. But she's better than he is because of those things, and she is to be believed instead of him.

"But you know something, ladies and gentleman," he said quietly and seriously, "when it comes down to it, when you really assess the matter, this is not necessary for this case because you do not have to believe Terry Harper. All you have to do is believe your ears, because you are a witness to the offense."

He looked over at Wanda again and said sternly and loudly, "You can hear her voice. You can hear how her emotions rise. You can hear the words she chooses to use. Witness the entire crime. And I think you're going to see that Wanda Holloway was quite serious about what she intended to do. You can tell by the tone of her voice."

Anderson turned back to the jury. The courtroom audience was as quiet as a church congregation, hanging on his every word.

"I'm not going to go through everything the defense talked about," Mike Anderson announced, to everyone's relief. No one wanted to hear the same old stuff again. "I'm not going to run down all those rabbit trails that have been set up. I won't do it—it's a waste of your time and a waste of this court's time. But the bottom line is, cheap jewelry? I don't know about you, but twenty-two hundred dollars is a lot of money, I think." Appealing to the common element of the jury was a wise move. The defense had undoubtedly alienated many with its talk of Wanda's wealth as a defense. He was referring back to Wanda's lawyers' presentation of evidence during the trial that Wanda had lots of jewelry worth more than the earrings she pawned off on Terry.

"But I submit this to you," he added. "When she's looking for that money, she knows she does not want to get caught. On the tapes," he went on, again looking at Wanda, who refused to look back, "she mentioned not wanting to get caught no less than sixteen times. Because her worst fear was to find herself in the position she's in right now. Her worst fear was not that two people might die, or that she'd have to pay twenty-five hundred dollars for mama, who ain't worth a crap," he spat the words out as hatefully as Wanda had on tape. "No," he said, shaking his head for emphasis. "Her worst fear was facing twelve people and having to try to figure out some way to weave and wind around the fact that she wanted two people dead in that tape!"

Anderson let his voice die back down from the near-thunder it had just assumed. "Now you might think," he said softly, "that this is such a weird reason to kill somebody. This is so bizarre, such a strange reason to have someone killed."

"But think about this," he suggested to the jury. "Can you give me a good reason for having somebody killed? Can you come up with an acceptable reason for capital murder?" Prosecutors had a way of sounding like preachers on many occasions, appealing to the moral uprightness of their audiences. Anderson was obviously an ace at it, perhaps because of his undergraduate days at Texas Lutheran College.

"Okay," he finally added, as if to say he knew that there were, after all, some standard reasons for murder. "Greed? I think we have that here. Jealousy? We have that here. Blind ambition? We have that here. And pure hatred? Yes, we have that here."

"This is not about cheerleading, folks," Anderson said with assurance. "This is about someone who hated two other people so much that it gnawed at her day and night. It gnawed at her to the point of obsession. It gnawed at her to the point of bothering everybody who could get within earshot of her with this talk of cheerleading."

"What's the deal with the money?" he asked the jury to consider. "You saw her testify, you can realize she's not a stupid person. She was a person eaten up with an obsession, so she made mistakes. She said herself, 'I've been talking about it for two years with C. D.' But where in the world is C. D. to tell us this didn't happen?" thundered Anderson, raising his arms in wonderment. "Why ain't he here?" In Texas, it is common for lawyers to adopt the folksy speech style of many of their witnesses and jurors, just as many wear cowboy boots to show they are good ole boys at heart, underneath their fancy speech and three-piece suits.

Again Mike Anderson turned toward the defendant. "And if Terry were as bad as she anticipated he was, we wouldn't be here, and neither would those two people back there on that second row," Mike said, pointing straight at Verna and Amber Heath. The jurors turned in their seats to once again view the would-be victims. "But for Terry," he continued, "we'd all be off doing whatever we do, and we would have gotten maybe a tiny message in the newspaper that two people died in a car wreck. And the only thing that Wanda Holloway would have been missing is a couple of earrings and maybe a little change."

It was a chilling thought, and Anderson wisely let it hang in the air before continuing his speech.

Anderson's close was to mop up the weak defense arguments. "In business terms," he said, switching his analysis, "when you have a contract, you have an offer, an acceptance, and an exchange of something valuable." It was the first lesson any law student learned in law school. "We had an offer here, we had an acceptance, and we had an exchange of value. She did her part, and by doing that, she pushed the button. It wasn't out of curiosity and it wasn't a joke. And the only thing that kept those two people from dying was the fact that Terry Harper decided one day that it was about time to do something right. Those people would not be here, and neither would we, if it were not for Terry Harper."

Still, the prosecutor conceded that Terry was no angel. "You may not like him," he went on. "You may not want to take him to lunch. You may not want to look upon his face ever again. But listen to what he said and compare it to what's on those tapes. You don't have to believe him, but there's no variance on those tapes. Just listen to them; they make you witnesses to this crime."

Then he reached his conclusion. "So I'm asking you to do this," he pleaded. "Remember the testimony that you heard, not the rabbit trails, not the conjuring, not the confusion, not the attempts to sway you off track. Just use the court's charge and do the only thing you can do and give some justice to these people. Give Verna Heath and her daughter a little justice, because this is the only place they can turn for it. And if you do that, I know you're going to come back with a verdict you can be proud of. Thank you."

Mike Anderson smiled politely and took his seat. Casey O'Brien patted him on the shoulder. It had been a beautiful closing argument, and he was congratulating his colleague.

Now it was up to the jury.

Since it was after twelve noon, Judge Godwin instructed the bailiffs to escort the jury to lunch before their deliberations began. The rest of the crowd did likewise, scattering to the hamburger stands and sandwich shops that ring the Harris County courthouses, which themselves cover a four-square-block area of downtown Houston. It was another hot summer day, with the sun beating down on the sidewalks and the temperature a sultry ninety-five.

At one thirty, the jurors entered the deliberation room and began discussing Wanda's fate. It would prove to be a long and stressful afternoon.

As the hours passed, the assembled crowd, waiting in the hallways, grew restless. All of the "main players," Wanda Holloway, Verna Heath, and their families, were safely seqestered away from the thronging media in private offices near the courtroom. The Harper brothers, along with their parents, worked the press in the hallways, although they could not discuss the case directly, since Judge Godwin's original gag order was in effect until a verdict was reached and recorded. Marla Harper was not in sight, however.

Stanley Schneider was the only one of the four attorneys who strolled the halls chatting with reporters. He, too, followed the judge's orders and did not directly discuss the case. He used the opportunity to talk of upcoming cases he had on his agenda, though, hoping to attract some more media attention. Publicity is as vital to lawyers as clients in a city with as many attorneys as Houston, and in fact can make or break a trial lawyer's career. Schneider was smiling and confident as he talked in the halls.

After 5:00 P.M., many in the crowd begin to drift off. Curious visitors from faraway suburbs were anxious to get home before dark; others simply tired of the wait and knew that the verdict would be broadcast on all the television news stations, since the video camera was still in the courtroom waiting for the moment the jurors returned. As the length of time the jurors remained out increased, speculation grew in the crowd that they must be having trouble reaching a consensus of guilty. There was talk of a hung jury, or an acquittal.

At 6:26 P.M., the jurors buzzed the courtroom that they had reached a verdict. Everyone eagerly hustled into the courtroom and took a seat; the defendant was led in looking somewhat pale and strained, for a change. The wait was obviously wearing on Wanda. Judge Godwin took his seat and admonished the crowd once more, "All right, members of the audience, whatever this verdict is, I do not want any demonstrations or any outburst, emotional or otherwise. If you cannot control yourself, please leave the room now." Even Judge Godwin looked suspenseful as he asked Herbert Schuett, the jury foreman, for his verdict.

Schuett respectfully approached the bench and handed the judge a piece of paper on which the jury had recorded its remarks to the four statements from which they could choose a verdict. They had been asked to choose one of four answers: Wanda Holloway was either guilty or innocent of solicitation of capital murder, or she was guilty or innocent of solicitation of aggravated kidnapping.

Unfortunately, the jury got mixed up—the instructions had been too legally technical and incomprehensible. When Schuett handed the judge the group's answer, Judge Godwin studied it for a moment. Wanda Holloway stood at the defense table, ready to hear what fate had been decided for her. She held her head high, but seemed to tremble slightly. A long minute passed, and then Judge Godwin said, "Mrs. Holloway, will you please be seated."

The jury had made a mistake and had answered in some way that violated the instructions given them. The judge asked that they be returned to the deliberation room to reconsider their verdict, but did not explain to them what the problem was.

No one else knew either. It was a mystery. And it certainly was anticlimactic after the long wait, but all things considered, it was perhaps a fitting touch to the strange goings-on of the entire trial. Even the television news broadcasts across the city, still in progress, had dramatically announced seconds before that the verdict was in, only to have to report minutes later that there was some kind of problem, and there was still no verdict.

Judge Godwin and the attorneys then got into a lengthy private discussion of whether the judge should properly send along further instruction to the jurors to explain why he had rejected their answer. The defense attorneys said he should not, the state's attorneys didn't mind if he did.

Before the argument could be settled, however, a note arrived from the jury foreman asking, "Can we find the defendant guilty of only one? Page 8, paragraph 3, Herbert Schuett, foreman of the jury." Schuett was referring to the instructions, which had said in a complicated way that they could only find Wanda Holloway guilty of either one charge or the other.

Judge Godwin announced to the four attorneys that he was sending a brief answer: "Yes!"

Only minutes later, the jury once again buzzed the court that it was heading back with its verdict. One more time, everyone rushed into the courtroom. Wanda again took her place at the defense table, between her two attorneys, both of whom offered her a hand on either shoulder for support.

Again Herbert Schuett approached the bench, and again Judge Godwin read the proffered piece of paper and passed it to the bailiff. He read, "We, the jury, find the defendant, Wanda A. Holloway, guilty of criminal solicitation for capital murder, as charged in count one of the indictment."

Wanda's knees seemed to give way but otherwise she maintained her composure. Her mother, Verna Webb, rushed to her side to comfort her, and soon she was surrounded by well-meaning friends and relatives. Reporters ran from the room to begin to jockey for position to interview the attorneys and other witnesses as they left the room. Simultaneously, the news was broadcast on television, interrupting regularly scheduled programming like *Family Feud* and *Entertainment Tonight*.

"She's guilty," screamed viewers jubilantly across the city. Poor Wanda; hardly anybody liked her.

Because Texas is one of several states that has what is known as a bifurcated criminal trial system, Wanda's sentencing for her crime would be carried out in a separate proceeding the next day, although the same panel of twelve would decide her punishment. During the punishment phase of trial, the character of the defendant can be made an issue, and witnesses are often called to testify as to a defendant's reputation in the community. Because she had not yet been sentenced, and was still free on her earlier-posted twenty thousand dollars, Wanda could leave the courthouse that night, and was quickly whisked away out a side door. Those who accompanied her later said that Wanda seemed calm, but her mother, Verna Webb, was a wailing, emotional wreck who had to be forcibly restrained in the parking lot so she could be put in a car for the return trip to Channelview.

Back in the courthouse, a podium had been erected in the third-floor lobby of the annex building to allow attorneys and witnesses a forum from which to offer their comments. It was brightly lit with television lights and surrounded by photojournalists and their cameras.

Verna Heath, with her husband Jack on one side and her daughter Amber on the other, was among the first to make a statement. She addressed the crowd with a prepared remark created with the help of her lawyer, Bob Shults.

"My family and I are grateful for the risks taken by so many law enforcement people to keep us safe," she said in her Texas drawl. "We will never be able to adequately thank Detective George Helton and the other sheriff's officers, the prosecutors, Judge Godwin, and Terry Harper for their help and protection," she said piously.

Then she got in her two-cents worth about the media coverage. "But my family and I were not only victimized by Wanda Holloway, we have also been victimized by certain members of the media," she said with an angry look. "These and other legal considerations will not permit me or my family to give any further interviews." With that, she stepped from the podium and made her way out of the courthouse with her family.

Troy McKinney snarled an angry, "No comment," as he passed the waiting podium. Trial law is like any other game—it's no fun to lose, and some are poorer sports than others. Mike Anderson made a brief statement about how thankful he was to the attentive jury and added some other familiar platitudes. Because the trial was not completely concluded yet, the jury was still under a gag order from Judge Godwin and none of its members could offer comment.

On the morning of Wednesday, September 4, a smaller crowd

gathered for the punishment phase of Wanda Holloway's trial. Wanda looked drawn, but still had on full makeup and a demure black and white print dress with a lacy white collar. On this morning she was accompanied by her daughter, Shanna, who seemed much more sophisticated than she had the previous January. Her hair appeared to be tinted a lighter shade of blonde, and her makeup was more professionally applied. Her modeling lessons were paying off. Verna Heath, scheduled to testify for the state's portion of the proceeding, was again present, but she looked as if she had had a long night.

The purpose of this phase was to allow the jury to decide what Wanda's sentence should be. Since solicitation of capital murder is a first-degree felony, they could decide on anything from five years to life in prison for Wanda Holloway. But because she had no previous convictions, the jurors could also recommend a probated sentence that would allow her to resume her life in Channelview, albeit under the court's supervision. As in the guilt/innocence portion of the criminal trial, the state put on its witnesses first, followed by the defense.

The prosecution began by calling a series of four Channelview women who all swore they knew the defendant. In demonstrating character, Texas Rules of Evidence dictate the form of the questions that can be asked. The standard questions are: "Do you know this person? Do you know his or her reputation in his or her community for being a peaceable and law-abiding citizen? Is that reputation good or bad?" Reference to specific instances of conduct are forbidden unless certain criteria are met.

All four women called to the stand said they knew Wanda's reputation, and it was bad. On cross-examination, however, all four admitted to Troy McKinney that they were good friends of Verna Heath's. The defense attorney wanted the jury to see why the women might be biased in their assessment of his client. Two of the women were Nancee Carter and her mother, Edie. Nancee was the girl who had beaten Shane Harper out for the position of band major, and knew firsthand how mean Wanda Holloway could become when someone bested one of her children.

Verna Heath was the last state's witness. She took the stand, armed with a handkerchief against tearful episodes, and answered Mike Anderson's questions. She related how this incident with Wanda had affected her and her family greatly, that she had had trouble sleeping ever since she heard the news the previous January. "I've had nightmares at night," she told the jury. "And when I get in my car, I'm afraid to start the engine." She had become wary of all strangers, too, she said. And explained, "Every time I look at somebody I don't know, I wonder if they are following me."

Verna also said that she was no longer able to be as good a mother to her children as she formerly had been, and that her children had been affected as well. "Amber's personality went from happy-go-lucky, smiling child to feeling like everything she did was guarded," Verna explained. "She does not have the same smile on her face." Her sons grades had dropped dramatically in their school work, and her baby, Blake, only three, had become introverted and clinging. "When we go somewhere," she tearfully told the jury, "When we went to the mall, he said, 'Here Mom, take this Ninja Turtle sword and keep it so nobody will get you.'"

Troy McKinney asked Verna on cross-examination if she had sought any counseling for her problems. She admitted she had, but said she had only been twice.

"Why?" he asked, implying she really wasn't all that distressed if she'd only been two times for professional assistance.

"It cost too much money," she forthrightly admitted. Her children had not been sent for counseling either, she told McKinney, except to their preacher at the Truth Tabernacle Pentecostal church. Most fundamentalist Christians don't have much truck with all that psychoanalysis bullcorn. God could set anybody right who sought His help.

The state rested its case. The defense began by putting C. D. Holloway on the stand, although he had been conspicuously absent during the main portion of the trial. Looking strained and grim, C. D. hoisted his hulking mass onto the witness stand and told the court he was married to Wanda Holloway, and was upset about the previous day's results. "I don't feel well about it," he said. "I love her, like her to be with me, and I don't think she is guilty." C. D. spoke in such a muted voice that he was asked to repeat his statement.

Mike Anderson, during his cross-examination , asked C. D. about cheerleading, and whether he had discussed it with his wife. "Didn't you think all this folderol about cheerleading was a bunch of crock?" he asked C. D.

Holloway answered carefully, "I thought it was maybe over-discussed, and too much importance put on it at times."

"Did your wife ever come to you and ask you for twenty-five

hundred dollars?" queried Anderson. C. D. admitted she had not. He also told the court that he and Wanda had never, "absolutely not," discussed killing Verna or Amber Heath.

Wanda's father, the stern Cleven Webb, even took the stand to beg for mercy for his daughter. When asked how he felt about his daughter, he told Stanley Schneider, "I love her very much." It was not clear why the defense witnesses all testified to their love for Wanda; that seemed irrelevant now, unless the attorneys were hoping the jury would have mercy on all these poor people who were about to lose their wife, friend, and daughter to the jaws of the Texas Department of Criminal Justice.

Finally Wanda Holloway was put on the stand. She looked appropriately tearful and contrite. Troy McKinney began by asking her if she had ever been convicted of a felony in this or any other state. She said she had not.

"How do you feel about the verdict?" he then asked his client.

"I don't agree with the verdict," Wanda said in her heavy twang, and meekly added, "But I can accept it. I'll have to do as the jury tells the courts to do, I have to abide by it." She began to weep quietly, dabbing at her eyes.

McKinney asked Wanda how her life had been changed since January 30, 1991. "It's been a total nightmare," she cried. "For everyone involved, the community, everyone."

"And how do you think it has affected Verna Heath?" asked McKinney, who wanted his client to express her remorse.

"I'm sure it's totally destroyed her life and her family's and I feel just terrible about that," Wanda said through her sobs.

"Are you asking this jury to give you probation?" queried McKinney.

"Yes," Wanda begged, turning to face her judges. "I think they should, because this trial has been enough to punish me. If Verna Heath were here, I would tell her I'm sorry, and I would take it all back. I never meant for her or Amber, either one, to be hurt."

Wanda was no longer imperiously cool. She was facing life behind bars, and she was begging for mercy.

Mike Anderson approached Wanda to ask a few cross-examination questions. "What if the situation were reversed?" he first asked her. "Would you ask a jury to give probation to someone who had said about you and your daughter, number one, if the little girl's legs just come up all screwed up. Would you ask for probation for someone who said that?"

"I hope that I could," Wanda said, looking up at him earnestly. "I've already told the jury that a lot of that was just talk. I was just mouthing. I never..."

"So you'd ask for probation for someone who said your daughter was a bitch, and made you sick to your stomach?" he continued to press, reminding the jury of Wanda's hatred.

Again Wanda simply said, "I would hope that I could."

Finally Mike Anderson approached the witness with a photo taken shortly after her arrest. It showed Wanda with a wide grin, followed by her grinning attorneys. "It appears you were not very remorseful in this photograph, does it not?" he asked her. She remained quiet.

"Are you crying in this photo?" he kept on.

"No, sir, I'm not," she had to admit.

"In fact, you're smiling."

"Yes, sir, I am, under the instructions of my attorneys," Wanda said defensively, her tears momentarily stopped.

Anderson passed the witness, and McKinney took one more stab at trying to make his client appear sorry for her crime.

"Are you ashamed or embarrassed by what's happened?" he led her.

"Yes, sir," she readily piped up. "I am totally humiliated. I've embarrassed my family and the Heaths. The Heaths are horrified, my community is horrified, my church members are horrified, it's just a nightmare!"

After that, each side's attorneys gave brief summary arguments for the punishment each side thought appropriate. Mike Anderson emphasized how Wanda's actions had affected the Heaths irreparably, and how all she had to say now involved herself. "I am really sorry that she's embarrassed," he said, mocking Wanda's choice of words. "I'm so sorry that this is embarrassing for Mrs. Holloway. It's 'me.' It's 'I.' Everything that you hear from Mrs. Holloway revolves around Mrs. Holloway," he said scornfully. Then he added, "I'm not even going to talk to you about probation because the very idea is ridiculous." He then made an impassioned plea for a life sentence.

Troy McKinney emphasized his client's previous law-abiding record, and her sincere remorse for what had since happened. He described what probation would entail—that Wanda would not be scot free, but would have to remain under continuing supervision of probation officers throughout whatever term the jurors agreed upon. He implored the jury to consider letting Wanda remain with her family, not just for their sake, but so that she could somehow make amends to the Heaths. He pleaded for mercy for Shanna, who, like Amber Heath, was an innocent victim.

"How is hurting another child going to help Verna and Amber Heath?" he passionately asked the jury. "The goal of sentencing is punishment, and Wanda Holloway has already been punished because you've found her guilty. She walks down the street now and people know who she is because of this. Putting her in prison is not really going to punish her any more. It will be vengeful, but it won't really punish her any more."

The jury retired before lunch to make its decision. It was not an easy one. Jurors would later report that the group was hotly divided between those who wanted to send Wanda to prison for life and those who wanted to put her on probation. But within an hour and a half, they had reached their decision, and brought it into the courtroom.

Judge Godwin looked at the jury's recommendation and handed it to the bailiff to be read aloud. Everyone leaned forward in their seats to hear the fateful final decision: "We the jury, having found the defendant guilty of solicitation for capital murder, assess her punishment in the Institutional Division of the Texas Department of Criminal Justice for fifteen years, and further assess a fine in the amount of ten thousand dollars."

Wanda put her face in her hands and leaned forward on the table as her attorneys hovered nearby. Shanna, on the first row, began to cry. Her mother was going to jail.

Later, jurors were besieged by the press to explain their actions thoughout the trial. The fifteen-year sentence, many reported, was a compromise reached because various factions couldn't decide between life in prison and probation. The fifteen-year term was picked as a form of poetic justice, because Wanda herself had talked on the tapes of sending Verna Heath to Cuba for "fifteen years." They all, to a person, expressed great relief the trial was over.

Juror Tim Evans, a forty-year-old X-ray technician, summed up their feelings. "There was deep sleaze in this trial," he said later. "To us, everybody should be flushed or something. You wanted to take a shower every time you left the courtroom." Ultimately, he said, it had been the tapes that had convicted Wanda, since most of the other witnesses were "not worth listening to."

Laura Mitchell, a fifty-three-year-old Houston nurse, echoed Evans's remarks. "I don't see how anybody could have listened to those tapes and found Wanda anything but guilty. We heard them over and over, and the more we heard them, the more certain I was that she was guilty. It was kind of scary, to hear that voice of hers." It's not every day that the average person hears unadulterated evil.

Garrett Livingston, a retired sixty-one-year-old Houstonian, more or less agreed. "The tapes were all there was to it. Who could hear someone laugh and giggle about killing a child and not find her guilty?" Livingston had nothing but scorn for the would-be victims in the case as well. "I felt no sympathy for any of them, other than the children, the two girls it all centered around. The whole group is a bunch of dysfunctional people. That Terry Harper is a hillbilly, no doubt," he said emphatically.

Tim Evans said the same thing about the Harpers. "Those guys are just scum," he said, shaking his head with disgust. "Just disgusting. Terry Harper, when he was asked how many times he'd married Marla, couldn't even say 'twice.' He had to say 'twicet.'" Bad grammar—the ultimate condemnation.

Juror Raymond Baker, a forty-five-year-old manager for South-western Bell Telephone Company, said of the whole business, "This trial showed humanity at its best and its worst. That Wanda Holloway definitely has mental problems. A normal person would not have those thought patterns."

Nevertheless, Wanda was led away to the Harris County jail that afternoon by court bailiffs. There, her attorney Stanley Schneider later said, his client finally "lost it." "She cried and cried," he reported. "I was really worried about her."

She had, in an ironic twist of fate, just accomplished for her own daughter what she had set out to do to Amber Heath: caused her to lose her mother.

_____**14**

Try and Try Again

As luck would have it, Wanda was not separated from Shanna for long. In fact, thanks to certain provisions of Texas law, Wanda was back in Channelview at her home on Mincing Lane within twenty-four hours of her incarceration.

In Texas, any defendant who has been sentenced to fifteen years or less and who also files notice of an appeal may be released from jail on an appeals bond. Since Wanda had received that exact cut-off point of a sentence, Stanley Schneider immediately filed notice of a pending appeal with the court and went to work on bailing Wanda out. By 1:30 P.M. on September 5, a smiling Wanda Holloway left the jailhouse in the company of her attorneys after they posted a seventy-five-thousand-dollar bond on her behalf.

The jurors, when they heard the news, were furious. They had given her the fifteen-year term simply because Wanda had herself talked of banishing Verna Heath from Channelview for that length of time. They were completely unaware of the provision of the law that allowed her to walk only hours later. One said angrily, "If we had known that, we would have given her fifteen years and one day, just to make sure she did some time."

But it is forbidden in Texas for jurors to be told how soon a defendant might be released on parole or on this type of bond while they are deliberating. They are not supposed to be considering those technicalities, the theory goes, but only what sentence the defendant deserves.

Stanley Schneider had sneaked Wanda out a backdoor of the jailhouse to avoid the throng of cameras that had been lying in wait for her at the main entrance. He whisked her into his car and off to his office at Greenway Plaza on the southwest side of Houston, where C. D. was waiting with his Lincoln Town Car to take his wife home.

"He was pissed," said Stanley later of C. D. "He didn't like losing. He said he'd never lost anything before in his life."

The offices of Schneider and McKinney were immediately deluged with requests for interviews with Wanda from every media outlet that had covered the trial. The first one they consented to was a special, live, forty-five-minute television interview to be broadcast the following Friday night, September 6, on Houston's *Channel 2 News*.

Wanda was to give her first one-on-one interview ever to that station's Ron Reagan, no relation, who had covered the trial from the beginning.

While Wanda prepared for the interview that Friday night, the Channelview Falcons football team prepared for its first game of the season, against Magnolia High, a school located in a small town to the west of Houston. It could have been a scene right out of H. G. Bissinger's best-seller, *Friday Night Lights*: The school band was playing, anxious parents chatted in the stands, the drill team waited to perform, and the concession stand was selling Frito pies and giant dill pickles. It was a perfect night for high-school football—a little breezy, not too warm, a hint of coming rain in the air.

The gathered teenagers and their parents seemed oblivious to the scandal that had just rocked their community. The high school was attempting to conduct business as usual, although certain precautions had been taken against the expected onslaught of media. Principal Will

Bigott stood guard at the press entrance to the field behind the high school on Sheldon Road and warned all comers that the press would be restricted to a certain seating area and would not be allowed to approach any of the cheerleaders, football players, or drill-squad members.

Many photographers had showed up hoping to snap a picture of Amber Heath, who was to have performed at her first football game as a high-school cheerleader. They left disappointed, because she was nowhere to be seen. She had been kept home by her anxious parents, who wanted to spare her the ordeal of being in the spotlight.

Before the game began, Principal Bigott led the crowd in a school prayer, which concluded, "God protect the players and the cheerleaders." It seemed an especially appropriate plea to the Almighty, given the circumstances of recent weeks. It also seemed incredible to see the Channelview cheerleaders, with their ponytails and blue and gold short skirts and sweaters, and realize how badly someone had wanted her daughter to be one. They really didn't look that special.

Just down the road from the school, at the Sheldon Road Ice House, roughneck refinery workers guzzled chilled beer and talked about the case of Wanda Holloway. Most were disgusted that she had walked free. And most were angry that their community had been besmirched by her actions.

"They've painted us out to be the sleaziest town in America," said one man with missing teeth. "But it's not, and it just isn't fair."

A lady named Roylene, with peroxided hair, sat at the bar and mused, "They should have give her probation, and let her work in this community, picking up paper, picking up trash. She's embarrassed our community and owes it to us. That would be her best punishment."

"I think they should have throwed her in jail," interjected Mary, the establishment's owner, standing behind the bar. "She may have more money, but that don't make her any better than us," she added. "We're hard-working people."

Roylene added, "Not buttholes, like they've made us out."

Others in the crowd went along with the defense theory. A forty-five-year-old pool player who looked like he was sixty-five, a guy called Dirty Dean Webb, said, "To tell the truth, I think she was set up. I think her ex-husband set her up to get the kids."

Another old man agreed, and said, "That Terry Harper, he worked for me at Phillips before it blew up. Back then, he was on drugs and cocaine, and I think he still is. I seen his eyes on TV the other day, and he looked to me like he was still using them drugs. I think he was just trying to make more money to support his drug habit."

Wanda still had a few supporters, after all. But when she went on the air at 10:30 that night, after the ten o'clock news show, she may have alienated any she had left.

She sat on camera and smiled broadly, her pointy nose looking like the Wicked Witch of the West's. Her makeup was painted on thickly, as usual, and her hair permed into perfect coils around her head. She showed no hint of remorse.

She spoke in her own defense, and told Ron Reagan, who gently questioned her, "If wanting something good for your kids is greedy, then yes, I'm greedy. But that's what parents are for, to see that their children's needs are met."

Whose needs was she really trying to serve, though, many wondered. Hers? Or Shanna's? She certainly hadn't furthered Shanna's chances.

Reagan asked Wanda about her experiences at the jail two nights before. Wanda began to weep, tears streaking her pancake makeup as the camera moved in for a close-up. "It's something everyone needs to see," she said, crying as she spoke. "Especially teenagers. I can't imagine what it would be like to spend fifteen years in a place like that."

At the very thought, she began to weep copiously, and Reagan paused to let her compose herself. Her own experience had not been too awful, though, she explained. "The matrons there were very nice to me," she said. "They put me in a secluded room, but the mattress was a little roughy [sic]." The only tears Wanda Holloway ever shed seemed to be for herself.

When asked about how Shanna was faring, Wanda seemed to perk right up. "She's a little more introverted, I guess is the word," Wanda explained. "But she's going to a psychiatrist. She doesn't want to, but she goes. Shanna told me she doesn't need to anymore."

Wanda went on to explain that she had not taken the kids for counseling herself because, "I didn't want to because of the expense of it."

Reagan asked Wanda if she was planning to get any therapy. "Why, no," Wanda answered, seeming surprised.

When asked if maybe she now thought she had been too involved in her children's lives, Wanda said hurriedly, "I never have tried to live through my child. That talk has come from the fact that we are so close. We even have a lot of the same clothes. A lot of hers are too trendy for me, but I wear them anyway," she added with a giggle. "We're the exact same size!"

When confronted with the way she sounded on the tapes, Wanda looked only slightly chagrined. "I did not do right by Shanna on those tapes," she admitted. "I did not do right by the Heaths. I am sorry, and I never ever meant for them to be hurt. I just hope someday I can forgive them."

Shouldn't it have been the other way around? Maybe Mike Anderson was right in his closing argument when he said that to Wanda, everything revolved around "me" and "I." Even now, after her conviction, she still felt as if someone had wronged her.

But she added, "Yes, I have some hatred and some meanness, but I am not a vengeful-type person."

The same night that Wanda went on the air locally, her ex-husband, Tony Harper, along with his attorney, Paula Asher, flew to Washington, DC, to appear on the *Larry King Show*. Also on the evening's were Dr. Kit Harrison and Wanda's lawyer, Troy McKinney, who appeared via remote hook-up. Terry Harper had been invited as well, but the state's attorneys asked him not to go on for fear he might unwittingly aid the defense in its appeal. King talked to McKinney first, who looked almost freakish on television, with his long, thin face and his gapped teeth. He continued to insist his client was an innocent victim of the Harper brothers, and said, "They set out with a preconceived goal, and they carried it to fruition."

When Larry King wanted to know why Wanda had never called the police, McKinney answered, "That's an extremely good question. She felt like she was in over her head, and she wanted it to end, and she figured the easiest way out was to just give Terry the earrings and be done with it."

"So, unequivocally," King said, "she did not want anyone hurt?"

McKinney shook his head emphatically. "Ya know," he said in his Texas drawl, "it seems strange to me that people could believe that something as generally unimportant as cheerleading could drive someone to ask someone else to commit murder, and yet no one can believe that two brothers could get together and plot this thing out."

Since Wanda's conviction, he added, he had received dozens of phone calls from supporters. "The most common thing I've heard," he said, "is that there's got to be something a little bit messed up when someone who just talks about killing somebody gets a prison sentence, while people who actually kill and rob and commit violent crime spend little or no time in prison."

When Tony appeared, Larry King asked him if he had been surprised when he heard about his ex-wife's arrest. "Not really," he said with a shrug. "Wanda's a very determined lady, she has always been determined. She follows things through. She is a very thorough lady."

Those two television appearances would prove to be only the first of many for both Wanda and her ex-husband. Before the month of September was out, almost everyone involved in this case would have criss-crossed the country to make appearances on such shows as *Geraldo*, *Oprah*, and *Donahue*. The last aired a special two-part series, with Tony Harper appearing one day, accompanied by Shane, and Wanda appearing the next, accompanied by Shanna. Both went on with their lawyers, who were eager to get in on the act.

After hitting all the national forums, Wanda made the local rounds. She and Troy McKinney even went on a Houston radio talk show, and received a barrage of critical calls from listeners. Wanda didn't mind, though. She just gave her little trademark giggle when one particularly incensed phoner told her he thought she sounded like "a hateful witch."

Verna Heath did her share, too. She and her husband and Amber went on the *Maury Povich Show* the same day Wanda went on *Donahue*. The case was over, but it was still all over the airwaves. On Maury's show, little Amber related how awkward it was for her to have to deal with Shanna Harper at Channelview High after all the scandal. It was especially hard, she said, because she was elected president of the freshman class, and Shanna had been elected vice-president. Poor Shanna was always an also-ran, it seemed.

Amber's mom, Verna, allowed as how she thought it was rather tacky of Shanna to seek the vice-presidential spot, "In light of all that's happened." It sounded as if Verna Heath thought Shanna should just refrain from all school activities out of deference for poor Amber's feelings.

By the end of September, there was hardly a tabloid television venue the two families had not covered. Wanda and her contingent made no secret of the fact that they were hoping Shanna might be discovered by a Hollywood agent while on one of the shows, and they had hired a somewhat notorious Houston attorney, Earle Lilly, to represent the girl's interests should Hollywood come knocking at the door. Now that cheerleading seemed permanently closed to Shanna Harper, Wanda had enrolled her in modeling classes and was hoping she might attain an acting career. Even then, after the harsh lesson of the trial and the conviction, Wanda could not see the error of her ways. She was still shamelessly promoting her daughter.

The only participants in the story who didn't rush out to talk to the media were the prosecutors and the police. Mike Anderson and Casey O'Brien kept a discreet distance from the publicity. Anderson, in fact, left town for a fishing trip to Costa Rica, and scrupulously avoided reporters when he returned. Detective Helton and Sergeant Blackwell had to stay out of the limelight: As undercover men, they could not risk being identified on television or in photos.

Toward the end of September, Stanley Schneider and Troy McKinney announced that they were filing, in addition to an appeal, a motion for a new trial. Such motions are usually somewhat standard procedure; this one was a little different, however, because it claimed that Wanda Holloway's entire trial and conviction were legally null and void. The reason? One of the jurors, Daniel Enriquez, thirty, had been serving out a sentence of deferred adjudication for possession of cocaine at the time he sat on Wanda's jury. Technically, that meant Enriquez was still under indictment for the felony crime of possession of cocaine, and such people are barred by Texas law from jury duty. Texas law had been clear on the matter for over one hundred years: The seating of such a juror is absolute error.

And "absolute error" means that no way, no how, no matter what, does the result of the so-afflicted trial stand.

A hearing on the motion for a new trial was set for November 7, 1991. The minute Schneider had filed the papers in Judge Godwin's court, setting forth the grounds for the motion, the state's attorneys hastened to double-check the information. To their chagrin, they discovered that the defense attorneys were right. Juror 11, Daniel Enriquez, was currently on deferred adjudication. According to Texas law, that rendered him ineligible for jury duty. Johnny Holmes, the handle-bar mustachioed head district attorney of Harris County, publicly announced, "We may have been outlawyered." He knew, and the prosecutors knew, that they should have caught the problem before allowing Enriquez to be empaneled.

They launched an extensive investigation into how such a mistake could have been made. Suddenly, some of the odd events of voir dire began to make sense. Casey O'Brien remembered remarking to Anderson how odd he thought it was that the defense had no objection to empaneling Enriquez, who had answered on his juror questionnaire that he thought Wanda was guilty.

The state's only excuses for not catching the error were that 1) They had had to read over 125 voluminous questionnaires in a hurry before beginning the selection process; and 2) Even though Enriquez had truthfully recorded his previous sentence for possession of drugs, Anderson thought that meant he had already served out his deferred adjudication. Prior to the very beginning of jury selection, Judge Ted Poe, who was conducting it, had asked the entire venire if anyone was then on probation. Enriquez did not raise his hand. So when the topic arose later, Anderson just assumed the man was eligible.

Other curious facts emerged, which strongly suggested that the defense attorneys had been completely aware of Enriquez's ineligibility to serve when they allowed him to be empaneled. These facts enraged the state's attorneys and the D.A.'s appellate division, which would be in charge of the state's appeal. It didn't seem right, or fair, or just, that McKinney and Schneider could sit back and let Enriquez take a seat on the panel, wait for a verdict, and then file a motion for a new trial based on his disqualification. It smacked of snakes under rocks, waiting for their chance to strike. And most everyone knew that if Wanda had been found innocent, Schneider and McKinney would never have mentioned the fact that the result was void.

State appellate attorney J. Harvey Hudson painstakingly researched the facts and the law around this incident. He found several witnesses, clerks in Judge Poe's office, who remembered that a few days after the news of Enriquez's illegal empanelment was announced, Schneider dropped by the courtroom. Poe's clerk, Elaine Stolte, recalled that she asked Schneider about how Enriquez came to be seated. She claimed in a sworn affidavit given to Harvey Hudson that the lawyer had smiled and said, "I knew he was on probation, Mike knew he was on probation, and we even had a bench conference about it." No such conference was recalled by Mike Anderson, who swears it never took place.

More telling are the minutes of the voir dire. When Judge Poe noticed Enriquez's answers on his questionnaire about the potential juror's feelings toward Wanda, and his opinion that she was guilty, the judge called the man before the bench for questioning. He wanted to determine if Enriquez could set his personal opinions aside and listen to the evidence.

Judge Poe asked, according to the records, "Have you reached a conclusion about her guilt or innocence?"

Enriquez responded honestly, "I've not reached a conclusion, but I'm leaning one way, toward guilty."

Poe then asked, "Are you telling us that you could not be a fair or impartial juror in this case?"

Enriquez answered, "I don't think I could be fair and impartial."

Judge Poe then looked quizzically over at the defense table and asked, "Mr. McKinney, any questions?" Such responses from a juror are grounds to strike for cause. But oddly, McKinney simply said he had no questions for the man, and Enriquez was thus empaneled.

As Harvey Hudson wrote later in his appeals brief, "Counsel's actions would at first glance appear to be an act of gross incompetence. However, the attorneys in this case are highly skilled and possess considerable experience in the field of criminal defense. The only rational explanation is that they were aware of Mr. Enriquez's status of deferred adjudication."

In the meantime, still other new developments in the case arose. First, a man named Calvin Stout, who claimed to work as a paralegal in Houston, came forward "out of the blue" to announce that back in January of 1991 Terry Harper had approached him looking to buy an ounce of cocaine. According to Stout, who was also a known police informant, Harper had related that by the end of the month he would have enough cash for the purchase because he "was setting up his ex-sister-in-law." Stout swore in an affidavit given to Schneider and McKinney that later in January Terry Harper approached him again and said he wouldn't have the cash for the drugs, after all, but could give him a pair of earrings instead.

The defense immediately added Stout to its reasons for seeking a new trial, because he was a new witness who had come forward before thirty days had elapsed after the trial. The only problem was, Stout was a known liar. And it is certainly an odd coincidence that just two days after Wanda's conviction, Stout was calling collect from the Harris County jail to Stanley Schneider's office. Stout also seemed suspiciously eager to cash in on his new position as a player in the weird case of

Wanda Holloway. After speaking with Wanda's lawyers, Stout got himself a lawyer, who promptly began calling media representatives, both local and national, offering to allow interviews with Calvin for a price. Such offers, which no one accepted, did not do much to improve Calvin Stout's credibility.

When Harvey Hudson investigated Stout, he came up with many witnesses willing to give affidavits to the effect that Calvin Stout was a notorious liar. Some said that although he was a mere paralegal, Stout had often held himself out as an attorney. It was certainly beginning to look as if Stout might be some kind of trumped up witness-for-hire, since some of the character witnesses discovered by the state testified that Stout had, on previous occasions, offered to give testimony for money in cases in which they were involved.

In another surprising, or maybe not so surprising, development, Marla and Terry Harper reconciled for the umpteenth time. Shortly after moving back into the trailer on Elspeth Street, Marla announced publicly that she had made a big mistake when she testified against her husband during Wanda's trial.

She told the *Houston Chronicle* in late October, 1991, "I went in there and said some bad things about my husband. I overreacted—I acted on my fear and my pain, and he was strongly misjudged. I owe him a public apology." She would not be a defense witness in any future trial of Wanda Holloway, she announced firmly.

On November 7, 1991, the motion for a new trial for Wanda Holloway was given a hearing in Judge Godwin's courtroom. Schneider and McKinney produced their evidence that Daniel Enriquez was disqualified as a juror. Harvey Hudson made an impassioned plea that, because of their foreknowledge of that fact, the defense should be barred from now seeking relief because of it. He said, "This juror gave answers on his questionnaire that would have alerted any competent defense counsel that he was not likely to make a good defense witness. He had been a victim of crime; he said he'd seen extensive pretrial publicity; he said he was leaning toward finding her guilty," he told Judge Godwin. Hudson continued, "I will vouch for those two being competent counsel."

Everyone on the D.A.'s staff was all too aware of how competent Stanley Schneider was, especially when it came to tripping up the prosecutors on technicalities. So that left only one possibility: Schneider and McKinney had known about this absolute error all along, and had hidden it throughout the trial like a crooked poker player might hide an ace in his pocket.

One witness to the voir dire in the case had even remembered Stanley Schneider boasting during jury selection that he "already had built-in error in the case."

Nevertheless, the law was clear: absolute error means just that— absolute error. Judge George Godwin had no real choice in the matter. He issued his ruling, and said, "We have a void conviction. And I don't like that." He frowned and signed his order mandating that Wanda Ann Holloway be given a new trial. Once again, the state of Texas had been Stanley Schneiderized. His impish grin to reporters after the hearing proved his delight in that fact. Maybe he and his partner were no great orators, maybe the jurors hadn't bought their flimsy arguments, but when push had come to shove, they had been the winners.

But as they say in the sports world, it ain't over til it's over, and it ain't over til the fat lady sings. In this situation, the fat lady is a Texas appeals court, where the case of Wanda Holloway now waits to be ruled upon.

The state of Texas filed an appeal arguing that the motion for a new trial should not have been granted because of the extensive evidence that the defense counsel more or less "arranged" the absolute error by remaining silent in the face of their knowledge of same. There is a rule in courtrooms known as the "contemporaneous objection" rule, which says that, if an attorney fails to object to evidence at the time it is introduced, he or she cannot later raise an objection to the admission of that evidence. Harvey Hudson, in his appellate brief, urged the higher courts to consider this incident in the same light. He also suggested that the higher court should consider reinterpreting an old line of cases on this subject, which Hudson claims, in a complicated legal argument, were originally misapplied by the courts. It is well settled in Texas law that the seating of an unqualified juror is absolute error.

Because of the heavy backlog of cases on appeal, no one knows when the state's appeal might be ruled upon. But even if the appellate court decides that Wanda does not deserve a new trial, her attorneys will move in another direction. They have also filed notice to appeal her conviction by the tainted jury, on the grounds that the trial judge should have allowed the testimony of several witnesses to be presented to the jury, especially the women who were scheduled to swear that

Terry and Tony Harper, had, on earlier occasions, asked them if they were interested in hiring a hit man. If the courts reverse Judge Godwin's decision, this second appeal will still have to be decided before a new trial is held.

In short, it could very well be years before the ultimate fate of Wanda Ann Holloway is decided.

Meanwhile, she is as free as a bird, living in her little home with C. D. and Shanna, going to church, visiting her parents, doing all the things she did before anyone had ever heard of her. About the only thing that has changed in her life is that now, wherever she goes, people stop and do double takes as they recognize the Cheerleader Mother from Hell. Because of that notoriety, friends of Wanda's say she has had to quit shopping at the nearby malls and instead must drive in to Houston to buy her fancy clothes. Now she goes to the Galleria instead of Baybrook Mall, and has modified her appearance to avoid recognition. She dyed her hair blond and cropped it short.

As for the Heaths, they have gone about their usual business, too. Verna still teaches her twirling and dance classes and Amber still remains one of the most popular girls in the freshman class at Channelview High.

The Heaths did, however, decide to get even with Wanda for all the trouble she'd caused. Just short of a year after Wanda's trial, the Heaths filed a civil lawsuit against Wanda Holloway. They asked for damages for the mental anguish and invasion of privacy they had suffered as a result of Wanda's actions.

Wanda's attorney, Troy McKinney, after learning of the suit, said that he thought it mighty hard to claim invasion of privacy when the plaintiffs themselves made the talk-show circuit to discuss their private lives.

The suit was coincidentally filed just days after HBO announced that its planned cable movie on the case was to begin shooting. The film's title indicated its relatively comic approach to the bizarre scenario: "The Positively True Adventures of the Alleged Texas Cheerleader-Murdering Mom."

Terry and Marla Harper are still living in their trailer, sometimes happily and sometimes not. Occasionally, they will be stopped on the street, or while shopping in places like Sam's Discount Warehouse or the local K Mart. People will ask where they've seen their faces before, and Terry and Marla proudly relate the parts they played in the drama of Wanda Holloway. But for the most part their moment in the spotlight appears to be over.

And Channelview will always be Channelview. The smoke and fumes still rise from the refineries, and the ship channel still stinks. The churches are still crowded on Sundays, but so are the ice houses. Life goes on.

Only once in a while do the locals give much thought to what happened in their community. Every now and then, maybe while watching the girls at the high school jump and shout as they perform their cheers for the Channelview Falcons, someone will remember, vaguely, Verna Heath's plaintive question to Detective Helton when she learned of Wanda's arrest, "Why, why, over cheerleading? For a child to not have a mother? Why?"

Still no one knows the answer. And so they hastily put the question out of their minds and go on clapping and applauding and admiring the girls on the field like nothing had changed.

Elsewhere in Harris County, people continue to hire hit men for strange, even trivial reasons. Not long after Wanda's case was sent to the appeals court, a fourteen-year-old Houston boy was sentenced to twenty years for his part in a plot to kill a friend's sixty-three-year-old grandmother. The woman's grandsons and daughter had ordered the hit, the boy explained to police, because Granny wouldn't buy the kids a basketball goal. The fourteen-year-old gunman, hired for a mere one hundred dollars, sneaked into the family home one afternoon and took a shot at Granny while she sat and watched television. Lucky for her, the kid just winged her. He later said he was supposed to shoot the grandfather, too, but couldn't get a shot off at the old man because he was out back in the shed.